Econometric Modelling in Theory and Practice

Econometric Modelling in Theory and Practice

Proceedings of a
Franco-Dutch Conference
held at Tilburg University, April 1979

Edited by

Joseph Plasmans

Sponsored by
the French Embassy at The Hague
and
the Office for International Relations of Tilburg University

1982
MARTINUS NIJHOFF PUBLISHERS
THE HAGUE/BOSTON/LONDON

Distributors:

for the United States and Canada
Kluwer Boston, Inc.
190 Old Derby Street
Hingham, MA 02043
USA

for all other countries
Kluwer Academic Publishers Group
Distribution Center
P.O. Box 322
3300 AH Dordrecht
The Netherlands

Library of Congress Cataloging in Publication Data
Main entry under title:

Econometric modelling in theory and practice.

Pref. and summary in French.
Includes index.
1. Econometrics--Congresses. 2. Economics--Mathematical models--Congresses. I. Plasmans, J. E. J. II. France. Ambassade (Netherlands) III. Katholieke Hogeschool. Office for International Relations.
HB141.E23 330'.028 81-18876
AACR2

ISBN-13: 978-94-009-7484-5 e-ISBN-13: 978-94-009-7482-1
DOI: 10.1007/978-94-009-7482-1

CONTENTS

PART V: INTERNATIONAL ECONOMETRIC MODELS

PREFACE

Charles de Gaulle commence ses Mémoires d'Espoir, ainsi: 'La France vient du fond des âges. Elle vit. Les Siècles l'appellent. Mais elle demeure elle-même au long du temps. Ses limites peuvent se modifier sans que changent le relief, le climat, les fleuves, les mers, qui la marquent indéfiniment. Y habitent des peuples qu'étreignent, au cours de l'Histoire, les épreuves les plus diverses, mais que la nature des choses, utilisée par la politique, pétrit sans cesse en une seule nation. Celle-ci a embrassé de nombreuses générations. Elle en comprend actuellement plusieurs. Elle en enfantera beaucoup d'autres. Mais, de par la géographie du pays qui est le sien, de par le génie des races qui la composent, de par les voisinages qui l'entourent, elle revêt un caractère constant qui fait dépendre de leurs pères les Français de chaque époque et les engage pour leurs descendants. A moins de se rompre, cet ensemble humain, sur ce territoire, au sein de cet univers, comporte donc un passé, un présent, un avenir, indissolubles. Aussi l'État, qui répond de la France, est-il en charge, à la fois, de son héritage d'hier, de ses intérêts d'aujourd'hui et de ses espoirs de demain.'

A la lumière de cette idée de nation, il est clair, qu'un dialogue entre nations est éminemment important et que la Semaine Universitaire Franco-Néerlandaise est une institution pour stimuler ce dialogue. C'est pour cette raison, que l'Université de Tilburg a organisé, pour la deuxième fois, avec beaucoup de plaisir et un grand enthousiasme cette Semaine Universitaire Franco-Néerlandaise, dans l'espoir que les deux nations se comprennent de mieux en mieux et coopèrent de plus en plus à la construction de l'Europe, cette famille de nations, qui viennent du fonds des âges.

Prof. Dr. J.J.J. Dalmulder

INTRODUCTION

From 23–27 April 1979, a 'Franco-Dutch Universitary Week' was organized at the University of Tilburg. The French Embassy at The Hague and the local Office for International Relations sponsored this meeting of leading Dutch and French economists originating from the academic world and from private institutions involved in research and planning, support from which is gratefully acknowledged.

The central theme was: 'Economic Power and Structuralism', and, more particularly: 'Power Structures and Construction of Sectoral, Regional and National Econometric Models', so the ideas and the experiences of a number of Dutch and French model builders were brought together. The result was a better understanding of the theoretical and empirical functioning of postwar western economies.

The conference began with some general lectures from Prof. Dr. Younès and from Dr. Ruys, on the microeconomic foundations of macroeconomic (dis)equilibrium theory and power structures. This theoretical analysis has been applied at sectoral level by Fouquet and by Courbis and his team, regional level by Courbis and Cornilleau, national level by Kooyman, Piganiol, Artus and Volle, and van de Klundert, and at international level by Plasmans. The conference was closed by a very lively and profound panel discussion about the theoretical and empirical aspects of economic model building and performance among some Dutch and French specialists in the field.

Although this book contains both theoretical and empirical issues, the emphasis is put on the empirical aspects being important for the description of the Dutch and French economies. Hence, economic theory applied on (aspects of) both western economies is the common starting point of nearly all the papers contained in this volume. Econometric estimation and validation of economic models, describing (parts of) both economies, are necessary phases to be passed.

Progress in economic theory or in economics in general and in econometric methodology or in econometrics in particular depends on at least three related activities:

(i) Development of tools to facilitate both the formulation and the testing of possible economic generalizations.

(ii) Collection or generation and accumulation of observations on economic processes and institutions.

(iii) Application of the tools and the observations to enlarge the body of established generalizations about economic modelling.

As regarding to (i), many statistical estimation, testing and prediction techniques have been developed during the last two decades. They can be used for many different kinds of econometric models, including linear and nonlinear interdependent structural models, models involving both qualitative and quantitative variables, models with time series complications, models for combined time series and cross-section data and models with random parameters. This research on statistical techniques and computer programs implementing them, a joint product of statisticians and econometricians, has been extremely important in the development of modern econometric modelling techniques.

The generation of observations on economic processes and institutions, mentioned under (ii), is subject to a continuous improvement owing to the permanent enlargement of statistical services and the progress of computer informatics.

Nevertheless, it should be kept in mind that the sample data used in econometrics come from the living laboratory of actual economic life. These data are generally not controlled nor repeated, and this makes statistical inference in economics especially difficult, for non-experimental. In this living laboratory, everything depends on everything else. The economy, in Walrasian spirit, can be represented as a system of simultaneous equations. They are generally non-linear, stochastic and dynamic.

This leads us to the econometric modelling phase itself, mentioned under (iii). The above called non-experimental model-building restriction dictates to a considerable degree the statistical models and search procedures included. Because there are many admissable economic models that do not contradict what we know about economic behaviour, there is in each applied venture a degree of uncertainty about the underlying economic model and, thus, about the correct statistical or sampling model.

Unfortunately, the sampling conclusions of much of traditional statistical inference, deal with the case of a known sampling model. The framework for a theory of statistical inference based on false models remains to be developed. This problem must certainly be faced in the future if we are to meet and cope with the problem of developing more efficient procedures for learning from finite samples of passively generated economic data.

In general, we can state that we would like econometric modelling to be as objective and person-free as possible, but an artistic element cannot be ignored in our science.

Although some economists look to parsimonious theory for the building of elegance and manageability into econometric systems, this rule of parsimony can be very misleading. It says that, between any pair of competing hypotheses, that specification should be accepted that explains a given data set at least as well as the other but uses fewer parameters. This rule can be quite misleading in the interpretation of certain small samples of econometrics.

It may lead us to accept a simple hypothesis that ignores the effects of some variables that have been quiescent during the sample period so that the true system was, in fact, more complicated than a parsimonious model suggested.

Parsimony appears to be at variance with the Walrasian concept that everything depends on everything else. To reach closer to the 'Walrasian ideal', we ought to be building more simultaneity into our models and going away, to the extent possible, from the simplistic systems of parsimonious reasoning.

But a strong warning should be made here! Large and simple models seem preferable to large and complicated models. In fact, a very disturbing feature of large, complicated models in the literature is that in (very) many cases they have no unique solution.

The above elements should be kept in mind when reading the conference papers. Before giving an overview of the detailed programme it should be stressed that the practical organization of this Franco-Dutch Conference was in the skilful hands of the abovementioned Office for International Relations of the Tilburg University. Particularly, the efficient and pleasant assistance of Miss Miek van Wanrooy and Messrs. Huub Meyers and Hans Smies, both at the conference and in connection with the many attendant social events, is very much appreciated, It should equally be noted that French and Dutch theologists, psychologists and jurists also met during this week.

The scientific economic program contained the following lectures, where it should be noted that the titles of the oral presentations may differ from the definitive titles in the written papers, although the contents are basically similar.

Wednesday, April 25 1979

10.00–11.30 h.	Prof. Dr. Y. Younès (Cepremap) 'The Microeconomic Foundations of Macroeconomic Theory'
11.30–12.30 h.	Dr. P. Ruys (Tilburg University) 'Disequilibrium in Economics and Econometrics'
14.00–15.15 h.	Prof. Dr. R. Courbis, A. Fonteneau, C. Le Van and P. Voisin (GAMA, Université de Paris X-Nanterre and CNRS) 'The MOGLI-Model: a short term–medium term pluri-sectoral dynamic Model of the French Economy'

15.15–16.30 h. Prof. Dr. M. Kooyman (University of Groningen)
'The GRECON Model for the Dutch Economy and its Prediction Performance'

Thursday, April 26 1979

9.30–11.00 h. Dr. J. Plasmans (Tilburg University)
'INTERPLAY: A linked Model for Economic Policy in the EEC'

11.15–12.45 h. Prof. Dr. B. Piganiol (Université Paris-IX Dauphine)
'An annual Economic Policy Model for France'

14.00–15.45 h. Prof. Dr. D. Fouquet (ENSAE, OCDE)
'The Dynamic Multisectoral Model DMS'

Friday, April 27 1979

9.30–11.00 h. Prof. Dr. M. Volle (ENSAE, INSEE)
'METRIC and its Experience for the French Economy'

11.15–12.45 h. Prof. Dr. T. van de Klundert (Tilburg University)
'The VINTAF II-model of the central planning bureau and its experience in the Netherlands'

14.00–15.15 h. Prof. Dr. R. Courbis and G. Cornilleau (GAMA, Université de Paris X–Nanterre and CNRS)
'The REGINA-model: a regional–national model for the French economy

15.30–16.30 h. Full session about economic model building and model performance with a panel comprising

- Prof. Dr. A.P. Barten (CORE, Catholic University of Louvain)
- Prof. Dr. R. Courbis (GAMA, Université de Paris X–Nanterre)
- Prof. Dr. T. Kloek (Erasmus University, Rotterdam)
- Dr. J. Plasmans (Tilburg University), president
- Dr. A. van Schaik (Tilburg University, Central Planning Bureau) and
- Prof. Dr. M. Volle (ENSAE, INSEE)

Joseph Plasmans

ABSTRAIT

Les colloques des économistes à la 'Semaine Universitaire Française' du 23 au 27 avril 1979 ont été organisés autour du thème: 'Pouvoir Economique et Structuralisme'. Le but était de rassembler quelques des meilleurs spécialistes de la France et des Pays-Bas en ce qui concerne la construction des modèles économiques nationaux, régionaux et sectoriels. Aussi bien des professeurs universitaires que des chercheurs des instituts spécialisés étaient présents.

Cette semaine fournissait une bonne plate-forme, aboutissant à un échange fructueux entre spécialistes francophones et néerlandophones. L'applicabilité des modèles dans la vie économique et sociale des pays occidentaux était amplement discutée.

La semaine commençait par quelques discours généraux qui apportaient des éléments fondamentaux sur l'analyse des modèles macro-économiques (comme Younès et Ruys). Surtout, l'analyse de (des)équilibre économique et la formalisation des structures de pouvoir ont été traitées ici. Par après, cette analyse théoretique était appliquée, aussi bien sur le plan sectoriel (Courbis, Fonteneau, Le Van et Voisin, Fouquet) que sur le plan régional (Courbis et Cornilleau), le plan national (Kooyman, Piganiol, Artus et Volle, van de Klundert) et sur le plan international (Plasmans).

DISEQUILIBRIUM CHARACTERIZED BY IMPLICIT PRICES IN TERMS OF EFFORT

P.H.M. RUYS

Summary

Processes or models using excess demand or supply as signals or variables are hampered by the fact that this excess is usually not observable. In this paper a solution is proposed by assuming that plans on the long side of any market (which need to be rationed) require effort from each individual agent to be carried out. The amount of effort used by each agent on a market is an indicator of his pressure on that market and, aggregated, of the size of the excess demand or supply. Using a transaction technology, prices in terms of effort can be derived which discriminate agents and oppress plans to the compatible level determined by agents on the short side of the market. No rationing institution is needed; this at the cost of some efficiency.

1. Introduction

Inflexibility of prices is the cause that some planned transactions cannot be carried out, and excess supply or excess demand prevails at some markets. Agents (that are demanders or suppliers) will be necessarily confronted with restrictions on their planned transactions and will thus be rationed. These rations will influence and probably alter plans on other markets and thus generate spill-over effects; the interdependence of quantity constraints is one of the characteristics of the general (dis)equilibrium models which are analysed here.

This type of model has been analyzed formally only recently, although the theory traces at least back to Keynes. The interest in this theory is revived by the study of an agent's decision in a disequilibrium situation in relation with Keynes' theory [13, 28, 6]. But also from other directions the relevance of disequilibrium situations was pointed out, which are implicit in a theory of price formation [3].

Microeconomic models were designed, showing that consistency of an economy with inflexible prices and rationing is no problem [45, 14], also when rules based on effective demand are followed [8]. It was shown that the allocations are not necessarily efficient, even relative to the fixed price, due to the fact that commodities are exchanged against money, market by market [18, 19].

These models served as foundation for simple macroeconomic models, such as developed by Malinvaud and Younès (1974), Malinvaud (1977), Böhm (1978), Muelbauer and Portes (1978), et al, resulting in régime- (or state-) dependent trade functions.

Further exploration in the direction of price dynamics, inventories, investments, expectations, etc. is momentarily done. But these (macro)-models have also served to design econometric models and methods in which equilibrium (rather than disequilibrium régime) has become a testable hypothesis. Firstly partial disequilibrium models have been developed, and recently general equilibrium models with spill-over effects were published [17, 25, 26].

All models mentioned above are based on quantitative rationing. Although there are some constraints on rationing, many procedures are admissible. But a similar problem arises as in the tâtonnement process of price forming: what kind of procedure leads to 'equilibrium' rations? Grandmont (1977) has remarked that a kind of auctioneer or institution is still indispensable.

In this paper I propose an equilibrium concept for which no rationing institution is needed, but which is based on self organization by individual agents. The central idea is that effort is needed to obtain trades if the agent is on the long side of the market. Effort is a nontransferrable personal commodity which can be gauged on social efficiency. The amount of effort needed per volume trade can be considered as an effort-price, which prices can be experienced directly by the agents on any market. These effort-prices determine constraints, which are the rations introduced in the above-mentioned models. The sign of an effort-price in a market corresponds with the state of that market (excess demand or excess supply). Thus effort-prices both indicate the state of the economy, and reduce plans to an admissible volume such that they are compatible.[1]

The organization of this paper is as follows. Firstly the disequilibrium model with quantity rationing is described. Then (sections 3 and 4) the effort-equilibrium is introduced and its existence proven. Some characteristics (viz. its asymmetric treatment of agents) and efficiency properties are given in section 5. A simple macroeconomic model is given as an example in section 6. Finally, the transaction technology is related with the theory of search, and an interpretation is given in terms of time.

Perhaps it is good to remind that the whole problem is based on the difference between two simple questions in a wage regulated economy: 'do you want this job?' and 'have you got a job?'.

2. Disequilibrium Allocations with a Rationing Institution

Consider an economy E with $m + 1$ marketable commodities, the first being money, $M := \{0, 1, \ldots, m\}$. Each commodity has a price, uniform on the market; the price vector p is an element of the set

$$\Delta := \{p \in R_+^{m+1} | p_0 = 1, 0 \leqq \underline{p}_k \leqq p_k \leqq \bar{p}_k < \infty, \quad k \in M\}. \tag{2.1}$$

The economy consists of h agents, indexed by $i \in H$, who trade commodities against money. A transaction of some agent, i, z^i, is equal to the difference between the commodity bundle desired by the agent after trade and the vector of initial resources, $z^i := x^i - w^i$.

The negative components of z^i are amounts supplied by i to the market, the positive components are received by i. Let $z_{k+} := \max\{0, z_k\}$, and $z_{k-} := \max\{0, -z_k\}$, then $z = z_+ - z_-$. Each agent chooses an optimal element in the set X^i of eligible commodity bundles for i. This choice is constrained by the money budget, $px^i = pw^i$, and possibly by quantitative constraints on transactions. The agent's preferences $\prec^i$ are defined on X^i, which include the commodity money. The model thus described is an intertemporal economy in which agents are able to shift money over time-periods to allocate consumption over time. This allocation will depend also on expectations about future earning power and future prices. Using standard dynamic programming techniques, preferences for commodities inclusive money can be derived for the actual period taken into consideration. Although the agent's preferences thus depend (through expectations) on actual prices and quantitative constraints, it is assumed here that they are independent.

This assumption is not essential and can easily be removed [18]. It is important to notice that the equilibrium concepts defined in this paper are temporary equilibria, i.e. only actual transactions are required to be compatible with each other; transaction plans in the future are not required to be consistent at this moment. Since it is transactions z^i rather than consumption bundles x^i which are the central objects of this analysis, the agent's choice is translated to the transaction set $Z^i := X^i - \{w^i\}$. The preferences are defined on Z^i by the preference relation $\prec^i$, or equivalently, by the preference correspondence $P^i(z^i)$ which associates with each z^i in Z^i the set of trades that are preferred by agent i to z^i. The budget constraint is given by $pz^i = 0$, or $pz^i_+ = pz^i_-$.

The quantitative constraints are given by a vector of lower bounds, $\underline{g}^i$, and a vector of upper bounds, $\bar{g}^i$, on transactions by agent i. It is assumed that there exists no quantitative constraint on money, or $\underline{g}^i_0 = -\infty, \bar{g}^i_0 = +\infty$, for all $i \in H$.

Any agent $i \in H$ chooses from the constraint set

$$B^i(p, \underline{g}^i, \bar{g}^i) := \{z^i \in Z^i | pz^i = 0, \underline{g}^i \leqq z^i \leqq \bar{g}^i\}$$

the maximal or optimal transaction vectors. The set of maximal elements from $B^i(p,g^i,\bar{g}^i)$ is called the *constraint choice correspondence* and is denoted by $f^i(p,g^i,\bar{g}^i)$. Notice that f^i_+ is the agent's demand correspondence, and f^i_- is the agent's supply correspondence under the given quantitative constraints.

A *disequilibrium allocation* in the economy E is a list of trades z^i, $i \in H$ (further denoted by z^H), a price p and an allocation of quantitative constraints g^H and $\bar{g}^H$, such that for each $i \in H$, $z^i \in f^i(p,g^i,\bar{g}^i)$ and $\Sigma z^i = 0$. This definition however, is hardly restrictive, as long as any consistent rationing system is allowed. Therefore two important institutional assumptions will be made: voluntary trade and a frictionless market.

An agent is said to *trade voluntarily* if he is not forced to buy or sell more than he wants, i.e. $g^i \leqq 0 \leqq \bar{g}^i$, for all $i \in H$.

In order to define a frictionless market, the state of any market will be defined. From the point of view of agent i, some market k cannot meet his demand (indicated by $+1$), can meet his demand or supply (0), or cannot meet his supply (-1). This can be made precise on two ways. Firstly, Drèze (1975) has used a binding constraint as a norm for the state of a market; let $z^i_k \in f^i(p,g^i,\bar{g}^i)$, then the state r^i_k is defined by:

$$r^i_k := \begin{cases} +1, & \text{if} \quad g^i_k < z^i_k = \bar{g}^i_k \\ 0, & \text{if} \quad g^i_k < z^i_k < \bar{g}^i_k \\ -1, & \text{if} \quad g^i_k = z^i_k < \bar{g}^i_k \end{cases}$$

Secondly, Benassy (1975) and Grandmont (1977) have used the concept of effective choice on some market k. The *effective choice* on market k by agent i is said to be the kth component of the maximal element(s) from the budget set $B^i_k(p,g^i_k,\bar{g}^i_k)$ in which the quantitative constraint on market k has been released. It is denoted by $\tilde{f}^i_k(p,g^i_k,\bar{g}^i_k)$. The state of market k as perceived by i is then defined by

$$s^i_k := \text{sgn}\,(\tilde{f}^i_k - f^i_k). \tag{2.2}$$

A market k is said to be *frictionless* if one of the following conditions is satisfied:

$$\begin{aligned} &\text{(Drèze condition):} && \text{for all} \quad i,j \in H: r^i_k r^j_k \geqq 0 \\ &\text{(Hahn-Negishi condition):} && \text{for all} \quad i,j \in H: s^i_k s^j_k \geqq 0. \end{aligned} \tag{2.3}$$

Since $r^i_k = 0$ implies $s^i_k = 0$, the Drèze condition implies the Hahn-Negishi condition. Under the assumption of a frictionless market, the state of some market cannot be perceived oppositionally by different agents, and depends on the existence of some agent with a binding constraint or an excess demand/supply: the *state of market* k, s_k, can therefore de defined by sgn Σs^i_k. The vector s of states of all markets in the economy describes the prevailing *régime* in the economy. Since the number of régimes may be great, viz 3^m, the occurence of a Walrasian equilibrium régime (with $s = 0$) is not so evident.

Definition. A disequilibrium allocation $(z^H, p, g^H, \bar{g}^H)$ in the economy E which satisfies the conditions of voluntary trade and frictionless markets is called *Drèze-equilibrium,* resp. a *K-equilibrium,* depending on the condition (Drèze, resp. Hahn-Negishi) chosen to define a frictionless market.

It may be noticed that the consistency condition on trades z^i above can be replaced by a consistency condition on constraints g^i, where $g^i = g^i_+ - g^i_-$ and $g^i = -g^i_-, \bar{g}^i = g^i_+$. This approach has been followed by Malinvaud and Younès (1974).

Which efficiency criterion may be applied? Following Drèze and Müller (1979) criteria can be defined on three levels: relative to the (market) consistency constraint, relative to consistency and price-budget constraint, and relative to additional quantitative constraints in any market. This can be made precise as follows: Let $P(z^H) := \Pi P^i(z^i)$, the set of allocations which are preferred to z^H by all agents. Given prices p, three sets of *admissible allocations* can be defined:

$$\mathscr{A} := \{z^H \in Z^H \mid \Sigma z^i = 0\}$$

$$\mathscr{A}(p) := \{z^H \in Z^H \mid \Sigma z^i = 0, \quad \text{and for all} \quad i \in H : pz^i = 0\}$$

$$\mathscr{A}_k(p, g^H, \bar{g}^H) := \{z^H \in \mathscr{A}(p) \mid \quad \text{for all} \quad i \in H,$$
$$j \neq 0, k : g^i_j \leqq z^i_j \leqq \bar{g}^i_j\}$$

The set of *Pareto optimal* allocations in E (first level) is defined by:

$$\mathscr{P} := \{z^H \in Z^H \mid P(z^H) \cap \mathscr{A} = \phi\}$$

The set of *efficient* allocations *relative to a price p* is defined by:

$$\mathscr{P}(p) := \{z^H \in Z^H \mid P(z^H) \cap \mathscr{A}(p) = \phi\}$$

The set of *market by market efficient* allocations relative to a price p in E:

$$\mathscr{P}(p, M) := \{z^H \in Z^H \mid \exists g^H, \bar{g}^H : \forall k \in M :$$
$$P(z^H) \cap \mathscr{A}_k(p, g^H, \bar{g}^H) = \phi\}$$

It has been remarked by Grandmont (1977b) that a K-equilibrium is efficient market by market. It may of course also have a higher level of efficiency, but then by coincidence or under special conditions. If a K-equilibrium is not efficient relative to the given price, it is due to the fact that recontracting by agents can only take place market by market. Since money is exchanged with commodities and direct barter is ruled out, no other information from other markets is available than the quantitative constraints perceived by the agents individually. A kind of interdependent rationing has been suggested by Drèze and Müller (1979) and results in a so called coupons-equilibrium. The necessary information from other markets is then obtained from a special coupons market on which uniform prices in terms of coupons are determined. Trading may not be voluntary any more, however. Examples of a K-equilibrium and a coupons equilibrium are given in fig. 4, which is drawn in the plane of admissible allocation relative to a given price p. The point K describes a K-allocation in which there is an excess supply on both markets. The demand z^j_{1+} of good 1 by agent j is perceived as a constraint z^i_{1-} on market 1 by agent i. Given this constraint, ith optimal supply of good 2 is equal to z^i_{2+}, which is again perceived as constraint z^j_{2-} by agent j on market 2. This example corresponds with a Keynesian situation in a simple macroeconomic model which is presented in the next section.

3. An Economy with Effort

The economy E which is introduced in section 2 is extended here such that every individual agent is endowed with a commodity 'effort' that can be used to obtain or promote transactions according to a given technology T in the economy $\bar{E}$.

The transaction technology relates trades (viz. on the long side of any market) with effort. Since agents are restricted by this technology, (shadow) prices in terms of effort can be defined for each allocation if the usual conditions are satisfied. An allocation is called an effort equilibrium if these prices sustain both the transaction technology and the agents' preferred sets of trades, which trades have to be compatible between agents.

An economy with effort consists of the following objects:

$$\bar{E} := \{N, H, (\bar{X}^i, \precsim^i, \bar{w}^i), \Delta, Q, T\},$$

respectively, the set of commodities N, the set of agents H, each characterized by a consumption set $\bar{X}^i$, a preference relation $\precsim^i$ and a bundle of initial resources; further a set of money prices Δ and of effort prices Q, and a transaction technology T.

There are $m+2$ goods, $\bar{x} := (x_0, x_1, \ldots, x_m, x_e) \in \mathbb{R}^n$. The last commodity is called *effort* and characterized by the following properties:

(a) It belongs personally to every agent, who has a limited positive capacity of effort, w^i_e, for all $i \in H$.

(b) Effort used, $z^i_e := z^i_e - w^i_e$, or $e^i := -z^i_e \geqq 0$, is able to promote a specific economic purpose, and is the only input in the transaction technology T in this model.

(c) Effort not used is consumed, $x^i_e := w^i_e - e^i$, and is called *ease*; it is strictly preferred by each agent.

(d) The social efficiency of effort has been gauged through the initial distribution $w^H_e := (w^1_e, \ldots, w^h_e)$. This implies that the amount e^i of effort used may not coincide with the personal perception of effort used. It also follows that a price of effort is uniform over all agents, although its height will be seen to vary.

Effort may be marketable (as services are), but in this section it is assumed not to be marketable so its price in terms of money equals zero. Call $\bar{z}^i := (z^i, z^i_e)$ agents ith *trade plan* and $\bar{z}^H := (\bar{z}^1, \ldots, \bar{z}^h) \in \mathbb{R}^{hn}$ a trade plan (not necessarily consistent) in $\bar{E}$. The following definitions and notations are used.

The economy's excess demand $z := \Sigma z^i$ has sign $s := \operatorname{sgn} z \in \mathbb{R}^{n-1}$. An individual $i \in H$ perceives a constraint on market $k \in M$ if the sign of his non-zero trade plan z^i_k is equal to the state on that market (the sign of the excess demand). A vector $z^{+i} \in \mathbb{R}^{n-1}$ with components consisting of those plans and zero otherwise, is called an agent's *long-side plan*, z^{+i}. An individual perceives no constraints on market k if the sign of his trade plan z^i_k is not equal to the state of the market. The vector $z^{-i} \in \mathbb{R}^{n-1}$ with those components from z^i which have a sign opposite to the state of the market and otherwise zero, is called an agent's *short-side plan*, z^{-i}. The vector of plans made by agent i on markets in equilibrium is denoted by z^{oi}. Notice that $z^i = (z^{+i} - z^{-i}) + z^{oi}$. Further, the *perceived state of the markets* by agent i is, $s^i := \operatorname{sgn} z^{+i}$.

Next, *total long-side plans*, are denoted by $z^+ := \Sigma z^{+i}$, and *total short-side plans* by $z^- := \Sigma z^{-i}$. Excess demand is thus expressed in terms of these plans:

$$z = z^+ - z^-.$$

Given a trade plan $\bar{z}^H$ in $\bar{E}$, the set of markets M can be partitioned in a set of disequilibrium markets M^+, with $z_k \neq 0$ for $k \in M^+$, and a set of equilibrium markets M^0.

Since trade plans are a function of prices p, so is the set is (dis)equilibrium markets.

In each disequilibrium market $k \in M^+$, the set of agents is partitioned in agents on the long-side, H^+_k, and agents on the short-side or with zero transaction plans, H^-_k:

$$H^+_k := \{i \in H \mid \operatorname{sgn} z^i_k = \operatorname{sgn} z_k \neq 0\}.$$

By using effort the agents $i \in H^+_k$ are supposed to be able to influence the trade plan $\bar{z}^H$. This also suppresses the desired trade volumes to the (minimum) levels, offered by the short side agents $i \in H^-_k$.

Effort-prices are thus oriented towards the direction in which expansion of a transaction is sought. Agents on the short side, H^-_k, are assumed not to use effort, neither for finding agents on the long side (frictionless market) nor for trying to trade a lesser volume than planned (voluntary exchange): see for example fig. 1, agent 2.

However, if an equilibrium between effort used and transactions obtained has been attained, then the distinction between the long and the short side of a market cannot be derived any more from a trade plan $\bar{z}^H$ in $\bar{E}$. It is replaced by a partition of agents in those who are using effort on market k and those

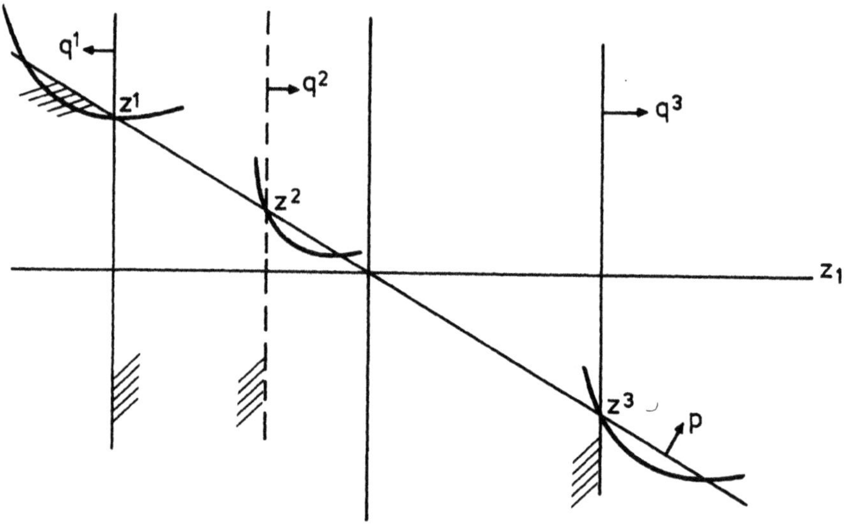

Fig. 1.

who are not. The assumption about the use of effort implies that this partition coincides with the other, so the same notation, H_k^+ and H_k^-, will be used.

Suppose an agent i uses an amount e_k^i of effort on market k, and let $q_k^i := e_k^i/z_k^i$ be called the *effective effort price* for i on market k. This price depends on two factors:

(i) the technology of agent i and the other agents in searching and obtaining transactions;

(ii) the state of the market, because no effort is needed if the agent is on the short side whatever be his technology.

The discussion about the technology can and will be postponed to section 6, if one accepts as a result from such a technology the emergence of *personal potential effort prices* $\hat{q}_k^i$. Under suitable conditions, e.g. if the pressure by one agent on a market is felt equally by all agents, then these prices may be *uniform* over all agents. It follows that an effective effort price is equal to:

$$q_k^i = \begin{cases} \hat{q}_k^i, & \text{if} \quad \hat{q}_k^i z_k^i > 0 \\ 0, & \text{if} \quad \hat{q}_k^i z_k^i \leqq 0 \end{cases} \tag{3.1}$$

Since the amount of effort e_k^i by agent i on market k is not assumed to be specified, condition (3.1) will serve as a definition instead.

Given a potential effort price $\hat{q}^i$ for an agent i, his 'effort-budget' is given by $\hat{q}^i z^i \leqq \hat{q}_e^i z_e^i$. Using (3.1) and the notation $e^i := z_e^i$, this inequality can be replaced by:

$$q_+^i z_+^i + q_-^i z_-^i \leqq q_e^i e^i. \tag{3.2}$$

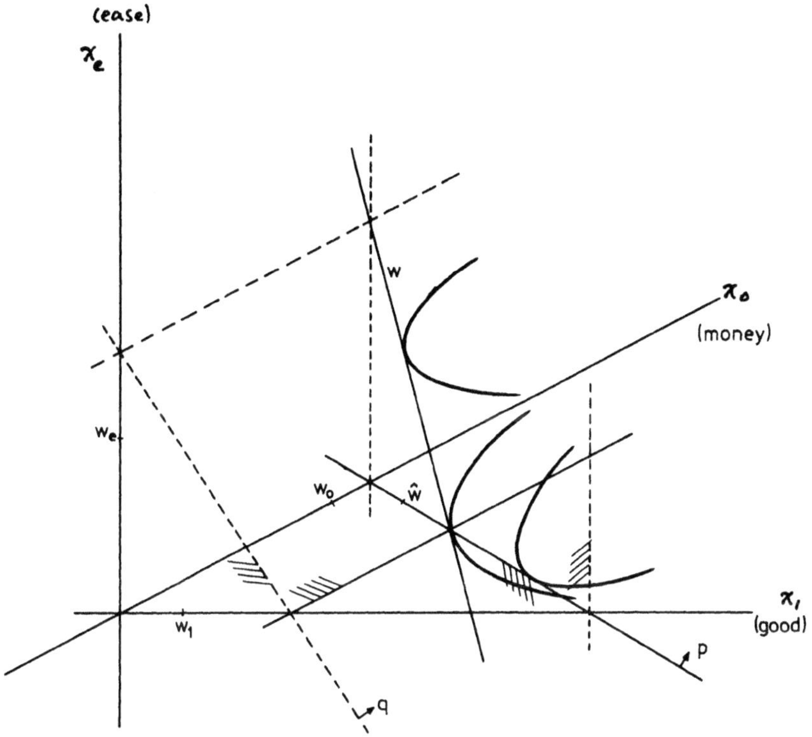

Fig. 2. The budgetset $\bar{B}^i(\bar{p}, \bar{q})$.

It should be noticed that (3.2) can be compared with the condition of voluntary trade in the sense that there is no restriction opposite in sign to the direction of effort used to realize a transaction: $q^i_+ z^i_- = q^i_- z^i_+ = 0$.

Given prices $(\bar{p}, \bar{q}^i)$ and $\bar{z}^i := (z^i, e^i)$, the budget set of an agent i is thus given by

$$\bar{B}^i(\bar{p},\bar{q}^i) := \{\bar{z}^i \in \bar{Z}^i \,|\, \bar{p}\bar{z}^i \leqq 0,\ q^i_+ z^i_+ + q^i_- z^i_- \leqq q^i_e e^i\}. \quad (3.3)$$

Let $\bar{P}^i(\bar{z}^i)$ be the set of elements in $\bar{Z}^i$ preferred to $\bar{z}^i$, which defines the preference correspondence $\bar{P}^i$ in $\bar{Z}^i$ for each agent i. The agents' *optimal choice* is then an element of the set

$$\bar{f}^i(\bar{p},\bar{q}^i) := \{\bar{z}^i \in \bar{B}^i(\bar{p},\bar{q}^i) \,|\, \bar{P}^i(\bar{z}^i) \cap \bar{B}^i(\bar{p},\bar{q}^i) = \phi\}. \quad (3.4)$$

Definition 3.5

For the economy $\bar{E}$ an *effort-equilibrium* $(\bar{z}^H, \bar{p}, \bar{q}^H)$ is a list of transactions z^H, an effort distribution e^H, a money-price $\bar{p} := (p, 0)$ with $p \in \Delta$, and a list of (effective) effort prices $\bar{q}^H := (0^H, q^H) \in: \mathbb{R}^{hn}$, such that:

(i) $\quad \bar{z}^i \in \bar{f}^i(\bar{p}, \bar{q}^i), \quad$ for $\quad i \in H,$

(ii) $\Sigma z^i = 0,$

(iii) $q^i_k q^j_k \geqq 0, \quad \text{for} \quad i,j \in H, \quad k \in M.$

Condition (iii) is evidently equivalent to the assumption of frictionless markets.

Given effort-prices $\bar{q}^H$, an agent is supposed to be able to increase his trade plan by increasing his effort. However, if all agents increase their effort on a specific market then this will certainly increase the effort-prices on that market, and leave the trade plans unchanged, presumably. If such a strategy is adapted for all markets simultaneously, then the social efficacy of effort, expressed in the price q_e, declines. More effort will then be used by everybody without changing much in the allocation. This behaviour is possible in a Nash game, and the existence of a Nash equilibrium implies that there exist an allocation at which no agent is inclined to change his actions, given the actions of other agents.

The following *assumptions* on the economy $\bar{E}$ are made:

A.1. $\bar{X}^i$ is a closed subset in $\mathbb{R}^n$ with $\bar{X}^i \subset \bar{X}^i + \mathbb{R}^n_+$.

A.2. $\bar{w}^i \in \operatorname{int} \bar{X}^i$.

A.3. The preference correspondence $\bar{P}^i$ in $\bar{X}^i$ defined by $\bar{\succ}^i$ has an open graph, is irreflexive and convex valued.

A.4. More of commodities money (x_0) and ease (x_e) is always strictly preferred by each agent.

A.5. The (potential) effort prices are uniform over all agents, i.e. $q = q^i$, for $i \in H$.

Assumption A.5. implies, of course, condition (iii) in the definition 3.5 of an effort equilibrium. It also follows that each agent on the long side of a market obtains a relative transaction volume that is equal to his relative effort used in that market.

4. Existence of an Effort-Equilibrium

Theorem. For an economy $\bar{E}$ with a transaction technology for effort, that satisfies A.1, to A.5 there exists an effort-equilibrium $(\bar{z}^H, \bar{p}, \bar{q})$.

Proof. The economy is converted into an abstract economy $\tilde{E}$ with $h + 2$ agents or players. A Nash-equilibrium in this economy exists if some conditions are met as specified by Schafer and Sonnenschein (1975): lemma 1. Next it is shown that this equilibrium corresponds to an effort equilibrium: lemma 2.

Define the effort-price set relative to an effort allocation e^H by

$$Q(e^H) := \{\bar{q} \in \mathbb{R}^n \mid q_0 = 0, \quad q_e = e - \|q\|, \quad \text{and} \\ \|q\| \leqq e\}$$

where

$$e := \sum_i e^i \quad \text{and} \quad \|q\| := \sum_{k=0}^{m} |q_k|.$$

The budget correspondence $\bar{B}^i$ in (3.3) is then redefined by

$$\bar{B}^i(e^H, \bar{p}, \bar{q}) := \left\{ \bar{z}^i \in \bar{Z} \;\middle|\; \begin{array}{l} pz^i \leqq 0, \\ q_+ z_+^i + q_- z_-^i \leqq q_e e^i \end{array} \right\}$$

The abstract economy

$$\tilde{E} := \{\tilde{H}, \tilde{X}^h, \tilde{P}^h : \tilde{X} \to \tilde{X}^h, \tilde{C}^h : \tilde{X} \to \tilde{X}^h\}$$

is defined as follows:

$$\tilde{H} := \{H, 0, e\}, \quad i \in H$$

$$\tilde{X} := \Pi X^h, \quad h \in \tilde{H}$$

$$\tilde{X}^i := \{\bar{z}^i \in \bar{Z}^i \,|\, \exists (\bar{z}^H, \bar{p}, \bar{q}) \in \tilde{X} : \bar{z}^i \in \bar{B}^i\}$$

$$\tilde{C}^i(\bar{z}^H, \bar{p}, \bar{q}) := \bar{B}^i(e^H, \bar{p}, \bar{q}) \cap \tilde{X}^i$$

$$\tilde{P}^i(\bar{z}^H, \bar{p}, \bar{q}) := \bar{P}^i(\bar{z}^i) \cap \tilde{X}^i$$

$$\tilde{X}^0 := \Delta$$

$$\tilde{C}^0(\bar{z}^H, \bar{p}, \bar{q}) := \Delta$$

$$\tilde{P}^0(\bar{z}^H, \bar{p}, \bar{q}) := \{\tilde{p} \in \Delta \,|\, \tilde{p}\bar{z} > \bar{p}\bar{z}, \quad \text{for} \quad \bar{z} := \Sigma \bar{z}^i\}$$

$$\tilde{X}^e := Q(\bar{w}_e^H)$$

$$\tilde{C}^e(\bar{z}^H, \bar{p}, \bar{q}) := Q(\bar{z}_e^H)$$

$$\tilde{P}^e(\bar{z}^H, \bar{p}, \bar{q}) := \left\{ \tilde{q} \in Q(\bar{z}_e^H) \;\middle|\; \begin{array}{l} \tilde{q}_+(z_+ + \bar{p} - \bar{\bar{p}}) + \tilde{q}_-(z_- + \bar{p} - \underline{p}) \\ > q_+(z_+ + \bar{p} - \bar{\bar{p}}) + \\ \quad + q_-(z_- + \bar{p} - \underline{p}) \end{array} \right\}$$

with $\bar{\bar{p}} := (\bar{p}, 0)$ and $\underline{p} := (p, 0)$, the upper and lower bound on prices.

An action $(\bar{z}^H, \bar{p}, \bar{q})$ is a Nash-equilibrium in $\tilde{E}$ if

(i) $$(\bar{z}^H, \bar{p}, \bar{q}) \in \prod_h \tilde{C}^h(\bar{z}^H, \bar{p}, \bar{q}), \quad \text{and}$$

(ii) $$\tilde{P}^h(\bar{z}^H, \bar{p}, \bar{q}) \cap \tilde{C}^h(\bar{z}^H, \bar{p}, \bar{q}) = \phi, \quad \text{for all} \quad h \in \tilde{H}.$$

Lemma 1. There exists a Nash-equilibrium $(\bar{z}^H, \bar{p}, \bar{q})$ in $\tilde{E}$, which lies on the boundary of the constraint sets.

Proof. The following 4 conditions have to be satisfied for existence:

(1) $\tilde{X}^h$ is compact and nonempty for all $h \in \tilde{H}$.
For $h \in H$: closedness from A.1 and boundedness from A.2.
For $h = 0$: by definition.
For $h = e$: by definition and from A.2.

(2) $\tilde{C}^h$ is nonempty, compact- and convex-valued.
For $h \in \tilde{H}$: by definition.

(3) $\tilde{C}^h$ is continuous.
For $i \in H$: since $\tilde{X}$ is closed it follows that $\tilde{C}^i$ has a closed graph; compactness of $\tilde{X}^i$ implies that $\tilde{C}^i$ is upper-hemicontinuous. Since $\bar{w}^i \in \text{int}\, \bar{X}^i$, which includes effort, $\tilde{C}^i(\bar{z}^H, \bar{p}, \bar{q}^H) \cap \text{int}\, \bar{Z}^i \neq \phi$. From standard arguments it follows that $\tilde{C}^i$ is lower hemi-continuous.
For $h = e$ again closedness and compactness of $\bar{X}$ imply that $\tilde{C}^e$ is upper hemi-continuous. If some e^e converges to 0, then $\tilde{C}^e(\bar{z}^H, \bar{p}, \bar{q}^e) \cap \text{int}\, Q^e(\bar{z}_e^H) = \phi$.
If, however, Σe^j converges to zero then any price sequence converges to zero: $Q^e(0) = \{0\}$. It follows that $\tilde{C}^e$ is lower hemi-continuous.

(4) $\tilde{P}^h$ is convex-valued and irreflexive, and has an open graph.
For $h \in H$: from A.3.
For $h \notin H$: by definition.

(5) Since from the definitions and A.4 follows that $(\bar{z}^H, \bar{p}, \bar{q})$ belongs to the closure of $\tilde{P}^h(\bar{z}^H, \bar{p}, \bar{q})$, the Nash-equilibrium lies also on the boundary of the constraint sets.

Lemma 2. A Nash-equilibrium in $\tilde{E}$ corresponds to an effort equilibrium in $\bar{E}$.

Proof. Suppose that for some $k \in M^+$, $z_k > 0$, resp. $z_k < 0$. Then the money price 'agent' puts $\bar{p}_k = \bar{\bar{p}}_k$, resp. $\bar{p}_k = \bar{p}_k$. Individual effort prices are then raised until $e = \Sigma\, \|q^i\|$, and $q_e = 0$.
Thus, for at least $i \in H^{+k}$, $qz^i > 0$. This contradicts with $qz^i \leqq q_e z_e^i = 0$.
Therefore, $z_k = 0$ for all $k \in M$.
The other conditions are trivially met. □

5. Characteristic of an Effort-Equilibrium

One of the main features of an effort-equilibrium is the *asymmetric-treatment* of agents on a market. A flexible market price expresses social scarcity and is neutral to all agents. This is not the case if the market price is fixed or inflexible. Then one has to distinguish traders on the long side of a disequilibrium market $k \in M^+$, and traders on the short side. The first group H^{+k} is discriminated to pay also, prices in terms of effort.

Let $\mu^i > 0$ be the marginal rate of substitution between money and effort, then (see fig. 3)

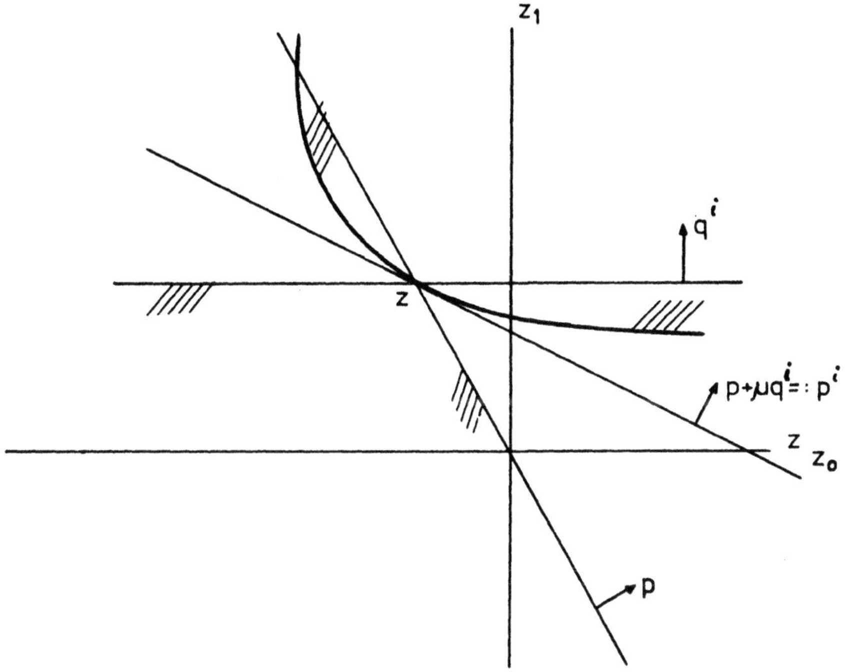

Fig. 3.

$$p_k^i := p_k + \mu^i q_k^{+i} := \begin{cases} p_k + \mu^i q_k^i, & \text{if} \quad i \in H^{+k} \\ p_k, & \text{if} \quad i \notin H^{+k} \end{cases} \tag{5.1}$$

With respect to *efficiency* the following can be said.

There are two reasons causing a loss in efficiency with respect to the equilibrium concepts defined in section 2. Firstly, the fact that using effort is at a cost of welfare; this cost is related with the fact that the rationing process corresponding with an effort-equilibrium is *self-organizing* and does not need to be carried out by a rationing institution (that is usually assumed to perform its activities without costs!). Secondly, the type of equilibrium is of *Nash,* which means that agents decide to use effort, given the use of effort by other agents. This makes an increase of effort by all agents possible without changing the allocation of trades much, which is evidently not very efficient. Therefore, the most one can say about efficiency is that an effort-equilibrium is *relative efficient,* firstly with respect to an effort allocation e^H, second with respect to a fixed price p determining the budget constraint, and thirdly to the market-by-market restrictions on transaction plans (see fig. 4).

Since an effort-equilibrium does not allow for compensation or interdependent rationing (which is typical for a coupons-equilibrium of Drèze and Müller, 1979), it is not relative-efficient at the second level (see section 2) unless in special circumstances.

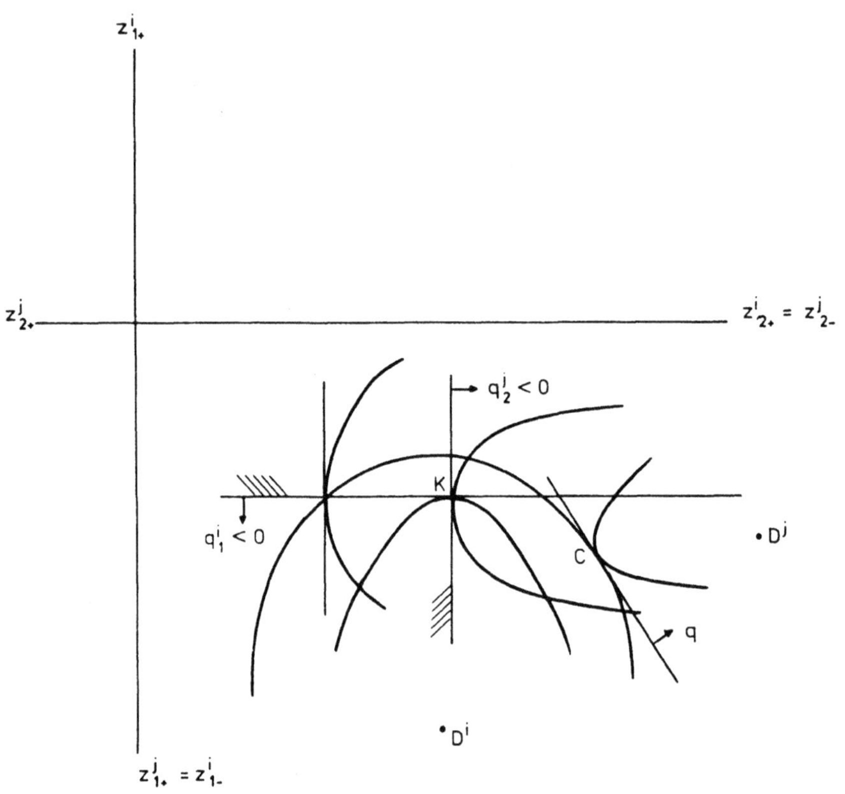

Fig. 4.

But neither is the individual agent passive in the allocation between markets. In fact, trade is not completely voluntary because some welfare has to be lost by using effort in order to obtain transactions.

However, if this effect has no influence on the composition of the bundle chosen, then an effort equilibrium is market-by-market efficient in the sense used by Grandmont. This condition is obtained by requiring separability of effort in the preference structure.

An agent's preference ordering is said to be *separable in effort* if the following equality holds for all $\bar{z} \in \bar{Z}^i$:

$$\bar{P}^i(z, z_e) = \{(\tilde{z}, \tilde{z}_e) \in \bar{Z}^i \,|\, (\tilde{z}, \tilde{z}_e) \in \bar{P}^i(z, z_e) \quad \text{and} \quad (z, \tilde{z}_e) \in \bar{P}^i(z, z_e)\}.$$

Definition. An effort equilibrium $(\bar{z}^H, \bar{p}, \bar{q}^H)$ in $\bar{E}$ is *relative efficient* with respect to the price p, the effort allocation e^H and market-by-market, if the disequilibrium allocation $(z^H, p, -z_-^H, z_+^H)$ is efficient market-by-market.

Property (efficiency)

(1) An effort-equilibrium is *relative efficient* in the sense mentioned above.

(2) If the preferences in the economy $\bar{E}$ separable in effort, then the set of trade allocations z^H in E that are sustained by a *K-equilibrium* is equal to the set of trade allocations $\bar{z}^H$ in $\bar{E}$ which can be sustained by an *effort-equilibrium.*

Proof.

(1) Suppose the effective demand on market k by agent $i \in H^{+k}$ is not equal to z_k^i, then $\Sigma z_k^i \neq 0$.

(2) Let $(z^H, p, g^H, \bar{g}^H)$ be a K-equilibrium. Then $g^H \leqq -z_-^H$ and $\bar{g}^H \geqq z_+^H$, and $(z^H, p, -z_-^H, z_+^H)$ is also a K-equilibrium. Choose $\bar{q}^H \in Q^H(e^H)$, for some $e^H \leqq w_e^H$, such that sgn $q :=$ sgn $(\Sigma q^i) =$ sgn r, defined above. Let $q_k z_k^i = q_e e_k^i$ whenever $q_k z_k^i \geqq 0$. Since $q_+ z_+^i + q_- z_-^i \leqq q_e e^i = q_e(\Sigma e_k^i)$, it follows that $z^i \in B^i(p, q)$ and $P^i(z^i) \cap B^i(p, q) = \phi$. Separability of $\bar{P}^i$ implies that for $(z^i, z_e^i) \in \bar{B}^i(\bar{p}, \bar{q})$, $\bar{P}(z^i, z_e^i) \cap \bar{B}^i(\bar{p}, \bar{q}) = \phi$. Thus $(\bar{z}^H, \bar{p}, \bar{q}^H)$ is an effort-equilibrium.
The inverse is easily checked. □

The main feature of a K-equilibrium is that all trades are against money and no information about other markets is obtained unless by the perceived rations. This character is also maintained in case of an effort-equilibrium, and although the use of effort is not independent of other agents, it is independent in the sense that no agent will withdraw from some market to be compensated in some other market. Only this type of interdependence can raise the level of efficiency.

The most important feature of an effort equilibrium, the asymmetry in the treatment of agents on the long side and on the short side of a market, has some important implications.

Firstly, a uniform indicator for social scarcity is ruled out, and composite *prices discriminate between the two groups* H^{+k} and H^{-k}, for each $k \in M$. Let $H^+ := \bigcup_{k \in M} H^{+k}$.

If the trade off between effort and money, μ^i for $i \in H^+$, is uniform for all agents, say μ, then the following values in equilibrium can be calculated, which are valid for agents as well as the economy:

consumption:	$px + \mu\bar{q}(\bar{w} + \bar{z}^+) = px + \mu[qz^+ + q_e x_e]$
initial wealth:	$pw + \mu q_e w_e$
trade value:	$pz + \mu[qz^+ - q_e e] = 0$

So both consumption and trade values depend on the class to which the individual belongs: H^+ or H^-, eventually specified by market.

Secondly, the asymmetry of effort prices *reveals the asymmetric pressure of excess on markets continuously*, even when these are reduced to zero by an equilibrium composition of money and effort prices. It can thus serve as an indicator of the size of disequilibrium (see Grandmont, 1977).

Let $f^i(p, q^+, e^i)$ be the trade function of agent i. Then q^+ indicates the vector of (uniform) effort-prices as far as these are active for agent i. Thus i maximizes $\prec^i$ over

$$\{z^i \in Z^i \mid pz^i \leqq 0 \quad \text{and} \quad q_+^+ z_+^i + q_-^+ z_-^i \leqq q_e e^i\}$$

The following *interpretation* may be clarifying. Consider the simple macro model below, and let effort be revealed by *time*.

6. An Example: a Simple Macroeconomic Model

The microeconomic foundations of macroeconomics can be illustrated by a *simple macroeconomic model* developed by Malinvaud (1977), Böhm (1978, 1980) and Muellbauer and Portes (1978).

Suppose there are two agents, a producer and a consumer, in an economy with three commodities: money, consumption goods and labor. Assuming voluntary trade and a frictionless market (which condition amounts to the minimum condition of supply and demand), there are 9 régimes imaginable in the economy. For it is assumed that the money market is always in equilibrium. Whether these 9 régimes are possible depends on the richness of the model constructed. Malinvaud (1977) and Böhm (1978) for example, did not allow producers to allocate money (and production decisions) over time, and found one corresponding régime to be impossible. Let the commodities consumption – goods and labor be denoted by x and l and both money and the wage rate be expressed in terms of the price of the consumption good, m and w. The constrained choice correspondences of agent 1, the consumer, are:

$$f_x^1(m, w, x, l, \bar{x}, \bar{l}) \quad \text{and} \quad f_l^1(m, w, x, l, \bar{x}, \bar{l}).$$

Voluntary trade suppresses the constraints x and $\bar{l}$ in the arguments. And, since the prices are supposed to be constant, m and w are also deleted in the arguments.

Next, the constrained choice correspondence is replaced by the effective choice correspondence, and called effective demand or supply according to their sign:

$$d_x(l) := \tilde{f}_{x+}^1(l) \quad \text{and} \quad s_l(\bar{x}) := \tilde{f}_{l-}^1(\bar{x})$$

where the constraints may be replaced by ∞ if no constraint applies. Any constraint is determined on a market by the minimum condition if there is excess supply or demand. If no constraint is perceived, the constraint is set infinity. On this way, the following table can be derived (the signs between brackets indicate the states of the commodity, resp. labor market as defined in 2.1).

It is evident that the spill-over effects of constraints from one market to the other depend on the prevailing régime in the economy. For example, in a

Table 1. Régimes in a simple macro model.

$d_x(l) = x < s_x(\infty)$	$d_x(\infty) = x < s_x(\infty)$	$d_x(\infty) = x < s_x(\bar{l})$
$s_l(\infty) > l = d_l(x)$	$s_l(\infty) = l = d_l(x)$	$s_l(\infty) = \bar{l} < d_l(x)$
Keynes: (–, –)	(–, 0)	Underconsumption: (–, +)
$d_x(l) = x = s_x(\infty)$	$d_x(\infty) = x = s_x(\infty)$	$d_x(\infty) = x = s_x(\bar{l})$
$s_l(\infty) > l = d_l(\infty)$	$s_l(\infty) = l = d_l(\infty)$	$s_l(\infty) = \bar{l} < d_l(\infty)$
(0, –)	Walras: (0, 0)	(0, +)
$d_x(l) > \bar{x} = s_x(\infty)$	$d_x(\infty) > \bar{x} = s_x(\infty)$	$d_x(\infty) > \bar{x} = s_x(\bar{l})$
$s_l(\bar{x}) > l = d_l(\infty)$	$s_l(\bar{x}) = l = d_l(\infty)$	$s_l(\bar{x}) = \bar{l} < d_l(\infty)$
Classical: (+, –)	(+, 0)	Inflation: (+, +)

Keynesian régime of excess supply in both markets, the 'equilibrium' transactions are determined by consumers' demand for goods and producers demand for labor. In a régime of Classical unemployment it is the producers' supply and demand functions that determine the allocation (and the constraints).

This dependence of demand and supply functions upon the prevailing régime constitutes the main problem in the so-called disequilibrium econometrics. It is not only the functional parameters which have to be estimated, but also the régime in which they are valid has to be determined from the sample data. One may say that equilibrium itself (as a special régime) has become a testable hypothesis [11].

This régime is determined by the signs of effort used in each market. The consumer a spends q_l^a units time to get a unit of a job and q_x^a units of time to get a unit of commodities. The total amount of time spent is equal to e^a.

For example, it costs 5 weeks (10% of a manyear) to get a job and 2 weeks to get a bundle of commodities, both for a year, and 10 weeks are used for these transactions ($= e^a$). If these are equilibrium values, then the joboffer, $-l$, with wage p_L has been got for $(-q_L)(-l)$ weeks, and the commodity bundle x with price p_x has been bought using $q_x x$ weeks. In this case, both constraints are supposed to be active for the consumer (a régime of classical unemployment).

If one can find a correct expression for effort, such as waiting time, research and communication costs, length of waiting lists, or do it yourself activities, imports from abroad, promotion and advertising, secondary (non pecuniar) conditions, legal restrictions (e.g. a law on selling agricultural properties), fringe benefits, etc., then these variables determine effort prices and reveal market pressures. Using these arguments one obtains a system of trade functions as described in table 2.

Since the sign of q indicates the state of a market, it is evident that the effort prices q describe similar régimes as the effective trade functions in table 1.

Table 2. Trade functions in a simple macro-model.

$d_x(-q_l) = z = s_x(-q_x)$ $s_l(-q_l) = l = d_l(-q_x)$	$d_x(0) = x = s_x(-q_x)$ $s_l(0) = l = d_l(-q_x)$	$d_x(0) = x = s_x(-q_x, +q_l)$ $s_l(0) = l = d_l(-q_x, +q_l)$
$d_x(-q_l) = x = s_x(0)$ $s_l(-q_l) = l = d_l(0)$	$d_x(0) = x = s_x(0)$ $s_l(0) = l = d_l(0)$	$d_x(0) = x = s_x(+q_l)$ $s_l(0) = l = d_l(+q_l)$
$d_x(+q_x, -q_l) = x = s_x(0)$ $s_l(+q_x, -q_l) = l = d_l(0)$	$d_x(+q_x) = x = s_x(0)$ $s_l(+q_x) = l = d_l(0)$	$d_x(+q_x) = x = s_x(+q_l)$ $s_l(+q_x) = l = d_l(+q_l)$

(money prices deleted; effort prices positive if sign neglected).

The effort prices *reduce* effective (and notional) *trades to the minimum of supply and demand* (see fig. 5). This is the last characteristic mentioned here. It is an essential feature of the type of disequilibrium models which have drawn attention recently. But it is not necessarily the wisest policy to push trade to the minimum position.

In fact, by supporting the minimum of demand or supply, one can raise trade to a higher volume. Support, if not given by monetary subsidies, can be given through rights or claims, and allows 'effort' prices without sign restriction. Such a mechanism is treated in Ruys (1980) and strongly resembles Drèze and Müller's (1979) 'coupons equilibrium'. Another natural effect of effort would be that it alters the decision of the trading partner towards the bid or demand of the partner using effort, thereby also raising the volume of trade. The reasons for revising a trade plan for a trader on the short side, however, can only be found in this model on other markets (spill over effects). It would be interesting to introduce *incomplete information* about the quality of the commodity in question (at a given price) from the part of a trader on the short side, which can be supplemented by the trader using effort. A host of ideas on this subject in a partial equilibrium frame work can be found in Akerlof (1970, 1976), Arrow (1973), Baily (1974), Riley (1975), Rosen (1974), Spence (1974, 1977), Stigler (1962) and the survey article by Hirschleifer and Riley (1979).

It is presumably in this aspect of uncertainty that the so-called régime of Keynesian unemployment contains only half the story Keynes has told. For, by reducing the uncertainty about expectation of producers, a chain of reactions is set up raising the volume of trade. This may be interpreted as lowering the price of production and so requires a dynamic analysis of the model of section 2 [9, 34]. One can, however, interpret this aspect in various ways, and expand the model accordingly.

7. The Transaction Technology and Some of Its Interpretations

A *transaction technology* T in $\bar{E}$ is a relation in the space of trade allocation plans $\mathbb{R}^{hn}$, with $\bar{z}^i := (z^i, z_e^i) = (z^i, -e^i) \in \mathbb{R}^{hn}$ satisfying the following

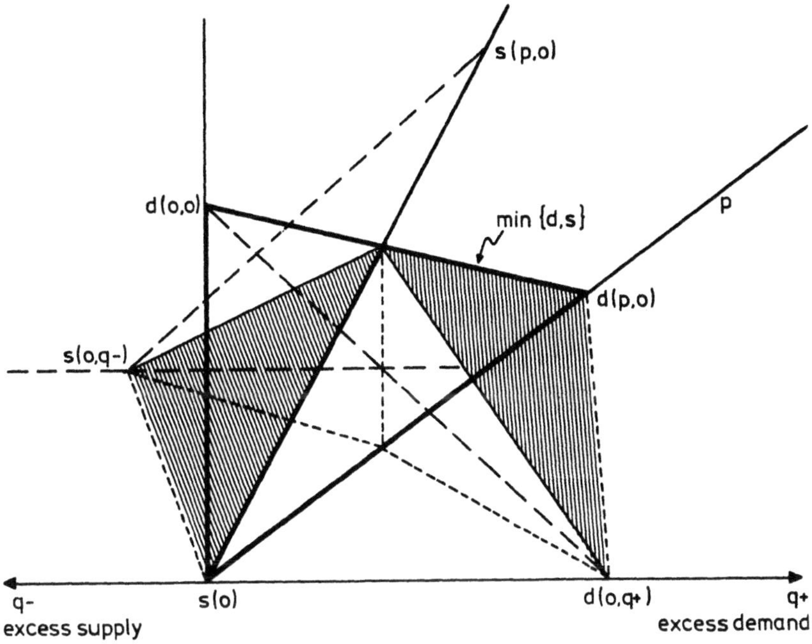

Fig. 5.

properties for each $i \in H, k \in M$:

($T1$) (on the use of effort) $\exists k \in M$: $z_k z_k^i > 0 \Leftrightarrow e^i > 0$, where $z_0 \equiv 0$.

($T2$) (no 'earning' of effort) $(-|z^i|, z_e^i) \leqq 0$.

($T3$) (monotonicity) $\bar{z}^H \in T$ and $(|\tilde{z}^i|, \tilde{z}_e^i) \leqq (|z^i|, z_e^i) \Rightarrow \tilde{\bar{z}} \in T$.

($T4$) (social interaction) if $\tilde{\bar{z}}^H, \bar{z}^H$ and $\tilde{z}_{(k)}^H = \tilde{z}_{(k)}^H$ then

$$\exists j \in H^{+k}: \tilde{z}_k^{+j} > z_k^{+j} \Rightarrow \forall i \in H^{+k}: \tilde{e}^i > e^i.$$

($T5$) (homogeneity of effort) $\bar{z}^H \in T$ and $\alpha > 0 \Rightarrow (z^H, \alpha z_e^H) \in T$.

($T6$) T is closed and convex.

A transaction technology is said to be *linear* if T is a convex cone.

In the sequel a linear transaction technology will be assumed to avoid unessential complications.

It follows that all markets are frictionless: $s_k s_k^i \geqq 0$ for all i, k, and that $s_k^i = 0$ is equivalent to i is not using effort on market k. Since $0^H \in T$, all transactions may be considered as voluntary.

It may be noticed that extra conditions on the transaction technology can be made, which make this theory applicable on various economic environments. For example, if for some good k and for all i, $w_k^i = w_k$ is given and not marketable, then k can be interpreted as a public good. For $i \in H_k^-$, $x_k^i - w_k^i = z_k^{-i} < 0$, and for $i \in H_k^+$, $x_k^i - w_k^i > 0$. The agents in H_k^+ are prepared to use effort in order to expand the supply of public good k. If the public good k is provided by a producer at a fixed price p_k, this model can be applied on Drèze's public goods with exclusion (1980). Another application is possible on Weddepohl's (1978) model on market shares.

The price set corresponding to the linear transaction technology T in $\bar{E}$ is the dual set T^* of T in $\mathbb{R}^{hn}$. From the properties of T can be deduced the following properties of T^*.

(T^*1) (by definition)

$$\forall \bar{z} \in T: \overline{qz} \leqq 0.$$

(T^*2) (on use of effort)

$$q_k^i z_k^i \geqq 0 \quad \text{for} \quad k \in M, \quad \text{and} \quad q_e^i z_e^i \leqq 0.$$

(T^*3) (no earning of effort)

$$q_+^i z_-^i + q_-^i z_+^i = q^i(z^{oi} - z^{-i}) = 0.$$

(T^*4) (monotonicity)

$$\bar{q}^H \in T^* \quad \text{and} \quad (-|\tilde{q}^i|, \tilde{q}_e) \geqq (-|\tilde{q}^i|, q_e) \Rightarrow \tilde{\bar{q}}^H \in T^*$$

(T^*5) (homogeneity)

$$\bar{q}^H \in T^* \quad \text{and} \quad \alpha > 0 \Rightarrow (q^H, q_e^H) \in T^*$$

(T^*6) (social interaction)

$$\exists j \in H^{+k}: \tilde{q}_k^j > q_k^j \Rightarrow \forall i \in H^{+k}: \tilde{q}_k^i > q_k^i, \text{cet. par.}$$

(T^*7) T^* is closed and a convex cone.

From (T^*2) follows that $\operatorname{sgn} q^i = \operatorname{sgn} z^{+i}$, $q_0^i = 0$, and $q_e^i \geqq 0$. Property (T^*3) implies that $q^i z^i = q^i z^{+i}$.

A compact subset of T^* is obtained if effort-prices are normed by total effort used in the economy. This is done by the following correspondence, where $e := \Sigma e^i$, and $\|q^i\| = \sum_k |q_k^i|$:

$$Q(e^H) := \left\{ \bar{q}^H \in T^* \mid \forall i, \quad q_e^i = e - \sum_i \|q^i\|, \right.$$
$$\left. \sum_i \|q^i\| \leqq e \right\}.$$

8. Some Interpretations of a Transaction Technology

Firstly, it will be shown that the *theory of search* can be applied to allow for an interpretation with individual choice under certainty. The theory of search is part of the economics of information, started by Stigler (1961) and until recently mainly interested in the economics of job search: see surveys by Lippman and McCall (1976) and (1979).

The basic model is oriented on a single commodity market in which a trade offer z (a wage or a volume) is a random variable with a known and finite probability distribution F. With each draw is associated a fixed cost c. Two important properties can be derived: (a) the reservation index (wage or volume) property, which classifies offers in acceptable and rejectable offers, and (b) the myopic stopping rule, which is calculated from F and c such that marginal expected gain equals marginal expected costs: $H(z) = c$, where $H(y) := \int_y^\infty (x - y)\, dF(x)$. Let z be the reservation index, then the amount of draws N until z is obtained is a geometrically distributed random variable: $P(N = m) = p(1 - p)^{m-1}$, with $p := 1 - F(z)$.

Its expected value $E(N)$ equals $1/p$, and the expected marginal cost $E(cN)$ equals $c/(1 - F(z))$. Assume that this value is identified by the transaction technology and represented by $q_k(z_k^i)$, where z_k^i stands for the reservation index. Then

$$(z_k^i, e_k^i) \in T_k^i := \left\{ (z^i, e^i) \mid \exists\, c^i : e^i = \frac{c^i E(N)}{e}, \quad c^i = H^i(z^i) \right\}.$$

Under this interpretation, the marginal cost of effort q_k is an expected value, related with the reservation volume index z_k through the transaction set T.

Whenever a trade can be realized as large as the reservation volume, search stops according to the stopping rule mentioned. The actual effort used on market k may differ from the expected value $q_k z_k$, but this difference is probably compensated by the differences on other markets, and the sum of these differences is either consumed as ease, or invested as extra effort used.

In this case, the actual allocation may differ from the equilibrium effort-allocation only for the commodity effort: consistency on the markets $k \in M$ is preserved.

It may be noticed that the probability distribution F depends on personal knowledge of factors such as: attributed skills for a job, knowledge of time and place of a trade, convincing capacities, relations, goodwill, claims, etc.; and on the pressure of other agents on a market. Applications of the theory of search on general equilibrium models are given by Butters (1977), Ioannides (1975), Kormendi (1979), Mortensen (1970) and Wharton (1975).

Another approach in this context consists of substituting the transaction technology T with effort as input by a *consumers technology,* in which activities are defined with specific inputs and outputs, and obeying certain rules.

One of the inputs is *time* which has the advantage over effort of being an objectively measurable and interpersonally comparable input that is both individually and socially constrained.

Activities for which time is needed are distinguished for some person as follows:

(a)	money earning activities	(wage labor, etc.);
(b)	commodity achieving activities	(nonpaid labor, etc.)
(c)	capacity developing activities	(creative and socially productive);
(d)	recreative/reproductive activities	(eventually destructive!)
(e)	reproductive activities	(mandate time; sleep etc.)

Although any agent has to take a decision about the allocation of time over these activities, this decision is highly dependent on the degree of social organization of the economy and the social efficacy of the various activities.

For example, if the degree of specialization is very low then most time will be spent on (b). But very high specialization and high wages will induce again a shift to (a), and to (c) and (d).

Activities (a) are usually institutionally oriented: the norm of productivity is given by an institution such as the market a production unit, etc.; income is its purpose;

(b) are domestic activities, activities to achieve commodities (search, deliberation, information, choice) public commodities (persuasion, etc.), do it yourself; money income is not a direct result (the norm of productivity is subjective);

(c) and (d) may be both final and instrumental activities, and may take place in combination with (a) and (b).

In order to minimize time spent in (a) or (b), somebody tries to maximize his income per hour, respectively, he buys time-saving products as domestic appliances and domestic goods, or he develops transaction promoting activities. Depending on the circumstances, there is a large degree of substitution between these allocations of time.

Anyway, the classical dichotomy between the disutility of wage labor and the utility of leisure time is not necessarily a correct view, and according to recent research consumers spend more time to achieve commodities (b) than to wage-labor time (a) (Becker, 1965 and 1972).

How is this all related with an effort-equilibrium? Assume that only search activities belong to (b), which cannot take place at the same time as activities (a). Suppose time for (c) and (d) can be added, then the consumers technology has been reduced to a *transaction technology*, in which time has been substituted for effort.

The following *example* of a simple transaction technology with individual choice and independent search functions is given:

Let a consumer be endowed with an amount t of time, a utility function u on commodities x, y and leisure time r, and a search function for commodity y; $s(y) = s$.

Both functions are regular (i.e. continuous, twice differentiable, increasing with decreasing derivative). Let the prices of labor time l, good x, resp. good y be w, p and q.

Then an optimum (x, y, r) is a maximum for u such that $px + qy \leqq wl$, $s(y) = s$ and $l + s + r \leqq t$.

There are four cases to be distinguished:

(1) Trade off between l, r and s:	$l + r + s \leqq t$
(2) Fixed search time $\bar{s}$:	$l + r \leqq t - \bar{s}$
(3) Fixed labor time $\bar{l}$:	$r + s \leqq t - \bar{l}$
(4) Fixed leisure time $\bar{r}$:	$l + s \leqq t - \bar{r}$

Let λ_1, resp. λ_2 be the marginal utility of money income, resp. of the time constraint, then the following table 3 can be set up:

Table 3. Characterization of the optimum of a rationed buyer.

trade off between:	good x		good y		good leisure r	
1. labor, search, leisure	$\frac{u_x}{\lambda_1 p}$	$=$	$\frac{u_y}{\lambda_1 (q + ws_y)}$	$=$	$\frac{u_r}{\lambda_1 w}$	$= 1$
2. labor, leisure	$\frac{u_x}{\lambda_1 p}$	$=$	$\frac{u_y}{\lambda_1 q + \lambda_2 s_y}$	$=$	$\frac{u_r}{\lambda_1 w}$	$= 1$
3. search, leisure	$\frac{u_x}{\lambda_1 p}$	$=$	$\frac{u_y}{\lambda_1 q + \lambda_2 s_y}$	$=$	$\frac{u_r}{\lambda_2}$	$= 1$
4. labor, search	$\frac{u_x}{\lambda_1 p}$	$=$	$\frac{u_y}{\lambda_1 (q + ws_y)}$	$=$	$\cdots$	$= 1$

An interpretation of the examples is that the economy consist of two sectors: the monetary and the time sector.

The *monetary sector* consists of activities by profit, nonprofit or public organizations; the *time sector* consists of activities as personal and domestic work; information, search and deliberation; volunteers and pressure groups, etc.

If social scarcity is measured only in monetary terms, then prices are (p, q, w), and income is $wl = px + qy$.

However, personal choice cannot be explained by these parameters if time is a constraint and considered scarce. Table 3 shows that if search is needed for commodity y, then prices become (depending on the trade-off-possibilities): $(p, q + ws_y, w)$, and 'full' money income[2] is $w(t - r) = px + qy + ws(y)$.

If the sectors remain separated, then w is substituted for $\lambda_2/\lambda_1 = \mu$, the marginal rate of substitution between both sectors.

Both prices and income can, of course, also be expressed in terms of time:[3] $(p/w, q/w + s_y, 1)$, and $t - r = (px/w) + (qy/w + s(y)) = l + s$. Then the money sector quote is expressed by $l/(l + s)$.

Suppose that labor and search time are fixed and scaled with prices $(p, q, \lambda_2/\lambda_1 = w)$ such that

$$\lambda_1 + \lambda_2 = 1 \quad \text{and} \quad \lambda_1 wl + \lambda_2 s = 1,$$

then two constraint sets can be defined:

$$B_1(p,q) := \{(x,y) \mid px + qy \leqq 1\}$$

$$B_2(0, sy) := \{(x,y) \mid 0x + s_y y \leqq 1\}.$$

Convex intersection or dual addition [40] of these sets gives (see fig. 3):

$$\lambda_1^{-1} B_1(p,q) \mathring{\cap} \lambda_2^{-1} B_2(0, s_y) =$$

$$= \{(x,y) \mid \lambda_1 px + (\lambda_1 q + \lambda_2 s_y)y \leqq 1\}$$

$$= B(\lambda_1 p, \lambda_1 q + \lambda_2 s_y)$$

The resulting constraint set B is determined by equilibrium prices (see table 3) and can be used to maximise u instead of both B_1 and B_2 with weights λ_1, resp. λ_2. Such a result is valid for all agents, and corresponds with (5.1); through multiplying these prices with λ_1^{-1} resp. λ_2^{-1}, one obtains prices in terms of money, resp. time: $(p + \mu q^+)$, resp. $(\mu^{-1} p + q^+)$. This approach is in my opinion closer to a *labor theory of value*, than the usual techniques to transform prices in labor values.

Restricting the attention again to an effort-equilibrium, it follows that the individual optimum represented in table 3 corresponds with a simple interpretation of an optimum in definition 3.4. If time can be measured, it characterizes the régimes in an economy, as given in table 2.

References

1. Akerlof, G.A. (1970), 'The market for "lemons": quality uncertainty and the market mechanism', Quarterly Journal of Economics, 48, 488–500.
2. Akerlof, G.A. (1976), 'The economics of caste and of the rate race and other woeful tales', Quarterly Journal of Economics, 90, 599–617.
3. Arrow, K.J. (1958), 'Toward a theory of price adjustment', in: P.A. Baran, T. Scitovsky, E.S. Shaw, eds, The Allocation of Economic Resources, Stanford University Press, Stanford.
4. Arrow, K.J. (1973), 'Higher education as a filter', Journal of Public Economics, 2, 193–216.
5. Baily, M.N. (1974), 'Wages and employment under uncertain demand', Review of Economic Studies, 41, 37–50.
6. Barro, R and Grossman, H. (1971), 'A general disequilibrium model of income and employment', American Economic Review, 61, 82–93.
7. Becker, G.S. (1976), The Economic Approach to Human Behavior, Chicago UP.
8. Benassy, J.P. (1975), 'Neo Keynesian disequilibrium theory in a monetary economy', Review of Economic Studies, 42, 503–523.
9. Böhm, V. (1978), 'Disequilibrium dynamics in a simple macroeconomic model', Journal of Economic Theory, 17, 179–199.

10. Böhm, V. (1980), Preise, Löhne und Beschäftigung, Mohr, Tübingen.
11. Bowden, R.J. (1978), The Econometrics of Disequilibrium, North-Holland, Amsterdam.
12. Butters, G.R. (1977). 'Equilibrium distributions of sales and advertising prices', Review of Economic Studies, 44, 465–491.
13. Clower, R. (1965), 'The Keynesian counterrevolution: a theoretical appraisal', in: The Theory of Interest Rates (eds: F.H. Hahn and F.P.R. Brechling), London: Mcmillan pp. 103–125.
14. Drèze, J. (1975), 'Existence of an exchange equilibrium under price rigidities', International Economic Review, 16, 301–320.
15. Drèze, J.H. and Müller, H. (1979), 'Optimality properties of rationing schemes', CORE Discussion Paper No. 7901, Louvain La Neuve.
16. Drèze, J.H. (1980), 'Public goods with exclusion', Journal of Public Economics, 13, 5–24.
17. Gourieroux, C., Laffont, J.J. and Montfort, A. (1980), 'Disequilibrium econometrics in simultaneous equation systems', Econometrica, 48, 75–96.
18. Grandmont, J.M. (1977a), 'Temporary general equilibrium theory', Econometrica, 45, 535–572.
19. Grandmont, J.M. (1977b), 'The logic of the fix-price method', Scand. Journal of Economic, 79, 169–186.
20. Hahn, F.H. (1978), 'On Non-Walrasian equilibria', Review of Economic Studies, 45, 1–17.
21. Hirshleifer, J. and Riley, J.G. (1979), 'The analytics of uncertainty and information an expository survey', Journal of Economic Literature, 17, 1357–1421.
22. Honkapohja, S. (1978), 'On the efficiency of a competitive monetary equilibrium with transaction costs', Review of Economic Studies, 45, 405–415.
23. Honkapohja, S. (1978), 'A re-examination of the store of value in a sequence economy with transaction costs', Journal of Economic Theory, 18, 278–293.
24. Ioannides, Y.M. (1975), 'Market allocation through search: equilibrium adjustment and price dispersion', Journal of Economic Theory, 11, 247–262.
25. Ito, T. (1980), 'Methods of estimation for multi-market disequilibrium models', Econometrica, 48, 97–126.
26. Kooiman, P. and Kloek, T. (1979), "Aggregation of micro markets in disequilibrium', Econometric Institute, Erasmus University Rotterdam.
27. Kormendi, R.C. (1979), 'Dispersed transaction prices in a model of decentralized pure exchange', in: S.A. Lippman and J.J. McCall (eds): Studies in the Economics of Search, North-Holland, Amsterdam, 53–81.
28. Leijonhufvud, A. (1968), On Keynes Economics and the Economics of Keynes, Oxford University Press, Oxford.
29. Lippman, S.A. and McCall, J.J. (1976), 'The economics of job search: a survey', Economic Inquiry, 14, 155–189.
30. Madden, P. (1979), 'The relationship between various fixed price equilibria', mimeo, University of Manchester.
31. Malinvaud, E. (1977), The Theory of Unemployment Reconsidered, Blackwell, Oxford.
32. Malinvaud, E and Younès, Y. (1974). 'Une nouvelle formulation générale pour l'etude des fondéments micro-economiques de la macro economie'. Cahiers du Séminaire d'Econométrie, No. 18, Centre National de la Recherche Scientifique, Paris, 1977, 63–112.
33. Mortensen, D.T. (1970), 'A Theory of wage and employment dynamics', in: E.S. Phelps, ed., Micro-economic Foundations of Employment and Inflation theory, New York.
34. Muellbauer, J. and Portes, R. (1978), 'Macro-economic models with quantity rationing', The Economic Journal, 88, 788–821.
35. Negishi, T. (1962), 'The Stability of a Competitive Economy: A Survey Article', Econometrica, 30, 635–69.
36. Radner, R. and Rothschild, M. (1975), 'On the allocation of effort', Journal of Economic Theory, 10, 358–376.

37. Riley, J.G. (1975), 'Competitive signalling', Journal of Economic Theory, 10, 175–186.
38. Rosen S. (1974), 'Hedonic prices and implicit markets: product differentiation in pure competition', Journal of Political Economy, 82, 34–55.
39. Ruys, P.H.M. (1978), 'Disequilibrium in economics and the appearance of another measure of value besides money', mimeo, Tilburg University.
40. Ruys, P.H.M. and Weddepohl, H.N. (1979), 'Economic theory and duality' in: J. Kriens, ed., Convex Analysis and Mathematical Economics, Springer, Berlin, 1–72.
41. Shafer, W. and Sonnenschein, H. (1975), 'Some theorems on the existence of a competitive equilibrium', Journal of Economic Theory, 11, 83–93.
42. Spence, A.M. (1973), 'Job market signaling' Quarterly Journal of Economics, 87, 355–359.
43. Siebrand, J.C. (1979), Towards Operational Disequilibrium Macro-Economics, Martinus Nijhoff, The Hague.
44. Stigler, G.J. (1961), 'The economics of information', Journal of Politic Economic, 69, 213–225.
45. Younès, Y. (1975), 'On the role of money in the process of exchange and the existence of a non-Walrasian equilibrium', Review of Economic Studies, 42, 489–501.
46. Wharton, J.B. (1979), 'The theory of search and equilibrium in a non-auctioneered market' in: S.A. Lippman and J.J. McCall (eds.), Studies in the Economics of Search, North-Holland, Amsterdam, 83–108.
47. Weddepohl, H.N. (1978), 'Increasing returns and fixed market shares', International Economic Review, 19, 405–414.

Footnotes

1. Implicit prices are also used by Hahn (1978); I also was inspired by the paper of Drèze and Müller (1979) who introduce a coupons-equilibrium with a higher level of efficiency. The term effort is also used (in a partial equilibrium context) by Radner and Rothschild (1975).
2. This term is introduced by Becker (1965).
3. For example $\mu^{-1}p$, or working time in hours in 1978 (1960) of a manual worker in Great Britain required to pay for: a bottle of whisky 3:30 (8:20), weekly rent 4:50 (4:20), a pound of sirloin 1:20 (1:10), a dozen eggs 0:20 (1:20), and 10 miles by train 1:00 (0:50). *Source: The Economist/Hansard,* March 1979.

THE MOGLI MODEL: A PLURI-SECTORAL ECONOMETRIC DYNAMIC MODEL OF THE FRENCH ECONOMY*

RAYMOND COURBIS, ALAIN FONTENEAU, CUONG LE VAN
and PASCAL VOISIN

Constructed in 1974–1978 by the authors at the G.A.M.A., the MOGLI model (*mo*dèle *gli*ssant) is a pluri-sectoral econometric dynamic model of the French economy which can be used both for short-term and medium-term forecasts and for simulations.

In this paper, we shall first give a general presentation[1] of the model (section 1) and then analyse simulations on the sample period and with multipliers (section 2).

1. General Presentation of the MOGLI Model

1.1. General Features and Structure of the MOGLI Model

Before analysing the main equations, it is useful to give a general outlook of the model. From a general standpoint, the main *characteristics* of the MOGLI model are the following:

(*i*) As a *pluri-sectoral* model, it analyses the production process in ten industries;[2] the behaviour of non-producing agents (households, administrations, financial institutions) is also described, with very often a disaggregated analysis of administrations.[3] Because of this disaggregation and also because of the fact that income distribution is analysed in a detailed way, MOGLI is a *large model,* with about 1300 equations.

(*ii*) The model having to be used as a forecast model, it has been interesting *to describe endogenously the behaviour of central government and of administrations* (especially with regard to public demand but also for taxation purposes) and of the *central bank* (with regard to the interest rate in the monetary market).

(*iii*) As a simulation model, it analyses with a fair amount of detail the main tools of *economic policy.* The specification of the relationships has been chosen in such a way that they are meaningful for both forecasting and simulation purposes.

*The version and results presented in this paper are those of the Mogli model January 1979. Some improvements have since been made to the main econometric relationships.

(*iv*) The MOGLI model is an *annual model,* but, as indicated above, we wanted to build a model which could be used for both *short-term* and *medium-term* analysis. It was therefore necessary to have first a pertinent and stable *specification of the relationships,* which are very often largely non-linear, while, at the same time, in a short-term model a linear approximation is convenient, and can be used in quite different situations. However the *structure* of a model has considerable relevance to its medium-term and long-term consistency. The MOGLI model is characterized by a *disequilibrium approach,* the economic path being described in disequilibrium terms. But – and from an economic point of view it is the most important feature of the model – the long-term path is also characterized by the continuation of disequilibrium (however the long-term steady-state solution is such that the disequilibria are, in relative terms, constant; see below).[4]

As indicated in Figure 1, both demand and supply play an important part but the dynamics of the interaction between internal and external factors is quite strategic in the medium and long term. *In the short term,* however, production depends on the evolution of demand (internal and external) and on the national market share between local production and imports. But the production level, because of the tension between supply and demand, has a feedback effect on foreign trade. The evolution of national prices depends on internal factors (unit costs, tension between supply and demand) and also, for manufactured goods, on the absolute advance (or lag) of French prices relative to foreign prices (which also have an influence on import levels). The rate of wage increase is determined not only by specific sectoral factors but also by the general price level increase and by the labour market situation.

In the medium term, the dynamics of the model are controlled by manufacturing capital accumulation (which determines the level of the potential output) and by the evolution of the absolute ratio for manufactured goods of national prices to foreign prices. Business investment is determined (with a lag) by self-financing possibilities, and as much by the interest rate as it is by the tension between supply and demand. Financial factors and costs/prices dynamics (which determine manufacturing profitability) have a great importance in the determination of medium-term time paths. Through their impact on prices and foreign trade, foreign prices largely influence internal evolution. The constantly recurring state of disequilibrium between foreign and national prices is determinant in the medium term dynamics of the model (as it is in the short-term dynamics). The evolution of the economy is not described as a series of states of equilibrium but as a series of states of disequilibrium. The MOGLI model contains three main indicators of disequilibrium:

- the capacity utilization rate for the manufacturing sector (disequilibrium between supply and demand for manufactured goods);
- the ratio between the number of vacancies and the number of unsatisfied demands for jobs (labor market disequilibrium indicator);

Structure of the MOGLI model

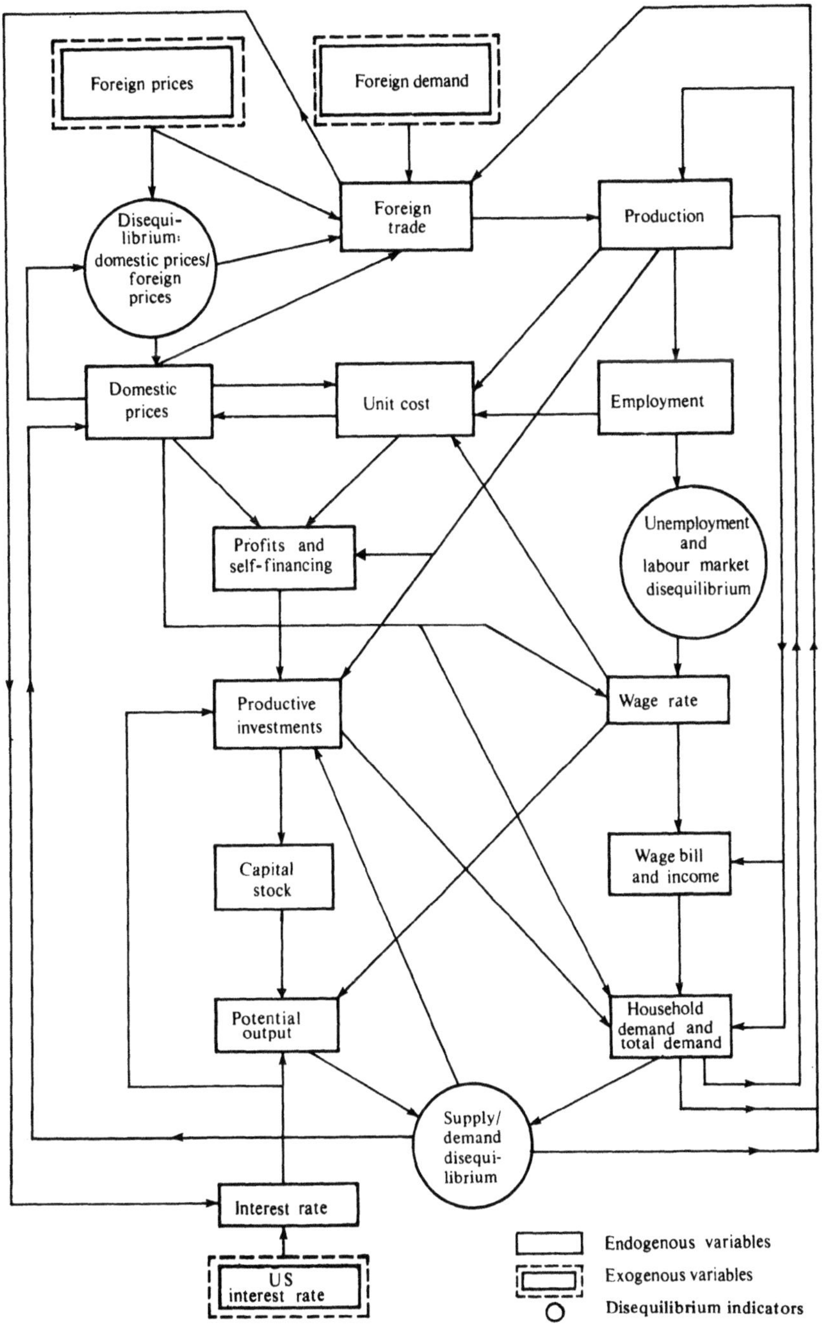

Fig. 1.

– the absolute advance or lag between the French price level (on the domestic market) and the foreign price level (import prices) for manufactured goods.

The first two indicators of disequilibrium are frequently used but the real novelty in the MOGLI model is the introduction of the third one which plays a key role in determination of the market share of local production and imports and of manufacturing sector dynamics.

1.2. Production

In the short term, production[5] is formally determined by final demand and foreign trade through a matrix of technical input-output coefficients which are projected by time trends. But supply possibilities and the level of potential output also influence, in the short term, the level of production. As indicated below (section 1.9), exports partly play the role of an adjustment variable, for they depend on unused capacity (or on output level, as far as foodstuffs industries are concerned). In this way the level of potential output has a strong influence on the level of production.[6]

In the medium term, the impact of supply is more important still, because of the cumulative impact exercised by the absolute advance (or the absolute lag) of French prices with respect to foreign prices (see section 1.9). Other things being equal, the growth rate of imports of manufactured goods is that much more important than the level of relative prices (i.e. the ratio production price on the national market, PQ, to the import price, PYM) is high. As this effect is cumulative, the price elasticity of manufactured imports relative to the ratio PQ/PYM – limited elasticity in the short term – progressively tends to become infinite.

This means that the model attempts to converge towards a state of equilibrium in which national and foreign prices would be equal, in which production would be determined entirely by supply (potential output level) and in which imports would be completely substitutable. This tendency is always disturbed but one can see the crucial role of supply possibilities on the evolution of output in the medium- or long-term dynamics.

1.3. Employment

Four different types of mechanism are used to analyse the employment by branch:[7]

(*a*) *In agriculture,* employment is either an exogeneous variable or – when endogeneous – is explained by the output level and the stock of capital.

(*b*) *In foodstuffs industries, energy, manufacturing, building and public works, transport and services,* the model determines as a first step the trend of hourly productivity and working time. For manufacturing for example, the productivity is determined as follows:

$$\dot{DH}4 = 0.00441 - 0.00139\ \text{TIME} + 0.0680\ \dot{QI}4,$$
$$\qquad (t = -6,9) \qquad (t = -2,5)$$

$$\text{M.C.O. (1960–1976)} \quad R^2 = 0.86 \quad \text{D.W.} = 2.19,$$

and

$$\dot{\pi H}4 = 0.425\ (\dot{QI}4) - 1.01\ \dot{DH}4 + 0.08\ \Delta\dot{\theta}4$$
$$(t = -8) \qquad (t = -2) \qquad (t = 2.2)$$

$$+ 2.5\ \dot{DHS}4 + 0.0618,$$
$$(t = 5)$$

$$\text{M.C.O. (1962–1976)} \quad R^2 = 0.91 \quad \text{D.W.} = 2.7$$

with DH4 = working time in manufacturing;
πH4 = hourly productivity in manufacturing;
QI4 = level of manufacturing output;
$\theta 4$ = investment rate in manufacturing;
DHS4 = DH if $|DH4| > 1.20\%$ and if $\Delta DH < 0$;
$\dot{X}$ = rate of growth of $X = \Delta X / X_{-1}$.

The desired level of employment can then be obtained and the actual level of employment is determined by progressive adjustment.

(*c*) *In communications and trade,* the actual level of employment is directly obtained from the average labour productivity.

(*d*) *For non-producing agents,* the model explains directly the employment of civil servants, of local authorities, of financial institutions and of households. Apart from this last case, the level of employment is determined by the level of the preceding year and by the gap between the expected and the actual level of the previous year.

Employment by activity is then decomposed between 'wage earners' and 'non-wage earners', and employment by branch is finally converted in sectoral terms for the determination of enterprises' accounts by sectors of activity.

1.4. The Labour Market and Unemployment

The level of unemployment is directly determined by an analysis of the variations of the labour market components. We found this way to be more efficient than determining unemployment using the difference between available working population and total employed labour. Finally we get:

$$\Delta\ \text{PDRE} = -0.67\ \Delta\ \text{RETR} - 0.49\ \Delta\ \text{ETER}$$
$$(-3.5) \qquad (-2.5)$$

$$- 0.53\ \Delta\ \text{ESEC} + 180$$
$$(-4.3)$$

$$\text{M.C.O. (1961–1976)} \quad R^2 = 0.84 \quad \text{D.W.} = 2.2.$$

with PDRE = unemployment;
RETR = number of non-working students plus intake for national service;
ETER = employment in the tertiary sector;
ESEC = employment in the secondary sector.

The available working population is calculated by adding the unemployment and the total employed labour.

1.5. Wages and Income

Wages paid to the different agents are determined by an analysis of the hourly per man wage rate, which is not similar for firms and non-producing agents.

The level of wages paid by enterprises is determined in two stages. First, a relationship describes the evolution of average hourly wages in manufacturing industries through a Phillips–Lipsey approach, whereby the rate of growth of average hourly wages depends on the unemployment rate and on the rate of increase of prices in the private consumption sector, but the link between wages and prices is non-linear for we assume that the more the inflation rate is increased the faster the growth of the wage rate will be.

More precisely, with quarterly data, we obtain the following relationship:

$$\dot{PWH} = \underset{(6)}{0.85\,\dot{PCM}} + \underset{(2.5)}{7.68\,(\dot{PCM})^2} - \underset{(-4.4)}{0.0048\log}\frac{DENS}{OENS} + 0.016,$$

M.C.O. (1959–1977; second quarter of 1968 excluded)

$R^2 = 0.75$ D.W. = 1.57 NOBS = 73.

with $\dot{PWH}$: rate of growth of average hourly wage (manufacturing and building industries); $\dot{PCM}$: rate of growth of consumer price index and DENS and OENS: unsatisfied demands for jobs and vacancies.

In a second step, the growth rate of average per man wages ($\dot{PWH}_i$) is calculated for each sector i. In most cases $\dot{PWH}_i$ is explained by $\dot{PWH}$ and by the relative ratio between the average wage rate of the sector and average wage for manufacturing and building industries. For example in the manufacturing sector we have:

$$\dot{PW4} = \underset{(4.7)}{0.852\,\dot{PWH}} - \underset{(-2.1)}{0.464}\left(\frac{PW4}{PWH} - 1\right)_{-1} + 0.0055,$$

M.C.O. (1960–1971) $R^2 = 0.71$ D.W. = 2.08.

For non-producing agents, wage rates are explained by indexation relationships.

Distribution of other incomes is described in a detailed way. For small businesses, income is determined by profits. Social security provided to households depends on demographic variables, the labour market situation and price increases. Various types of benefits are differentiated: sickness and maternity benefits, pensions, unemployment benefits, children's allowances and other grants and benefits.

For the long-term dynamics of the MOGLI model, determination of increases in wage rate plays an important role. As indicated above, we have schematically, a relationship such as:

$$\dot{\text{PWH}} = \alpha + f(\dot{\text{PC}}) + g(u, u_s)$$

where u and u_s are total unemployment and structural unemployment ratios.

However, for the steady-state growth solution, the increase in unit costs must be consistent with price increases (accordingly we have the necessary link – see below – between financing possibilities and investment). So, we must have

$$\dot{\text{P}} = \dot{\text{PWH}} - \dot{\pi} + \epsilon.$$

Therefore, we have

$$g(u, u_s) - \dot{\text{P}} + f(\dot{\text{PC}}) - (\dot{\pi} - \epsilon - \alpha) = 0.$$

But – as pointed out below – in the long term the increase in domestic prices is determined by that of foreign prices. In these conditions, the previous equation *determines, in turn, the equilibrium level of the unemployment* ratio for the steady-state solution (and a given level of structural employment); the steady-state path is characterized by a constant disequilibrium between labour demand and supply.[8]

1.6. Prices

Five different types of specifications are used to determine the production prices in the domestic market for the different industries.

(*a*) *For foodstuffs industries and building,* the rate of growth of production price is explained by the rate of growth of unit cost (cost per unit of output) – it includes intermediate consumption, wages, contributions to social security and indirect taxes – and by advance (or lag) between production price index and unit cost index.

(*b*) *For trade,* price is determined by an analysis of trade margin rates.

(*c*) *For rented housing,* evolution of prices is explained by the production prices in building industries (construction price indexation).

(*d*) *For transport and communications,* production prices are related to the general price level.

(*e*) *For manufacturing* industries, the evolution of production prices on the domestic market strongly depends in the short term on foreign competition conditions – measured by the non-structural gap between foreign and local prices on the domestic market – and on the tension between supply and demand (degree of capacity utilization). The incidence of unit cost is of less importance, a factor which emphasizes the importance of foreign competition in price formation. Finally we get[9]

$$\dot{PQ4}_t = \underset{}{0.024} - \underset{(-5.7)}{1.03}\ APPAE_t - \underset{(-3.2)}{0.199}\left(\frac{\widehat{PQ4}}{PYMTC4} - 1\right)_{t-1}$$

$$+ \underset{(1.3)}{0.188}\ \dot{IPR4}$$

$$\text{M.C.O. (1960–1971)} \quad R^2 = 0.97 \quad D.W. = 2.36$$

PQ4 and $\dot{PQ4}$ are, respectively, the level and the rate of increase of production price for manufactured goods on the domestic market; $\dot{IPR4}$ is the rate of increase of unit costs in manufacturing; PYMTC4 is the level of import prices for manufactured goods (taxes included); $\widehat{(PQ4/PYMTC4)}$ represents the value of the ratio (PQ4/PYMTC4) compensated for time trend and APPAE = (1 − UK)/UK where UK is the capacity utilization rate.

Once production prices have been calculated, the model determines the utilization prices (taking into account the trade margin rate and the import prices).

The above equation indicates that the increase of production prices for manufacturing depends on the rate of capacity utilization and the absolute gap or advance between French prices and foreign prices. But, as we shall see, in the long term, for the steady-state solution, PQ4 is determined by PYMTC4 and $\widehat{(PQ4/PYMTC4)}$ is constant (although not necessarily equal to 1). So, in these conditions, the $\dot{PQ4}$ equation in fact determines *the degree of capacity utilization.*

1.7. Fixed Investment by Firms, Stock of Capital, Potential Output

According to the different cases, firms' fixed investment by sector (which is exogenous for communications) is:

(*a*) determined by an 'accelerator' model for energy, construction and transportation;

(*b*) dependent on the profits of the sector for agriculture, services and trade, since there are a large number of small businesses in these sectors, and it is assumed that investment by these firms depends on the evolution of their income (or of their permanent income);

(*c*) linked to self-financing possibilities in food industries and the manufacturing sector ('self-financing behaviour'), but the self-financing rate – or more precisely the ratio of investment to self-financing – is not an exogenous variable but depends on several variables and particularly on the interest rate and the pressure of demand. For manufacturing industries, we get:

$$\frac{FCFVS4}{AUT4^*} + 2\,(0.05 - \dot{PIB})_+ = \underset{(6.4)}{2.07}\ GAINKAP^* + \underset{(1.4)}{1.12}\ \dot{PIB}$$

$$- \underset{(-3.4)}{1.74} \frac{1}{\text{GOULOT4}^*} + 2.77,$$

M.C.O. (1961–1974) $R^2 = 0.79$ D.W. = 2.4,

where FCFVS4 = investment (in fixed assets) in manufacturing (in value);
AUT4 = available self-financing possibilities;
$AUT4^* = 0.5\ AUT4_{-2} + 0.25\ AUT_{-1} + 0.25\ AUT$;
GAINKAP = difference between gross capital profitability and long-term interest rate;
$GAINKAP^* = 0.75\ GAINKAP_{-1} + 0.25\ GAINKAP$;
$GOULOT4^* = 0.5\ UK_{-2} + 0.25\ UK_{-1} + 0.25\ UK$ (where UK is the capacity utilization rate);
$\dot{P}IB$ = rate of growth of real gross domestic production;
$(0.05 - PIB)_+ = 0.05 - \dot{P}IB$ if $\dot{P}IB \leqslant 5\%$ and $= 0$ otherwise.

It is possible then to determine the capital stock from the level of investments and the rate of depreciation of capital. This determines in turn the level of potential production in manufacturing from the value of production per unit of capital (for a full utilization of capital stock), which depends on the relative cost of capital and labour and on expectations (regarding relative cost and interest rates).

1.8. Domestic Consumption

Total domestic consumption is directly determined by the average propensity to consume relationship CVM/R′, where R′ is the disposable income of households R, from which certain compulsory savings components have been subtracted ($R' = R - S_0$ with S_0 = self-employeds' fixed investment financing + repayments of loans for housing).

The ratio CVM/R′ is not affected by a linear trend as is the ratio CVM/R. We have:

$$CVM/R' = \underset{(5.2)}{0.36} \frac{CM_{-1} \times PCM}{R'} + \underset{(4.4)}{0.52} \frac{TAX}{R'}$$

$$- \underset{(-2.9)}{0.086} (\dot{P}CM - (\dot{P}CM)_{-1}) - \underset{(-2.1)}{0.010}\ \dot{D}ENS$$

$$- \underset{(-3.2)}{0.49} \frac{DENS}{PAI} + \underset{(9.8)}{0.56},$$

M.C.O. (1952–1976) $R^2 = 0.80$ D.W. = 2.1.

CVM = household consumption, current prices;
CM = household consumption, constant prices (1970);
$\dot{P}CM$ = rate of growth of consumption price index;

R' = disposable income less self-employed fixed investment financing and repayments of loans for housing;
TAX = direct taxes paid by households;
DENS = unsatisfied demands for jobs;
PAI = total labour force.

In this relationship, the positive incidence of consumption habits is dictated by the variable $CM_{-1} \times PCM/R'$. The influence of prices is taken in consideration through the difference between $\dot{PCM}$ and $\dot{PCM}_{-1}$. The negative sign associated with this variable corresponds to a 'real balance' effect. The influence of unemployment (DENS) is positive, for an increase in unsatisfied demands for jobs stimulates precautionary savings. The positive sign associated with the variable TAX/R' means that an increase in the tax burden on households has a greater proportional effect on savings than on consumption.

Once global consumption has been determined, real consumption for the different types of goods is obtained following the framework developed by Houthakker and Taylor.[10]

1.9. Foreign Trade

The general relationship used in the import and export functions has three different types of explanatory variables:

- the foreign demand (DE) or the national demand weighted by constant import components (DP);
- the relationship between foreign prices and national export prices (PET/PEX) or between import prices (taxes included) and production prices in the national market (PYMTC/PQ) – all these prices are in francs;
- the capacity utilization rate which has been compensated for incidence of exports on production.

For exports of manufactured goods, the relationship is:

$$\log EX4 = \underset{(12.2)}{0.70} \log DE + \underset{(4.1)}{0.65} \log \left(\frac{PET}{PEX}\right) + \underset{(3.5)}{0.55} \log \left(\frac{PET}{PEX}\right)_{-1}$$

$$+ \underset{(16.5)}{0.85} \log (1 - UK_c) + 12.1,$$

M.C.O. (1961–1976) $R^2 = 0.9996$ D.W. = 2.8.

Let us remark that the capacity utilization rate compensated for the influence of exports (UK_c) is very significant and has a strong influence on the volume of exports of manufactured goods. The manufacturing goods import function, as mentioned above in section 1.2, has a disequilibrium formulation.

As a first step, imports YM4* are determined by a short-term import function:

$$\log YM4^* = \underset{(14.3)}{1.75} \log DP4 - \underset{(-2.8)}{0.30} \log \left(\frac{PYMTC4}{PQ4}\right)$$

$$-0.59 \log \left(\frac{\text{PYMTC4}}{\text{PQ4}}\right)_{-1} - 0.09 \log \text{TIME} - 7.5,$$
$$(-4.1) \qquad\qquad (-1.9) \qquad\qquad (-6.2)$$

M.C.O. (1960–1976) $R^2 = 0.9988$ D.W. $= 1.7$.

The capacity utilization rate has not been introduced for this variable because it was not significant. However, we assumed that this rate would have an influence if it rose above the maximum observed in the past. The influence of relative prices is quite small, and appears with an average time lag of eight months.

In a second step, the result is corrected by the following relationship which allows in the medium term a consistency between national prices and foreign prices. This relation takes into account the *cumulative incidence* of an absolute advance (or an absolute lag) of French production prices (in the national market) PQ4 relative to import prices PYMTC4 (import taxes included).

$$\dot{\text{YM}}4 = \underset{(18.9)}{0.92} \left(\frac{\Delta \text{YM}^*}{\text{YM4}}\right)_{-1} - \underset{(-1.2)}{0.24} (\text{PR4}^*_{-1} - 1) + \underset{(2.0)}{1.03} \text{APPIB}^+$$

$$+ 0.031 \text{ DUM69},$$

M.C.O. (1961–1976) $R^2 = 0.93$.

where $\dot{\text{YM}}4$ = rate of growth of effective imports of manufactured goods;

$\Delta \text{YM4}^* = \text{YM4}^* - \text{YM4}^*_{-1}$;

$\text{PR4}^* - 1 = (\text{PYMTC4/PQ4} - 1)$ compensated for its structural trend over time (this variable which is *in level* has a cumulative impact);

DUM69 = dummy variable for 1969;

APPIB^+ = positive value of G.N.P. price index acceleration.

Export prices are determined by foreign prices, national prices, a weighted index of rates of exchange and an indicator of the tension between supply and demand. Import prices of manufactured goods alone are endogenous. They are a function of foreign prices converted into francs and imported raw material prices.

In the long term, the cumulative effect of PR4^* on imports in manufactured goods (YM4) is a very important mechanism because it tends to ensure consistency between the rates of increase of foreign and domestic prices. Let us assume that DP4 and PR4^* are constant. We have consequently $\text{YM4}^* = 0$, but according to the second relationship, YM4 will increase or decrease when PR4^*_t is respectively lower or greater than 1. So, all other things being equal, YM4 would change until $\text{PR4}^* = 1$. It means that the price elasticity would become infinite in long term.

The long-term steady-state solution implies *a constant gap between domestic and foreign prices.* Schematically we have:

$$\dot{\text{YM4}} = \alpha + \beta\dot{\text{DP4}} + \gamma\dot{\text{PR4}}^* + \delta(\text{PR4}^* - 1).$$

But for the steady-state solution we have[11] $\dot{\text{PR4}}^* = 0$ (i.e. $\dot{\text{PQ4}} = \dot{\text{PYMTC4}} + \bar{\epsilon}$) and $\dot{\text{YM4}} = \dot{\text{DP4}} = \dot{\text{QI4}}$. So, PR4* is such that

$$\text{PR4}^* = 1 - \frac{1}{\delta}[(\beta - 1)\dot{\text{QI4}} + \alpha].$$

In the long term, $\dot{\text{PQ4}}$ is determined by the increase in foreign prices; effective domestic production of the manufacturing sector is determined by capital accumulation and supply, and there is a complete substitutability between production and imports. So, in the long term, the steady-state path is characterized by a constant unemployment rate, and (for manufacturing) by a constant capital utilization rate and a constant gap between foreign and national prices.

1.10. The Behaviour of the Administration

The behaviour of administrations is described endogenously in terms of both taxation and expenditure (which is very unusual in French models). The following three groups are distinguished: central government, local authorities, and 'other administrations', which include the social security administration, 'OSPAEs' (semi-public bodies of economic action, such as those running ports and toll motorways), and private and international administrative bodies.

Public expenditure is chiefly derived from the public finance situation (growth of taxation receipts) and by an indicator of the stage of the business cycle (rate of growth, in real terms, of gross national product). For example the level of central government investment expenditure is obtained from the following relationship:

$$\frac{\text{FCFVAE}}{\text{PIBV}} = 0.687\left(\frac{\text{FCFVAE}}{\text{PIBV}}\right)_{-1} + 0.085\left(\frac{\text{TAXAER}}{\text{PIBV}}\right)_{-1}$$

$$-0.022\,\dot{\text{PIB}} - 0.013,$$

$$(1961\text{–}1974) \quad R^2 = 0.937 \quad \text{min at } \rho = -0.45.$$

For local authorities, investment expenditures are explained, besides by the variables mentioned above, by the level of central government investment expenditure (which has a negative influence).

Tax receipts are derived from a detailed analysis of the different types of taxes paid by the main economic units. Direct taxes paid by households consist mainly of income tax. Indirect taxes, which represent the main part of government receipts, are principally extracted from enterprises' accounts.

The evolution of the ratio between household income tax and disposable income of households depends on the evolution of real income per head, because of the progressiveness of income tax. As far as enterprises are concerned, tax on added value is obtained from an estimation of the tax base to which exogenous tax rates are applied. Corporate income tax is calculated from the tax base (taxable profit) to which institutional mechanisms of tax payment are applied. For social security contributions, a detailed analysis is also made.

1.11. Interest Rates

Since commercial banks in France are largely indebted to the Banque de France, this central bank can influence money supply behaviour directly. Consequently we describe directly the determination of interest rate in the money market (TICT) by a relationship which may be considered as a behaviour equation of the Banque de France:

$$\Delta \mathrm{TICT} = \underset{(7.5)}{0.77}\,\Delta \mathrm{TFEF} + \underset{(2.7)}{0.10}\,\dot{\mathrm{TXCHGE}} \underset{(-1.8)}{-0.05}\left(\frac{\dot{\mathrm{EXV}}}{\mathrm{YMV}}\right) \underset{(-1.4)}{-0.0079}\,\dot{\mathrm{OD}},$$

M.C.O. (1961–1977) $R^2 = 0.936$ D.W. $= 2.0$.

with TFEF = United States interest rate (federal funds interest rate);
TXCHGE = exchange rate;
EXV and YMV = total exports and total imports in current prices;
OD = reserves in gold and foreign currencies.

TICT determines in turn the short-term and the long-term interest rates, this latter having an impact on investment and on substitutions between capital and labour.

2. Simulations of the Model on the Sample Period

Full dynamic simulations on the sample period have been undertaken in order to test both the relationships between the model equations and their stability throughout the period. In the first place, we shall discuss the results of the dynamic simulations on the periods 1964–1973 and 1973–1976. We shall then proceed to the analysis of the relationships among the most important blocks of the model.

In the following paragraphs, the degree of uncertainty will be estimated through the average absolute percentage error (AVABSP).[12]

2.1. Dynamic Simulations of the model on the periods 1964–1973 and 1973–1976

2.1.1. First Period (1964–1973). Table 1 shows that the average absolute

Table 1. Average absolute percentage errors: dynamic simulations, 1964–1973 and 1973–1976.

	Simulation of the model (with exogenous interest rates), 1964–1973	Simulation of the model (with endogenous interest rates), 1964–1973	Simulation of the model (with endogenous interest rate and exogenous public expenditure) 1973–1976		Simulation by block(s) 1962–1973	Block number(s)
Gross national product	0.72	0.74	0.44	0.66		
Private consumption	0.65	0.79	0.43	0.54	0.4	
Fixed investment by firms	3.6	3.4	4.0	4.4	1.2	14, 15, 28, 35
Public investment	1.9	1.9			1.7	36
Public net consumption	2.4	2.3			1.6	36
Total exports	3.0	2.4	1.1	0.9	1.5	10, 21
Total imports	2.7	2.5	2.5	3.3	1.2	10, 21
Changes in inventories[a]	2.2	2.2	3.2	4.2		
GDP deflator	1.0	1.0	1.1	0.95		
Private consumption deflator	1.0	1.0	0.99	0.87		
Price index of fixed investment by firms	1.1	1.1	2.0	1.9		
Manufacturing goods production price	1.9	1.9	2.1	2.0	0.75	26
Manufacturing goods export price	1.0	0.9	1.4	1.3	0.8	11
Hourly wage rate	1.8	1.8	2.1	1.8	0.9	25
Household wage income	1.4	1.4	1.4	1.6		
Total employment	0.38	0.41	0.65	0.7	0.32	16
Unemployment (thousands)	44	46	80	89	46	20
Labour force	0.30	0.30	0.20	0.22	0.28	20
Manufacturing capital utilization rate	1.3	1.3	1.0	1.0	0.8	22
Short-term interest rate		0.47	0.76	0.70	0.40	42

[a]In billions of 1970 francs. Changes in inventories exogenous in 1975.

error (AVABSP) for the chief real aggregates stands at around 0.7% for GDP and private consumption, 2.5% for imports and exports, 3.5% for fixed investment by firms, and 2% for public investment and consumption. The predictions for the general level of prices (GDP deflator) and the hourly wage rate are less accurate (AVABSP equal to 1% and 1.8% respectively). These two variables are often overestimated especially at the beginning of the sample period because of the important part played by the later years in the estimation of the coefficients of the econometric equations.

The evolution of the labour market is correctly described (AVABSP = 0.4% for employment, 12% for unemployment). The utilization rate is accurately simulated (AVABSP = 1.3%) which tends to indicate that the capital accumulation dynamics of the model are well described. Table 1 also shows that prediction errors on main aggregates increase only weakly when interest rates are endogenous. The average absolute percentage error on the short-term interest rate is 0.5 points.

Figure 2 and Figure 3 give observed and simulated values of both the absolute level and the growth rate of real GDP and GDP deflator. It is easily noticeable that the predicted values of real GDP are alternatively higher and lower than the actual ones. In terms of growth rates, Figure 2 shows that the model anticipates the economic slowdown of 1968 by one year whereas the sharp upturn of 1969 spreads over 1969–1970 in the simulation. As far as GDP price index is concerned, only the slowdown of 1965 and the acceleration of 1973 are not correctly predicted.

2.1.2. Second Period (1973–1976). Two dynamic simulations have been made. In the first one, changes in inventories are exogenous in 1975 whereas in the second they remain endogenous. Results are provided in Table 1. Comments are as follows:

- real GDP, private consumption and foreign trade variables are predicted with a better precision than over the period 1964–1973;
- however, there is less precision in the prediction of changes in inventories,[13] employment and unemployment;
- residuals on fixed investment by firms are greater also, but this is mainly induced by a bad prediction of the investment price index;[14]
- production and export prices for manufacturing goods are generally underestimated: for 1975, this phenomenon can be explained by the high utilization rate; in 1976, the negative coercion of foreign prices tended to slow down the growth of the price index for French-manufactured goods.

Figure 4 gives real GDP and GDP deflator growth rates. The most important errors occur in 1975, when the model overestimates GDP by 1.8% with endogenous changes in inventories and by 1.1% when changes in inventories remain exogenous. This difference occurs because lower prices stimulate real private consumption, firms fixed investment and exports. However it is

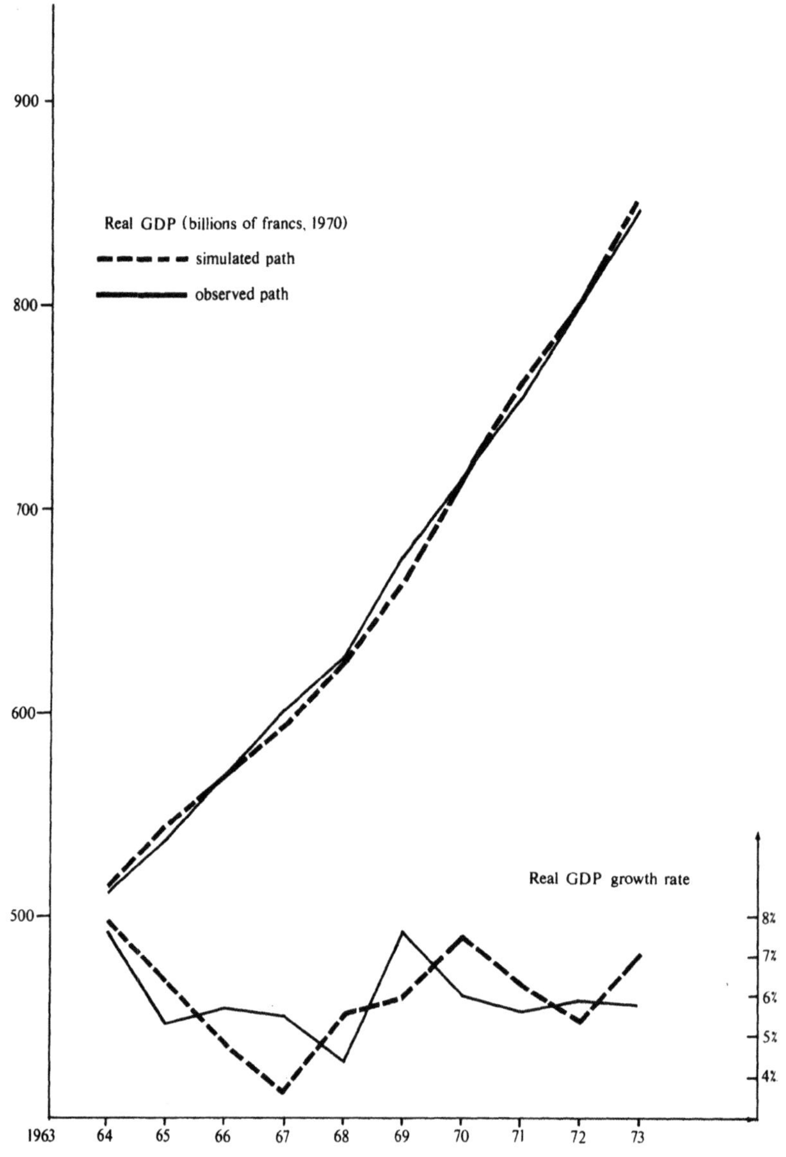

Fig. 2.

noticeable that predicted cumulative growth rates for real GDP and GDP deflator for the period 1973–1976 are very close to their actual values.

2.2. *Subset Simulations*

Subsets of the model have been solved in order to appreciate the influence of simultaneity. Table 1 gives the results of simulations by blocks. We shall now

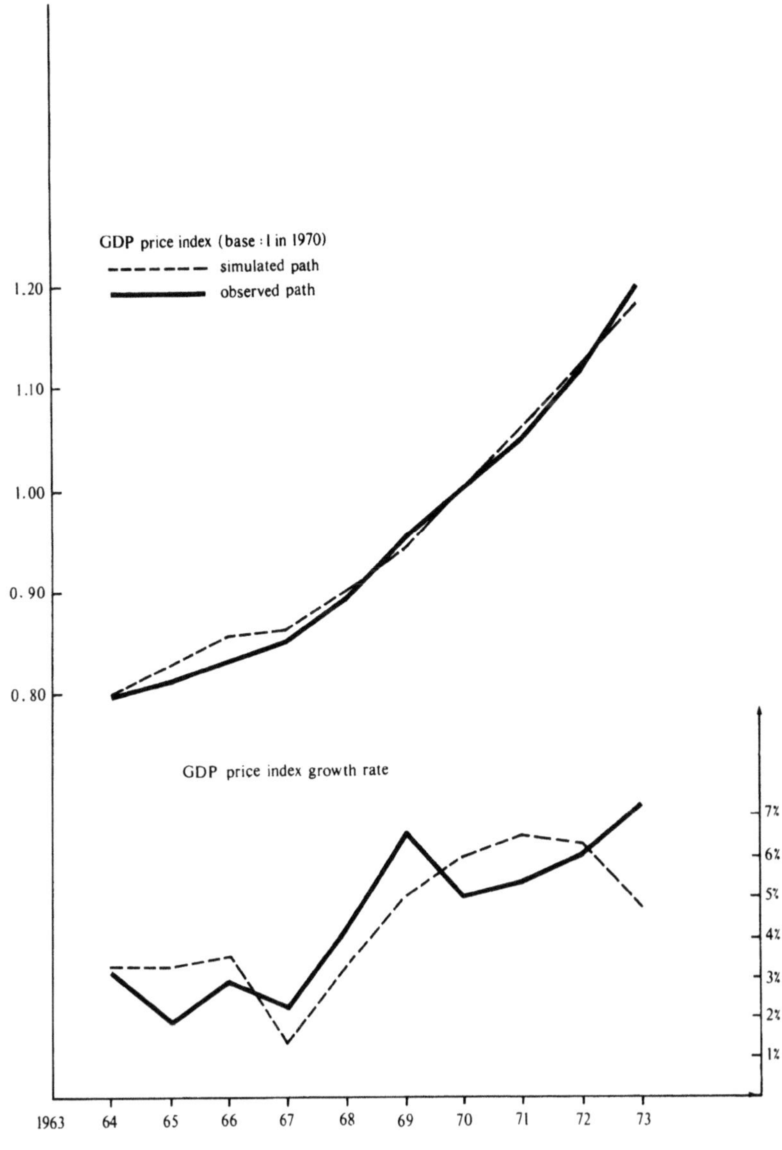

Fig. 3.

discuss the results obtained in solving simultaneously some important blocks of the model.

2.2.1. External Trade. Two dynamic simulations of this sector have been done. In the first one, imports of manufacturing goods are determined by a 'classical' short-term import function. In the second, the correction function

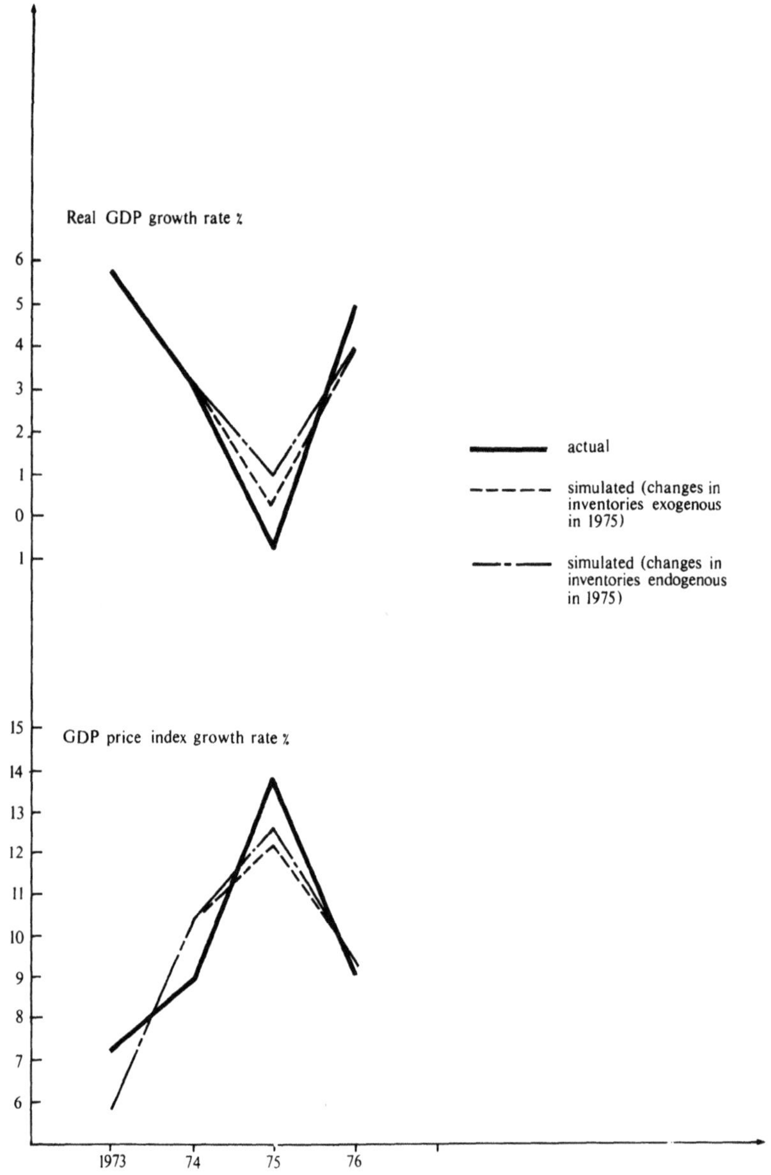

Fig. 4.

has been introduced (see Section 1.9). Table 2 shows that predictions are improved, especially when both relations are used for the recent years.

2.2.2. Production and Export Prices, Utilization Rate and External Trade. Considering the key role played by the utilization rate in the determination of production and export prices and in the calculation of export levels, it has

Table 2. Absolute average percentage errors for the external trade sector.

Simulation period	1962–1976	1971–1976
Manufactured goods imports		
– without 'correction' function	2.0	2.7
– with 'correction' function	1.5	1.5
Total imports (with 'correction' function)	1.2	1.4
Total exports	1.5	1.5

Table 3. Absolute average percentage errors for the production and export prices, utilization rate and external trade subset.

Blocks 21, 10, 26 11, 22	EX4	YM4	EX	YM	PEX4	PQ4	UK
Period 1962–1973	4.7	1.9	4.1	1.55	1.0	1.3	0.8
Period 1962–1976	4.6	2.2	4.1	1.6	1.2	1.3	0.9

EX4 : exports of manufactured goods, constant prices;
YM4 : imports of manufactured goods, constant prices;
EX : total exports, constant prices;
YM : total imports, constant prices;
PEX4 : export price of manufactured goods;
PQ4 : production price of manufactured goods;
UK : utilization rate.

worthwhile finding out prediction errors in this subset of the model. Table 3 shows that simultaneity mainly affects exports (AVABSP = 4.7% whereas AVABSP = 1.5% when the foreign trade block is solved as a whole as shown in Table 1).

2.2.3. Interest Rates, Capital and Investment. Compared to the results given in Table 1 (simulations by blocks), the errors obtained by solving this subset of the model are only slightly increased (Table 4). The good quality of this simulation is induced by the precision of the long-term interest rate determination.

2.2.4. Tensions in the Labour Market, Employment and Wages. There is a strong interdependence between employment, wages, and tensions in the labour market. Table 5 gives the absolute average percentage error for the most important variables.

2.2.5. Conclusion. The simulation on the sample period of this January 1979 version of the MOGLI model shows that, given the level of disaggregation and the small number of exogenous variables, the final results are quite satisfactory when compared to those produced by other similar models. Moreover, mention should be made that the two dynamic simulations presented have been obtained *from the same version of the model.* This result corroborates the fact that the theoretical basis of the MOGLI model is universal enough to

Table 4. Absolute average percentage errors for the interest rates, capital and investment subset.

Blocks 22, 28, 14, 15, 35, 42	FCF	KCAP	UK	TILT
Period 1962–1973	1.5	1.4	1.2	0.56

FCF : total firms' fixed investment;
KCAP : capital coefficient (in manufacturing);
UK : utilization rate (in manufacturing);
TILT : long-term interest rate.

Table 5. Absolute average percentage error for the labour market and wages subset.

Blocks 16, 20, 25	EBT	DENS[a]	OENS	PWH	SALM
Period 1962–1973	0.33	20.0	7.2	1.0	0.55
Period 1962–1976	0.39	32.0	11.4	0.82	0.56

EST : total employment of branches;
DENS : unsatisfied demands for jobs;
OENS : job vacancies;
PWH : hourly wage rate;
SALM : household wage income.
[a]Errors on DENS are absolute average errors in thousands.

adapt itself to a great number of economic situations. It has also become obvious that the three main indicators of disequilibrium of the model actually played a key role in previous economic evolution. In order to understand thoroughly the qualities of the model in simulation, we shall now examine the results of some characteristic multiplier runs.

2.3. Policy Simulations

All the multiplier runs in this section are based on a sample period control solution over the years 1970 to 1977, i.e. a period of 8 years. The following assumptions have been made for the various runs:

(*i*) an isolated increase in public investment;
(*ii*) an isolated increase in social security benefits provided to households;
(*iii*) an isolated decrease in social security contributions paid by corporations.

(All these isolated shocks were made only for the year 1970. Their magnitudes are about the same.)

The increase in public investment directly stimulates effective demand and production. So, in the short term, there is a strong impact on GDP. But owing to higher inflationary pressures in the labour market, there is an increase in wages and costs which reduces profits; consequently, there is a decrease of investment during the second year and the multiplier effect on GDP becomes greatly reduced (see Figure 5). For an increase in social benefits, the mechanism is similar, but the impact on effective demand (and GDP) is smaller because a part of the additional household income is saved. However, for the decrease

Real GDP multipliers (isolated shocks in 1970)

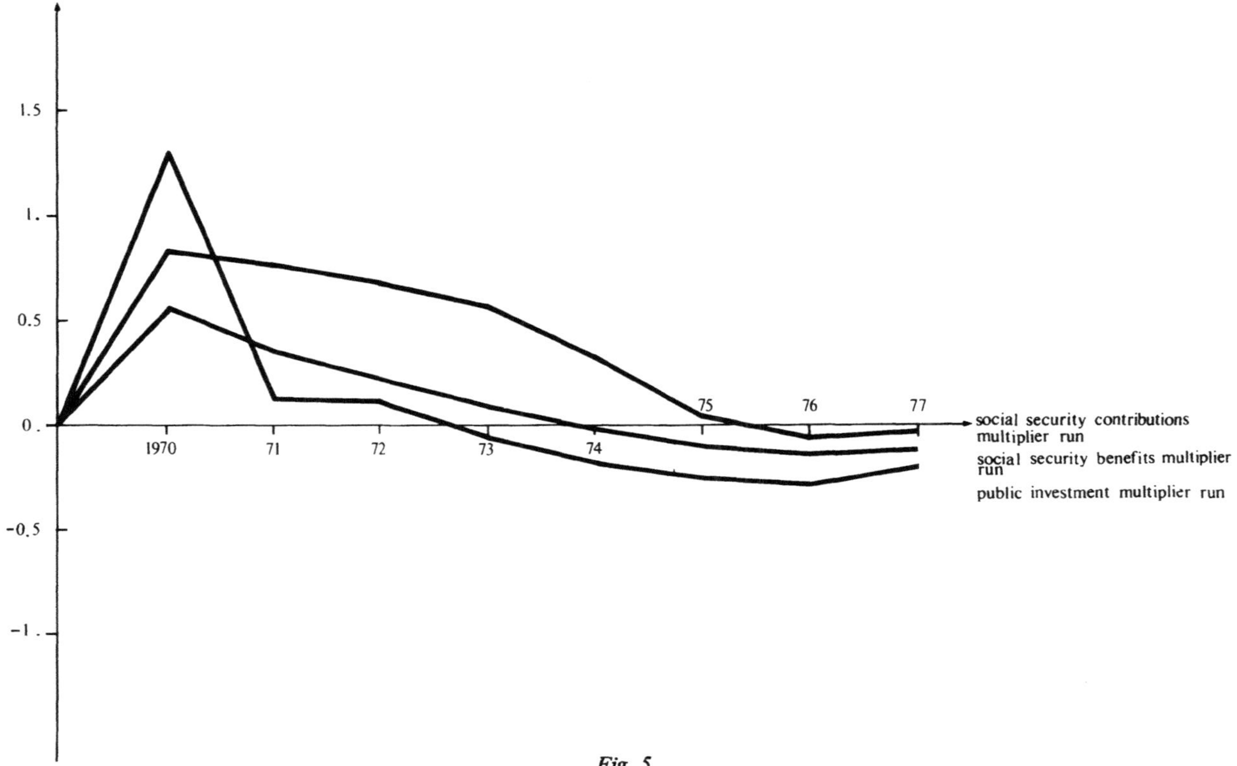

Fig. 5.

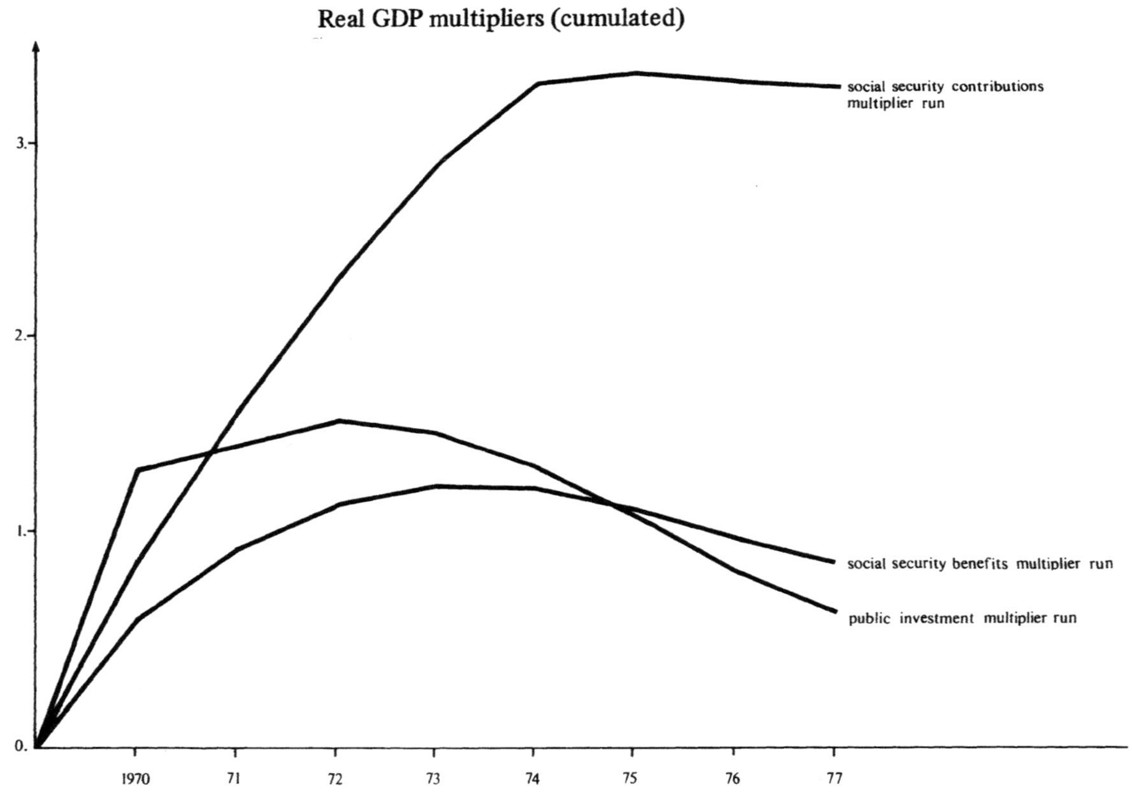
Real GDP multipliers (cumulated)
3.
2.
1.
0.
1970
71
72
73
74
75
76
77
social security contributions multiplier run
social security benefits multiplier run
public investment multiplier run

Fig. 6.

Real GDP cumulated multiplier response path for several starting years magnitude of the shock: 1 billion FF on public investment (at 1970 prices)

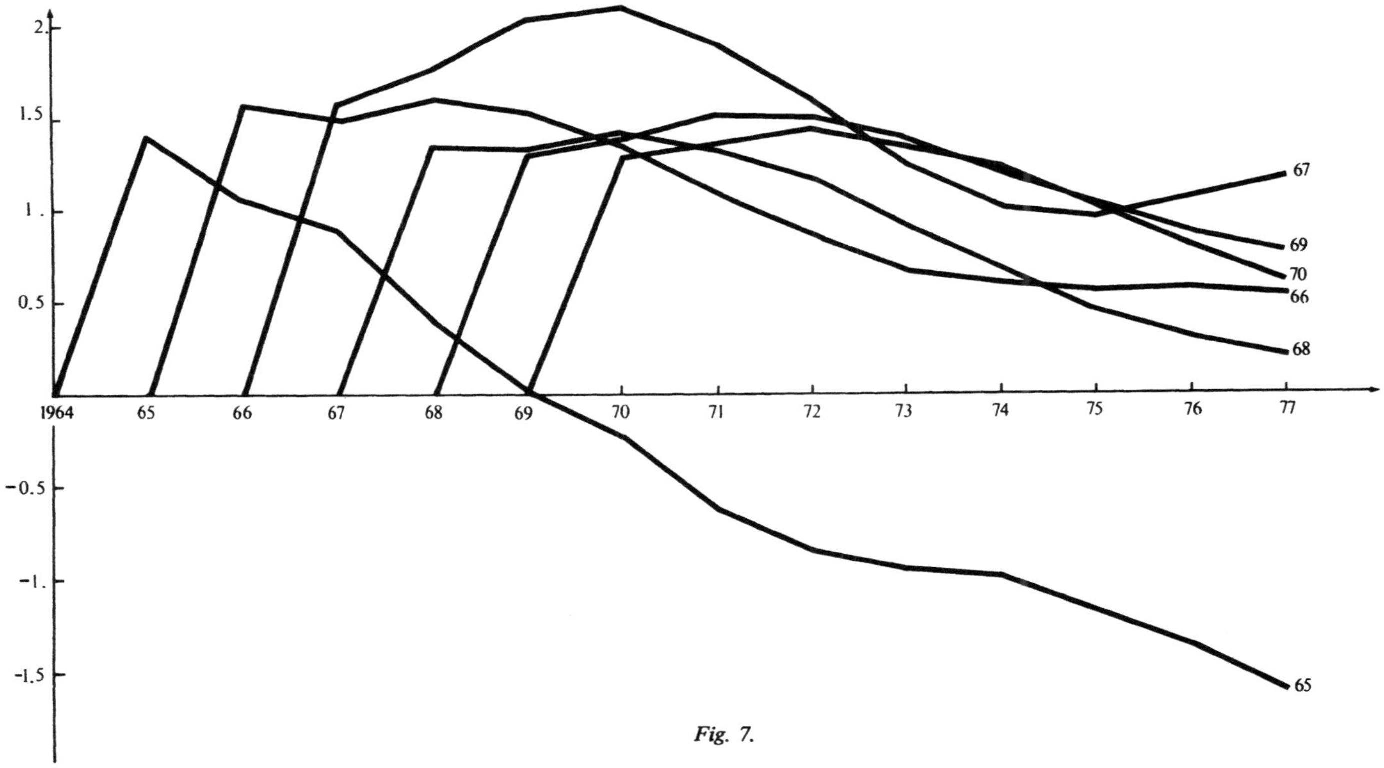

Fig. 7.

Real GDP multiplier (sustained shift)
Real GDP multiplier cumulated for an isolated shock in 1965
Public investment multiplier run

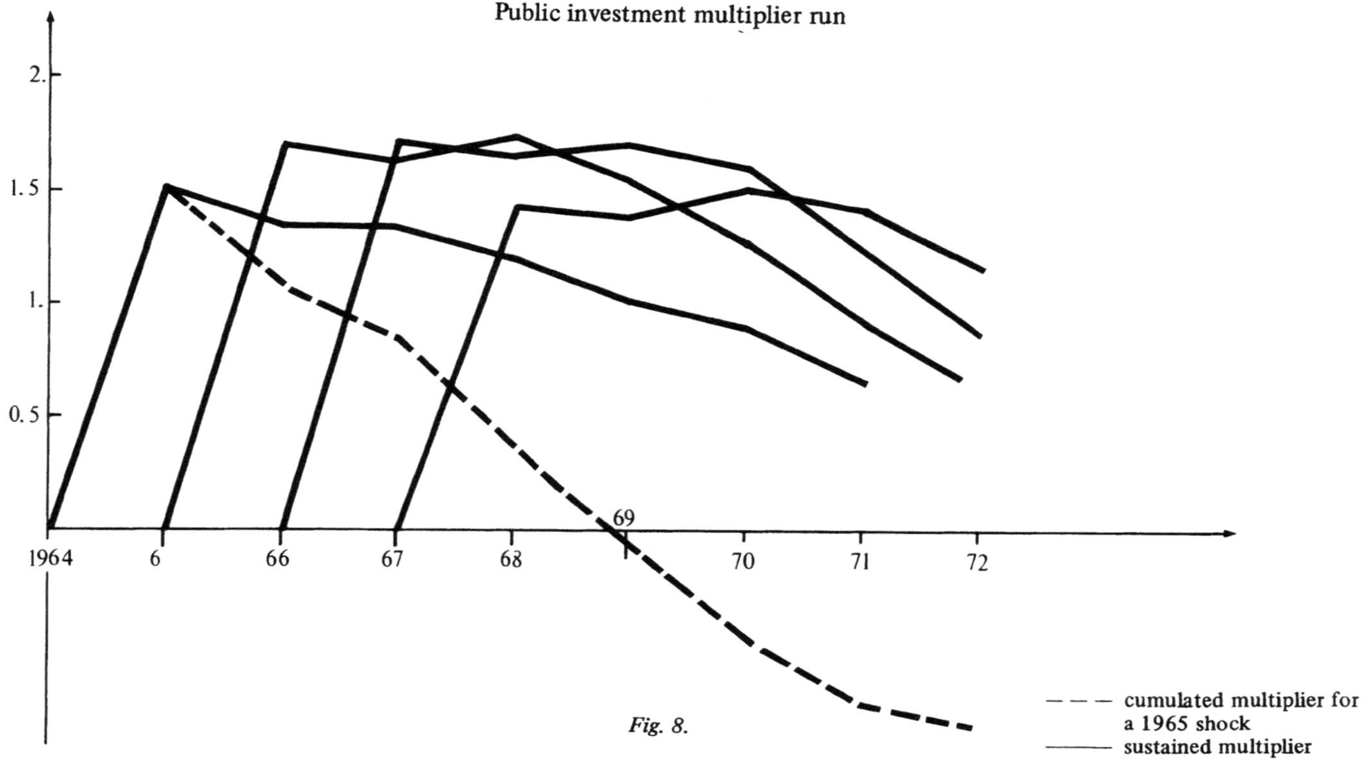

Fig. 8.

of social security contributions paid by corporations, the propelling forces are investment and supply. The unit costs are reduced and self-financing possibilities increase; there is both a slowdown of price increases (which improves purchasing power and household consumption) and a stimulation of investment. The stimulation of investment in manufacturing gradually increases potential production and this explains why there is a quite important effect on GDP for four years. Afterwards, increased inflationary pressures lead to a slowdown of business investment and the impact on GDP gradually vanishes.

The comparison (see Figure 5) of the three multiplier runs shows that an increase of public investment has the strongest multiplier effect on GDP for the first year, but that, for the following years, it is the reduction of corporations' social security contributions which has the greatest effect. In Figure 6 we give the *cumulative* effects: it is noticeable that the multiplier effect of demand-stimulating policies is quite low in the long term. On the contrary investment-stimulating policy leads to a strong multiplier effect on output in the longer term. It is also noticeable that in a highly nonlinear model such as ours, the response path of multipliers is not independent of the initial conditions in each year of the simulation, as shown in Figure 7, which gives normalized response paths of public investment multiplier runs for several years of commencement.

The nonlinearity of the MOGLI model also explains why the time path of response of the system to a sustained shift in a variable is not similar to the one observed in cumulating the results of an isolated shock in a single period (see Figure 8).

Endnotes

1. For a more detailed presentation see R. Courbis, C. Le Van, P. Voisin and A. Fonteneau, 'Le modèle MOGLI, modèle économétrique pluri-sectorel de prévision glissante de l'économie française', G.A.M.A. working paper 220, May 1978.
2. Agriculture, foodstuffs industries, energy, manufacturing, construction, transport, communications, housing (rented), services, and retail trade.
3. The activities of administrations are often divided into the following groups: 'central government', 'local authorities', 'social security' and 'other administrations'.
4. From the point of view of macroeconomic theory, the MOGLI model is grounded on a reformulation of the Courbis theory of economies in competition. See for this theoretical framework R Courbis, 'Une reformulation dynamique de la théorie des économies concurrencées', *Économie Appliquée*, forthcoming.
5. Agricultural production in real terms is, however, exogenous.
6. So, in the short term, if effective demand tends to become infinite, effective production tends to be equal to potential production.
7. In the French national accounting system, a 'branch' consists of all production units which produce the same type of products, whereas 'sectors' group together all the firms which have the same principal activity.
8. For such a determination (in the long-term steady-state solution), see R. Courbis, *Competitivité et croissance en économie concurrencée* (Paris: Dunod, 1975), Ch. 4.
9. This estimation has been made for 1960–1971 because of limited data for IPR4. But, more recently, it has been possible to update IPR4 to 1976 and to re-estimate the relationship; it appears that the coefficient of IPR4 is higher. We give here

however the previous estimation which corresponds to the one used in the model for simulations presented in the second part of the paper.

10. Houthakker and Taylor, *Consumer Demand in the U.S. 1929–60* (Harvard U.P., 1970).
11. See Courbis, 'Une reformulation . . . ,' *op. cit.*
12. AVABSP $= (100/n) \sum_{t=1}^{t=n} |(\hat{x} - x)/x|$ with $\hat{x}$: predicted value of variable x; x : actual value of variable x; n : number of periods of the simulation.
13. But the level of inventories at the end of the period is well described.
14. Statistical data for the estimation of investment price index equations were only available for 1959–1972.

THE DMS MODEL: VERSION 2

JEAN M. CHARPIN and DENIS FOUQUET

1. Introduction

1.1. From DMS–1 to DMS–2

The first version of the DMS[1] model was developed from 1974 to 1976 at the INSEE (Service des Programmes)[2] and has been presented in several articles and publications (c.f. [10, 11, 12] or, for an exhaustive presentation, including an analysis of simulations over the estimation period, [13]). Some of its characteristics and properties have also led to specific studies and publications [3, 8, 14, 15, 21, 22], including the construction and study of a very compact form of the model, Mini-DMS (cf. [23, 6, 7]).

This model, referred to as DMS–1, was built and estimated to be consistent with the former system of French national accounts concepts and series. However, since 1975 the French national accounts have been calculated and published according to a new system, the SECN (*Système élargi de Comptabilité nationale*), which is almost completely in line with the ESA (European System of Accounts). The change from one system to the other involved modification in the conceptual national accounts framework, and also modifications to the evaluation methods and to the set of basic statistics used in the evaluation process, which led to considerable variations in the levels and rate of growth of a number of national accounts series. For this reason, it was necessary to adapt the equations of the model to the new national accounts framework and to make a complete re-estimation of the model. This re-estimation was undertaken[3] as soon as historical series according to the SECN were available (March 1978) and was achieved only in December 1978.

The re-estimation did not bring about any fundamental modification in the general structure of the model, nor in the basic ideas which underlie this structure, which will be presented in section 2. However, some individual equations or groups of equations have been more particularly affected by this re-estimation, in some cases owing to the fact that some coefficients were no longer significantly different from zero (the main example being the influence of unemployment on wage rate increases, an influence which no longer seems supported by empirical evidence) but in most cases in order to improve some behavioural relations, which were not fully satisfactory in the first version of the model. The main areas where such modifications arose are in the determination of wages, households' saving behaviour, and external trade, but some other sectors have also been affected to a smaller extent. A complete description of the external account has also been added in the new version of the model. Moreover, consistently with the SECN, the operations of the large public corporations[4] have been isolated and their account is now extensively described. The description of the main behavioural equations of DMS, which is presented in section 3, takes into account these modifications and corresponds to the most recent version[5] of the model, DMS–2. The exact nature of the differences between the first and second versions will also be described in section 3.

Finally, we present in section 4 a dynamic simulation of DMS–2 in its present state (April 1979), over the period 1962–1975.

1.2. Uses of the Model

DMS was mainly designed to be used in the medium-term planning process as a successor to the Fifi model, which was used during the preparation of the VIth (1970–1975) and VIIth (1975–1980) five-year plans (for a description of Fifi, see [1, 2]), and some of its characteristics are clearly linked to this aim. For instance, the large size of the model – it includes approximately 2000 equations (there are about 1300 in DMS–1) – and its level of disaggregation (eleven categories of commodities, twelve industries, twenty-two categories of household consumption) are necessary in order to provide the various working parties of the CGP (Commissariat Général du Plan) with the detailed quantitative information on medium-term economic prospects they need. For the same reasons, the description of the economic policy instruments is most often explicit and very detailed, as, for instance, is the case in the treatment of taxes, social security contributions and benefits, subsidies, and so on.

DMS–1 has actually been used frequently either to produce medium-term projections or to study various economic policy projects. The main medium-term projections were made in relation to the 'adjustment' of the VIIth plan in February 1978 (cf. [9]) and to the first stage (*phase des options*) of the preparation of the VIIIth plan in February 1979, up to 1983 in both cases. A large number of studies of economic policy projects have also been performed for the CGP (see for example [24]) or other departments (see for example [25]).

The very first use of DMS–2, which was taking place at the time this paper was written (March–April 1979), was connected with the first fulfilment of an annual medium-term forecasting exercise undertaken at the initiative of the CGP and under the directorship of the BIPE (Bureau d'Information et de Prévision économiques), an exercise which included projections up to 1985 at three levels of disaggregation, the first of which corresponds to DMS.[6]

2. Main Features and General Structure of the Model

2.1. *Formal Characteristics*

DMS is an annual simulation model of the French economy, without any breakdown by region, aimed at producing medium-term (i.e. up to seven or eight years) projections and economic policy analysis.

2.1.1. Classifications Used. The institutional sectors described by the model are: enterprises, households, government, financial institutions, and the rest of the world. Whereas each of the other sectors is treated globally,[7] the enterprise sector is broken down into twelve sub-sectors which are:

1. agriculture,
2. food industries,
3. energy and utilities,
4. manufacturing: intermediate goods,
5. manufacturing: investment goods (including cars and other household durables),
6. manufacturing: consumer goods,
7. construction,
8. transport and communication,
9. housing services,
10. other non-financial services,
11. retail trade, and
12. financial services.

This classification of enterprises by sub-sectors, as well as the related classifications by industries (twelve industries) and by commodities (eleven categories), is used throughout the model. Complete accounts (including income flows, taxes, subsidies, interest paid, and so on) are described for each of these sub-sectors as well as for the large public corporations and for the four other sectors, allowing the determination of household disposable income and enterprise profits through accounting identities.

Flows of goods and services (external trade, changes in stocks, households' consumption[8]) are determined directly for each item of this classification, and a number of variables related to the production process and the determination of prices and wages are analysed independently for each of the twelve industries (gross fixed capital formation – GFCF, employment, capacity utilization, production prices, wage rates and so on).

Flows of goods and services by product and output by industries are linked through an input–output table, and groups of very simple equations are introduced to ensure, when necessary, the transition from one of these classifications to another (from industries to sub-sectors for value added and GFCF, from industries to commodities for GFCF, from commodities to sub-sectors for changes in stocks).

This breakdown to the enterprise sector, together with the description of all major entries of the national accounts, is sufficient to explain the very large number of equations in the DMS (among the 2000 equations of the model, 1400 are identities and only half of the econometric equations could be called 'important' behavioural equations).

2.2. Estimation

Behavioural equations have been estimated mainly by ordinary least squares using annual series (generally national accounts series) covering the period 1959–1975 or 1959–1976. In some cases, use has been made of Cochrane–Orcutt or Hildreth–Lu methods (correction for serial correlation). Given the annual data used and the length of the estimation period, no use has been made of Almon distributed lags. The data-processing management of the model is handled by the SIMSYS software (cf. [17]), first developed for the Canadian CANDIDE model.

2.3. General Structure of the Model

Figure 1 shows the general structure of DMS. Given the demand for commodities, gross output by industries is determined through an input–output table. For each of the three manufacturing industries, capacity utilization – derived from actual production and capacity, which depends only on past investments – plays an important role in the rest of the model (determination of wages, prices, investment, imports) as an indicator of the characteristics of the short-term equilibrium. Employment is then derived from actual production and wage rates and prices from unit labour costs and capacity utilization. The calculation of complete accounts for institutional sectors and sub-sectors results in the determination of households' disposable income and of enterprises' profits, which, together with prices, are the main explanatory variables for demand determination. The direct impact of unemployment on the level of household consumption, as well as the important feedback of profit rates on prices, must also be noted.

Up to now, DMS has not included the monetary and financial sector. However, the model is likely to be improved on this point fairly soon. Research is being performed to achieve this goal, along lines differing greatly from the classical IS–LM mechanisms. The basic ideas which are now being tested are the following: for each sub-sector, a 'desired' debt ratio is defined – it is assumed to be a function of the expected profit rate (+), the real interest rate (–) and the opportunity for long-term credit (+). The gap between the actual and the 'desired' debt ratio is assumed to influence firms in their price decisions, in their investment decisions and perhaps also in their wage policy.

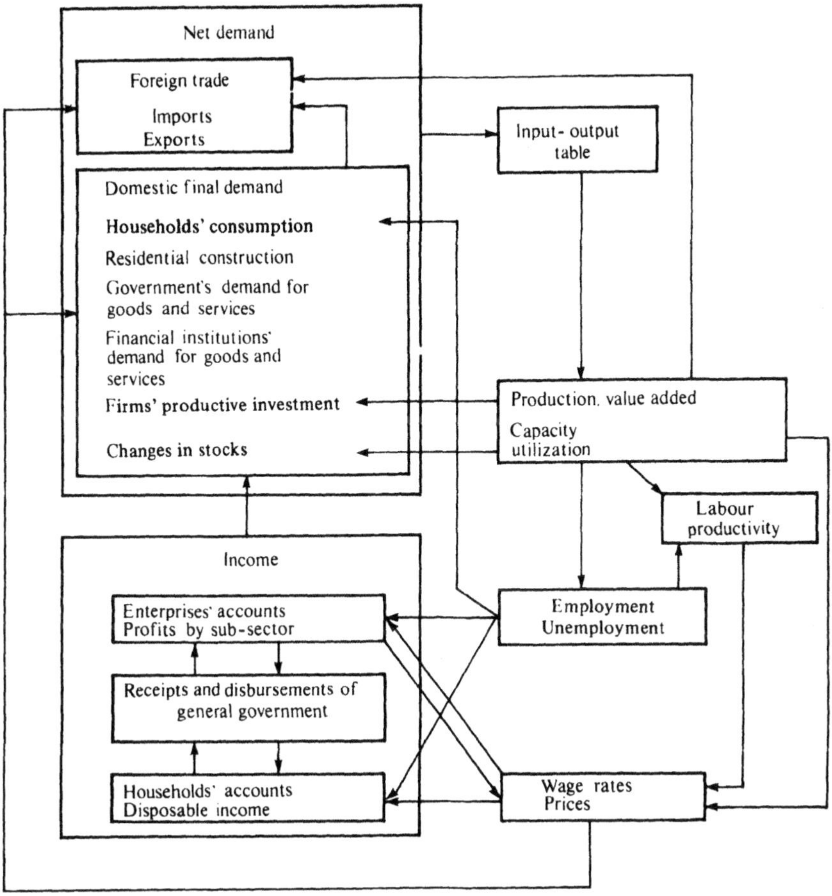

Fig. 1. General structure of the model.

2.4. An Important Economic Mechanism: Capital Accumulation Dynamics

DMS, being a medium-term model, is crucially concerned with the process of capital accumulation (particularly in manufacturing industries), which determines the evolution of supply capacity and therefore has a strong influence on medium-term growth (and even on the short-term equilibrium, through the external trade relationships and the mechanisms of market sharing between French and foreign producers). Though it neglects important features of the model (for instance the productivity cycle, and foreign trade) and describes only the behaviour of manufacturing enterprises, Figure 2 is useful for an understanding of the model's basic mechanisms. This figure is based upon the twofold nature of capital, which is both an investment and a factor of production; to these two aspects correspond two important endogenous variables of DMS, profit margin and capacity utilization. The two relations

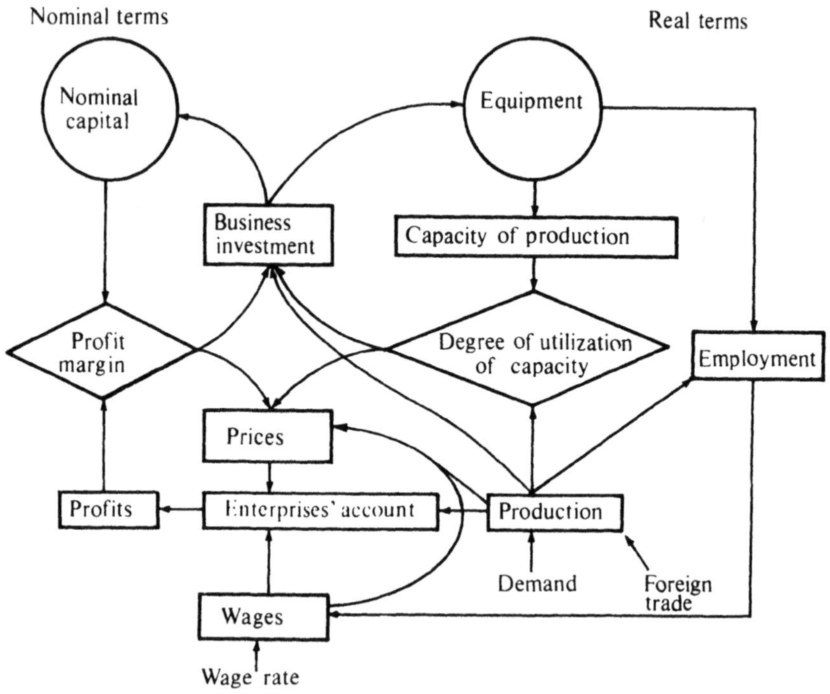

Fig. 2. Real and nominal dynamics of accumulation in a given manufacturing industry (demand and the wage rate depend on economy-wide variables).

determining capital accumulation and prices reflect the two roles of capital, as they both include an explanatory variables profit margin and capacity utilization.

The influence of the profit margin (which is almost always lagged in the reactions considered here) can be summarized as follows: a decrease in profit margins, and therefore of self-financing capacity, entails a decrease in investment and an increase in prices, which are the two main ways for firms to restore profitability (price increases being of course much more efficient in the short run). Both have a deflationary impact on real output.

Similarly, capacity utilization influences both investment and prices. Excess capacity tends to reduce investment, through a flexible accelerator mechanism, and to reduce the rate of growth of prices. The two effects have stabilizing consequences on the utilization of capacity.

3. Description of the Main Behavioural Equations

We will limit this presentation to those equations which we think to be important for an understanding of the model, with a particular emphasis on those which are very different from the corresponding equations of DMS–1.

3.1. Households' Consumption

The first step in the determination of households' consumption by product consists in the calculation of global consumption in constant prices, through a saving ratio equation. This equation has been modified substantially with respect to that used in DMS–1. The main characteristics of this modification are as follows:

(i) The savings ratio determined by this equation is adjusted for the financing of investment by nonincorporated enterprises and in order to take into account the influence on savings of households' investment in dwellings, and is equal to:

$$\mathcal{S} = \frac{\text{GS} - 0.4\ \text{HI} - \text{FFCEI}}{\text{DI} - \text{FFCEI}}$$

with GS = gross saving of households;
HI = households' investment;
FFCEI = financing of investment by nonincorporated enterprises;
DI = households' disposable income.

(The coefficient 0.4 has been chosen in order to maximize the coefficient of determination of the equation.)

(ii) The long term elasticity of saving with respect to disposable income is assumed to be equal to one (this elasticity was equal to 1.35 in DMS–1), which is a necessary condition for the stability of the model in the long run.

(iii) A positive influence of the short-term inflation rate on the savings ratio is introduced, according to a 'real balance effect' hypothesis – reverting to an idea already present in the very first estimation of a savings ratio equation for DMS [21].

(iv) A positive short-term influence of unemployment on saving is also introduced (a 'precaution' effect). The actual formulation of the savings ratio equation is:

$$\log \mathcal{S} = \underset{(7.8)}{3.88} \log \left(\frac{\text{RDIP}}{\text{RDIP}_{-1}}\right) + \underset{(3.5)}{0.26} \left(\frac{\text{UNE}}{\text{UNE}_{-1}}\right)$$

$$\underset{(12.0)}{3.50} \log \left(0.7 \frac{p}{p_{-1}} + 0.3 \frac{p_{-1}}{p_{-2}}\right) - 0.23\ \text{D}\ 69 - 2.72$$

$R^2 = 0.975 \quad \text{D.W.} = 1.84$

with RDIP = real disposable income per person;
UNE = unemployment;
p = price of households' consumption.

Total consumption is then broken down into 22 categories of goods and services through an equal number of behavioural equations, using as main explanatory variables total consumption at constant prices, lagged consumption of the product, and relative prices. Most of these equations follow the framework developed by Houthakker and Taylor [16], i.e.

$$\begin{cases} q_t = \alpha + \beta S_t + \gamma C_t + \delta p_t \\ S_{t+1} - S_t = q_t - \lambda S_t \end{cases}$$

with q_t = real consumption during period t;
S_t = status variable;
C_t = total real consumption[9];
p_t = relative price;

leading to the estimation form[10]

$$q_t = a + bq_{t-1} + c\Delta C_t + dC_{t-1} + e\Delta p_t + fp_{t-1}$$

This equation describes a 'stock' effect, i.e., a negative effect of consumption in previous periods on present consumption, if β is negative and, conversely, a 'habit' effect if β is positive. Table 1 below summarizes the main characteristics of these 22 equations.

3.2. Housing Construction

In DMS–1, the projection of residential construction was made in two steps (see [22]): (*i*) projection of 'long-run' desired investment in dwellings, and (*ii*) determination of a short-term adjustment to this long-run level as a function of the short-term evolution of the population over twenty years of age and of an indicator of the real cost of credit. This rather complicated treatment has been replaced in DMS–2 by a single equation explaining the rate of gross addition to the stock of dwellings by the average growth rate of population over twenty (averaged over five years), the average growth rate of real disposable income per capita (averaged over three years), and the real cost of credit.

$$\frac{\mathrm{HI}}{\mathrm{SD}} = \underset{(11.0)}{0.82} \left(\frac{\mathrm{HI}}{\mathrm{SD}}\right)_{-1} + \underset{(5.4)}{0.018}\, \bar{g}(\mathrm{POP}) + \underset{(2.3)}{0.4 \times 10^{-3}}\, \bar{g}(\mathrm{RDIP})$$

$$- 0.013\ \mathrm{RCC} + 0.4 \times 10^{-2}\ \mathrm{D68} - 0.5 \times 10^{-2},$$

$$R^2 = 0.992 \qquad \mathrm{D.W.} = 1.99,$$

with
SD $= 0.9885\ \mathrm{SD}_{-1} + \mathrm{HI}$;
HI = households' investment in dwellings (constant prices);
SD = stock of dwellings (constant prices);
$\bar{g}$(POP) = average growth rate of population over twenty;
$\bar{g}$(RDIP) = average growth rate of real disposable income per person;
RCC = real cost of credit (for a definition of this variable, see [21]).

Table 1. Detailed households' consumption relationships.

	Product[a]	Functions of households' consumption[b]	Model[c]	Relative price effect	Other variables[d]	'Stock' or 'habit' effect[e]	Short-term elasticity[f]	Long-term elasticity[f]
1. Agricultural products	1	F	log	Yes			0.14	0.14
2. Food	2	F	HT	Yes		N	0.33	0
3. Water, electricity, gas and household fuels	3	Ho	HT	No	HIV	STO	1.42	1.30
4. Petrol, oil and lubricants	3	T	*	Yes			0	0
5. Pharmaceutical products	6	He	HT	No			0.75[g]	1.75
6. Intermediate goods	4	Ho	log	Yes			0.83	1.23
7. Automobiles	5	T	HT	Yes	p4	STO	5.3	1.49
8. Household appliances	5	Ho	HT	Yes	D62–63		0.44[g]	4.2
9. Other investment goods	5	R	log	No	D69		0.71	1.62
10. Clothing	6	Cl	HT	Yes			0.84	0
11. Furniture and household textiles	6	Ho	HT	No	D69	N	1.29	1.43
12. Books, newspapers, magazines	6	R	log	No			0.72	0.72
13. Other consumer goods	6	R	HT	No		HAB	1.05	1.42
14. House maintenance and repair	7	Ho	log	No			1.16	1.16
15. Transport	8	T	HT	Yes		HAB	0.71	0
16. Communication	8	T	HT	No	D74	N	2.36	0
17. Rent	9	Ho	log	No			1.37	1.37
18. Medical services	10	He	log	No	D68		0.52	1.57
19. Hotels, cafés, restaurants	10	R	HT	Yes	D68	STO	0.66	0.43
20. Automobile maintenance and repair	10	T	log	Yes			0.08[h]	0.90[h]
21. Other non-financial services	10	R	HT	No	D68	N	0.63	0
22. Financial services	12	R	log	Yes			1.63	1.63

[a] Refers to the 'standard' classification by product, see Section 2.1.1.
[b] F = food, Cl = clothing, Ho = household, He = health, T = transport, R = recreation and others.
[c] HT = Houthakker–Taylor, log = formulations in logarithmic form, * = other formulations.
[d] HIV = indicator of average temperature in winter, p4 = price of petrol, oil and lubricants.
[e] HAB = 'habit' effect ($\beta > 0$), STO = 'stock' effect ($\beta < 0$), N = neutral ($|\beta| < 0.05$); no 'stock' or 'habit' effect is indicated if $\lambda = 1$, i.e. if $S_t = q_{t-1}$.
[f] With respect to real income.
[g] With a one-year lag, the instantaneous effect being nil.
[h] With respect to the consumption of automobiles.

3.3 Firms' Fixed Investment

As explained previously, the two main explanatory variables for firms' fixed investment are an accelerator and the rate of profit, with a time lag between zero and one year. Furthermore, actual investment is assumed to be linked to the 'desired' investment through Koyck's distributed lags, which involves the introduction of the lagged endogenous variable in the estimated equation.

For the industries for which the capacity utilization is calculated (i.e. the manufacturing industries) the accelerator effect is measured by the variable $(\dot{Q}^{(e)} + (\beta u - \bar{u})/u)$, where $\dot{Q}^{(e)}$ is the expected rate of growth of production, u is the capacity utilization, and $\bar{u}$ its average value over the estimation period (considered as the 'desired' value). For the other industries, the accelerator effect is measured only by $\dot{Q}^{(e)}$.

This formulation is applied to investment in machinery and equipment (at constant prices) for all industries except agriculture, energy, transport and communication (where fixed investment is exogenous), and trade. Table 2 gives the results of the econometric estimations. Investment in construction is determined as a function of investment in machinery and equipment, following the formulation:

$$\frac{\mathrm{IC}}{\mathrm{KC}} = a\left(\frac{\mathrm{IC}}{\mathrm{KC}}\right)_{-1} + b\,\frac{\mathrm{IH}}{\mathrm{KM}} + c,$$

with IC = investment in construction (at constant prices),
KC = capital stock in construction (at constant prices),
IH = investment in machinery and equipment (at constant prices),
KM = capital stock in machinery and equipment (at constant prices),

For the trade industry, a global investment equation is introduced, explaining the ratio of total investment at current prices to the capital stock at current replacement costs by present and lagged values of the profit margin π:

$$\frac{\mathrm{I}}{\mathrm{K}} = \underset{(7.7)}{0.38}\left(\frac{\mathrm{I}}{\mathrm{K}}\right)_{-1} + \underset{(7.1)}{0.176\pi} - \underset{(-5.3)}{0.167(\pi - \pi_{-1})} + \alpha \mathrm{D71} + 0.39,$$

$$R^2 = 0.89 \quad \mathrm{D.W.} = 2.28.$$

3.4. Changes in Inventories

Changes in inventories are determined for each product (i.e. here only for the first six items of the standard classification: agriculture, food industries, intermediate goods, investment goods, consumer goods)[11] and separately for materials and supplies (including stocks in wholesale and retail trade) and for finished goods. The formulation used in DMS–1 described changes in stocks

Table 2. Firms' fixed investment in machinery and equipment.

Endogenous variable: IM/KM	$\left(\frac{IM}{KM}\right)_{-1}$	$\alpha\dot{Q} + (1-\alpha)\dot{Q}_{-1} + \beta\left[\gamma\frac{u-\bar{u}}{u} + (1-\gamma)\left(\frac{u-\bar{u}}{u}\right)_{-1}\right]$	α	β	γ	π	π_{-1}	FISC	Dummies	Constant	R^2	D.W.
Food industry	0.55 (2.4)	0.115 (1.9)	1	0		0.34[a]		−0.139 (2.7)	D75	0.0147	0.75	2.01
Intermediate goods	0.62 (3.2)	0.096 (3.1)	1	1	0.6		0.35 (2.2)		D62, D64	0.010	0.91	1.06
Investment goods	0.50 (4.8)	0.123 (3.2)	1	1	1		0.26 (4.0)		D69–D68	0.032	0.92	2.35
Consumer goods	0.49 (5.0)	0.261 (7.3)	0.62	0.59	1	0.23 (2.5)				0.025	0.96	2.02
Services	0.83 (9.8)	$0.48\dot{Q} + 0.40\dot{Q}_{-1}$ (2.2) (1.6)				0.64 (3.4)			D70	0.072	0.95	2.27

IM : investment in machinery and equipment.
KM : capital stock in machinery and equipment.
$\dot{Q}$: growth of value added.
u : capacity utilization.
$\bar{u}$: average capacity utilization.
π : profit margin.
FSIC : indicator of the short-term effects of variations in the tax legislation.
[a] constrained by the condition insuring the compatibility with a steady state growth path, that the sum of the coefficients of $(IM/KM)_{-1}$, $\dot{Q}$ and π be equal to one.

as the sum of a partial adjustment to a desired stock (linked to expected demand) and involuntary stocks (equal to the difference between expected demand and actual demand). This formulation was not very successful when applied to the new national accounts series; it had a very poor statistical fit. Furthermore, this model includes the lagged endogenous variable as one of the explanatory variables with a coefficient $(1-k)$, where k is the 'damping factor' characterizing the partial adjustment to desired stock: the expected sign (+) of $1-k$ was not obtained in a number of regressions.

For these reasons, a more empirical approach has been used, in which the explanatory variables of changes in stocks are:

(*i*) changes in demand (or production, depending on the statistical fit);

(*ii*) the acceleration of the price of the product (explaining a speculative behaviour in changes in stocks of finished goods).

Table 3 below gives the results of the estimations.

3.5. External Trade

In DMS–2, as in DMS–1, the imports and exports equations include three main categories of explanatory variables, which are (*i*) a demand variable (domestic demand in the case of imports, and an indicator of foreign demand in the case of exports), (*ii*) a relative prices variable, and (*iii*) the degree of capacity utilization in the domestic industry concerned. Although the basic concepts are still the same, the way in which they are formulated in DMS–2 constitutes an improvement over the DMS–1 equations.

3.5.1. Demand Variables. The indicator of real foreign demand is a weighted average (the weights being equal to the relative importance of the individual partner countries in French exports) of total imports – of the product under study – of the six main partner countries of France in foreign trade (Germany, Belgium, Netherlands, Italy, United Kingdom, United States). However, this indicator has proved to be insufficient in recent times and an additional variable, $(1 + D^0/D)$, with D = demand indicator for industrialized partner countries, and D^0 = total imports by non-industrialized countries, has been introduced in order to take into account the effects of the growing purchasing power of non-industrialized countries.

3.5.2. Relative Price Variables. The variable used in DMS–1 was the ratio of weighted foreign domestic prices to French domestic prices. This proved to be a relatively inadequate process for the measurement of competitiveness, and has been replaced by the ratio of foreign domestic prices to export prices in export equations. An additional term, equal to the ratio of export prices to domestic prices, is also introduced in export equations in order to take into account a 'marginal effect' on the behaviour of French exporters: this results in a splitting into two parts, $\log (Pf/Pd) = \log (Pf/Px) + \log (Px/Pd)$, of the previously used relative prices variable. Furthermore, these variables are

Table 3. Changes in inventories

	'Demand' variable used (D)	D	D_{-1}	$\ddot{P}_m$	Constant	R^2	D.W.
Finished goods							
Energy	PR–SF		0.014 (0.3)	566.7 (3.7)	222	0.69	0.97
Intermediate goods	PR–SF		0.028 (1.8)	4897.7 (5.2)	740	0.72	1.78
Investment goods	PR	0.235 (7.6)	0.172 (5.2)		–	0.79	1.65
Consumer goods	PR	0.057 (2.1)	0.037 (1.0)		221	0.31	2.28
Materials and supplies							
Energy	PR–SM–SF	−0.060 (−2.2)	0.079 (2.7)		188	0.47	1.54
Intermediate goods	ICP	0.384 (11.8)			–	0.82	1.22
Investment goods	PR	0.234 (6.5)	0.057 (1.5)		−665	0.78	2.07
Consumer goods	PR	0.312 (5.3)	−0.082 (−1.4)		1001	0.70	2.06

PR = production,
SM = changes in stocks of materials and supplies,
ICP = intermediate consumption of the product,
SF = changes in stocks of finished products,
$\ddot{P}_m$ = acceleration of import prices = $(P/P_{-1}) - (P_{-1}/P_{-2})$.
All variables are evaluated at constant prices.

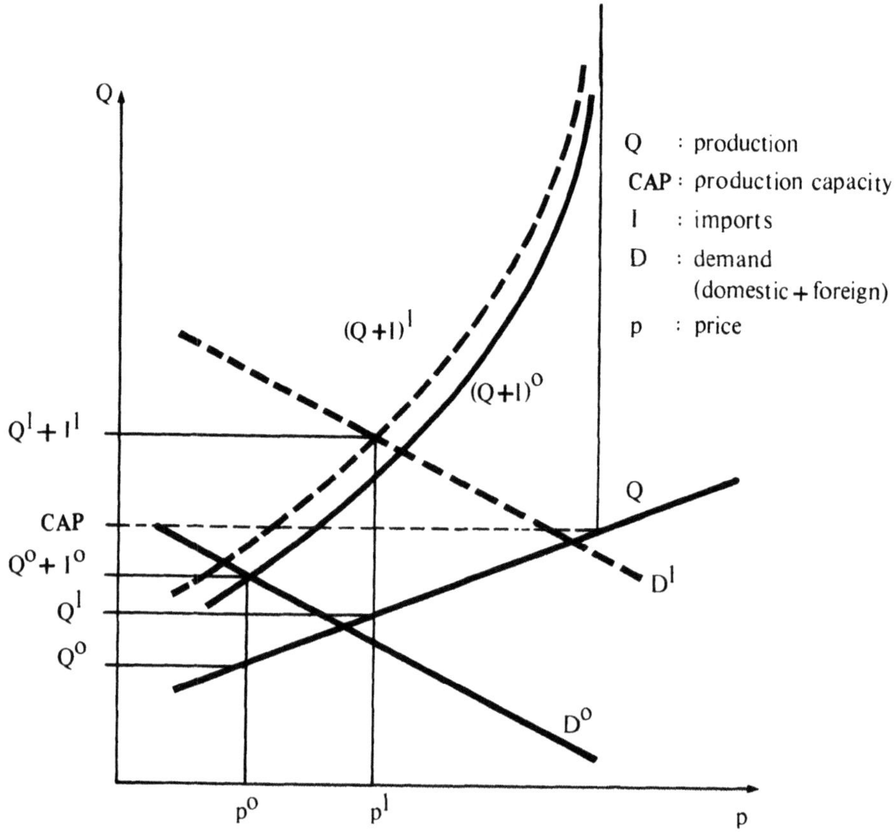

Fig. 3. Respective effects of an exogenous increase in demand on production and imports.

expressed as deviations from trend (trend due in particular to the specific composition of the basket of exported goods) in order to suppress any collinearity with the demand variable.

3.5.3. Capacity Utilization. In the export equations, the variable used is $\log u'$ (expressed as deviation from trend) with $u' = (Q - X)/\mathrm{CAP} = u(Q - X)/Q$ (Q = production, X = exports, CAP = production capacity, u = capacity utilization), which indicates the proportion of the production capacity which is not used to satisfy domestic demand.

In the import equations, the variable introduced is $\log(1 - u)$ (with a negative coefficient). The presence of this variable, i.e., of a non-linear relationship between imports and capacity utilization, in which imports increase indefinitely when capacity utilization tends to one, in the import equations induces an important stabilizing mechanism in DMS: the closer the capacity utilization is to one, the higher is the proportion of an exogenous increase of domestic demand which will lead to an increase of imports and not to an increase of domestic production, resulting in an elasticity of production to demand tending to zero when the capacity utilization tends to one (see Figure 3). This clearly prevents non-realistic values of the degree of capacity utilization (i.e. near or greater than one) being obtained.

In the case of imports of agricultural and food industries products, where no capacity utilization is calculated, a similar effect[12] is introduced through the ratio of actual production to its trend (in agriculture), or through a modulation of the elasticity with respect to demand by the average rate of growth of production in recent years.

Imports of energy are calculated as the difference between demand which is endogenous, and production, which is exogenous.

3.5.4. Econometric Results. Table 4 and Table 5 give the main results of the econometric estimation. The results for the import equations suggest the following comments.

(*i*) The coefficients of log D are roughly equal to one (as compared to 1.7 in DMS–1). This result has been obtained by introducing a time trend in the equation, but the importance of this autonomous trend in imports (10% annual growth for consumer goods) is not fully emphasized. The actual elasticity of imports to demand, including the influence of the degree of utilization of capacity, remains greater than one, but is much lower than in DMS–1.

(*ii*) The relative price variable appears to have a significant effect on imports of consumer goods, although the global effect on imports remains low, as in DMS–1.

3.6. Production Functions

In each of the three *manufacturing industries,* the production functions are derived from a clay–clay vintage model including a formalization of the productivity cycle (see [4]). They describe the links between equipment and production capacity on the one hand, and between actual production and employment on the other.

This model can be written as follows:

$$\mathrm{CAP}_t = \alpha(1+a)^t \sum_{v=t-m_t^*}^{v=t-1} E_v \qquad (1)$$

$$Q_t = \alpha(1+a)^t \sum_{v=t-m_t}^{v=t-1} E_v \qquad (2)$$

$$N_t^* = \frac{\alpha}{\alpha'}\left(\frac{1+a}{1+a'}\right)^t \sum_{v=t-m_t}^{v=t-1} \frac{1}{(1+b')^v} E_v \qquad (3)$$

Table 4. Exports of products of manufacturing industries.

Products	D	$1 + D^0/D$	$\left(\frac{Pf}{Px}\right)^a$	$\left(\frac{Pf}{Px}\right)^a_{-1}$	$\left(\frac{Px}{Pd}\right)^a$	u'^a	Constant	Dummies (D . . .)	R^2	D.W.
Intermediate goods	1.15	1.19	1.45	1.13	1.4	−1.45	9.44	0.08 D73[a]	0.997	
	(50.6)	(3.3)	(3.2)	(3.3)	(2.9)	(1.6)		(1.9)		
Investment goods	1.15	0.38	0.39			−2.43	10.29		0.999	1.9
	(32)	(1.8)	(3.7)			(5.8)				
Consumer goods	1.02		0.64	0.63		−1.51	9.71	0.055 D67[a]	0.998	1.7
	(65.7)		(3.5)	(3.3)		(5.1)		(2.3)		

D = demand indicator, industrialized countries,
D^0 = demand indicator, non-industrialized countries,
Pf = foreign price,
Px = export price,
Pd = domestic price,
u' = capacity utilization, rectified for export content of output,
All variables, excluding u', are at constant prices and in logarithmic form.
[a]Variables expressed as deviation from trend.

Table 5. Imports of products of agriculture, food industries and manufacturing industries.

Product	DD	$Q/\bar{Q}$	$1-u$	P_m/P_d	Time	Dummies	R^2	D.W.
Agricultural products	1.177 (5.8)	−1.46 (−4)				D67, D68	0.89	1.22
Food	$2.4 - 0.77\bar{\tau}$ (34) (4.1)					D67, D73	0.99	2.54
Intermediate goods	1.007 (4.5)		−0.106 (1.5)		0.06 (5.0)	D62	0.99	2.11
Investment goods	1.016 (3.9)		−0.227 (1.7)		0.069 (4.0)	D64	0.99	1.76
Consumer goods	0.947 (2.2)		−0.36 (2.0)	−0.775 (3.2)	0.102 (2.9)	–	0.99	1.88

DD = domestic demand, including changes in stocks,
Q = production,
$\bar{Q}$ = production trend,
u = degree of utilization of capacity,
$\bar{\tau}$ = average rate of growth of production over three years (food industry),
P_m = foreign price,
P_d = domestic price.
All variables, excluding $Q/\bar{Q}$ and time are at constant prices and in logarithmic form.

$$\frac{N_t}{N_{t-1}} = \left(\frac{N_t^*}{N_{t-1}}\right)^{\lambda}, \tag{4}$$

$$u = Q_t/\text{CAP}_t \tag{5}$$

with E_v = investment in machinery and equipment completed at date v,
Q_t = actual production,
CAP_t = capacity of production,
N_t^* = 'normal' employment,
N_t = actual employment,
m_t = age of the oldest equipment in use,
m_t^* = age of the oldest profitable equipment (generally exogenous),
u_t = capacity utilization.

The method of estimation used minimized the sum of squared residuals referring to actual employment, m_t being chosen in such a way that the residuals of (2) are nil; in all other respects, the method is very similar to that described in [4]. This procedure does not explicitly take into account the relationship between the labour productivity on equipment of vintage m_t^* and the real wage rate, which proves to be essential in determining the importance of labour-saving-embodied technical progress (b') as compared to disembodied technical progress (a').[13] However, this relationship has been used implicitly in such a way that the implicit mark-up[14] on equipment of vintage m_t^* is roughly constant over the estimation period. Table 6 gives the numerical values of the parameters thus obtained.

In the *other industries*, the model used is simpler and combines the representation of a productivity cycle (an equation similar to (4)) with the determination of 'normal' employment by an exponential trend of labour productivity, i.e., with WH = weekly hours of work,

$$\log\left(\frac{N}{N-1}\right) = a + \lambda \log\left(\frac{Q/\text{WH}}{N-1}\right) + b_t,$$

where λ is the 'damping factor' of equation (4). It may be noted that the λ coefficients for intermediate goods and construction are much lower than in DMS–1, where their respective values were 0.28 and 0.76 (see Table 7).

3.7. Prices

The econometric price equations determine the price of value added; a mechanical repercussion of the input prices on output prices is supposed, i.e., any change in the value of inputs results in an equal change in the value of output. This is somewhat different from what was done in DMS–1, where the behavioural equations concerned the output prices, with an elasticity of

Table 6. Production functions in manufacturing industries (estimation period: 1960–1975).

	a (%)	a' (%)	b' (%)	λ	Average value of m_t	Average value of m_t^*	Average value of the implicit mark-up rates
Intermediate goods	−0.8	2.2	4	0.18	11.0	13.8	9.3 (7.9 over 1960–1973)
Investment goods	−0.8	4.4	2	0.44	11.0	15.3	10.6 (10.1 over 1960–1973)
Consumer goods	−1.9	3.6	3	0.36	11.0	15.5	9.4 (8.5 over 1960–1972)

Table 7. Parameter (λ) of the productivity cycle in non-manufacturing industries.

Industry	Construction	Transport, communication	Services	Trade
λ	0.37	0.15	0.22	0.23

output prices to input prices determined by an econometric adjustment, and not put a priori equal to the ratio of intermediate consumption to production.

The other characteristics of the price equations remain unchanged, and the explanatory variables are

(*i*) capacity utilization;

(*ii*) the rate of growth of unit labour cost (however, it is supposed that a negative growth rate of unit labour cost does not result in a negative impact on the rate of growth of prices);

(*iii*) the profit rate, lagged by one year.

Thus, the price model is mainly based on a mark-up on costs, with additional influences of the demand pressure on available supply (u) and the financial situation of firms (π_{-1}). This model is used for the three manufacturing industries, construction and services (see Table 8).

For food industries and energy, the price equations determine the growth rate of the output price, which enables the introduction of mechanical repercussions of specific taxes (on tobacco, alcohol and petroleum products). Furthermore, in the case of energy, prices are determined separately for mineral fuels, electricity and petroleum products as functions of unit labour cost and import prices of petroleum and mineral fuels.

The price of agricultural products and the relative prices of transport and communication services are exogenous.

Wage Rates

In DMS–2, as in DMS–1, the wage rates – defined as the ratio of total wages paid by a sub-sector of enterprises to the number of man-hours worked per week in the corresponding industry – are determined independently of enterprises for most of the industries or sub-sectors.[15] The formulation used in DMS–1 was a very classical one: the growth rate of the nominal wage rate was explained by the growth rate of the price of households' final consumption and by an indicator of the tensions on the labour market,[16] and occasionally by some additional variables (rate of change in labour productivity, ratio of the net new credit in the economy to total gross domestic product).

This approach was completely unsuccessful with the new series, and on the new estimation period. Various alternative indicators for the tension on the labour market have been tried without any satisfactory results, the least disappointing being the one previously used in DMS–1. The reason for this is quite clear: the year 1975 was characterized simultaneously by a sustained growth, or even by an acceleration of the real wage rate, despite the very important increase in unemployment. It is then not possible to obtain any coherent effect on wages of an indicator based on unemployment in a sample including 1975.

The solution finally adopted consists of using an indicator of the tension on the labour market which is not based on a measure of unemployment. Such an indicator has been previously proposed for the French economy (cf.

Table 8. Price equations.

	U	$0.5\,(\dot{ULC} + \lvert\dot{ULC}\rvert)$	$\pi_{-1} - \bar{\pi}$ (%)	$\dot{P}_{IC}$	Constant	Dummies	R^2	D.W.
Food industries[a]		0.29	–0.52	0.23	2.7	D61, D68	0.92	2.07
		(2.4)	(2.5)	(2.0)				
Intermediate goods	2.0	0.93	–3.1		–1.76	–	0.72	2.19
	(3.5)	(5.4)	(1.7)					
Investment goods		0.67	–0.81		0.62	D74	0.91	2.58
		(4.7)	(2.4)					
Consumer goods	0.88	0.57	–1.43		–0.71	D74–D73	0.87	2.17
	(3.0)	(6.7)	(2.9)					
Construction		0.62	–0.32		2.00	–	0.65	1.5
		(3.9)	(1.7)					
Services		0.40	–0.60		4.06	–	0.50	1.97
		(2.7)	(1.4)					

The endogenous variable is the annual growth rate of the price of value added.
[a]Output prices, adjusted for the specific tax on tobacco and alcohol.
U = degree of utilization of capacity,
ULC = unit labour cost,
π = profit margin,
$\bar{\pi}$ = average profit margin over the estimation period,
P_{IC} = average price of intermediate consumption.

Table 9. Determination of the wage rates.

	$\dot{p}$	$(u_5)_{-1}$	Constant	R^2	D.W.
Food industry	1.09 (3.8)	0.45 (1.2)	−32.0	0.82	1.1
Intermediate goods	0.85 (3.4)	0.81 (2.5)	−61.4	0.86	2.2
Investment goods	0.68 (3.1)	0.72 (2.5)	−53.1	0.84	2.7
Consumer goods	0.76 (3.4)	0.64 (2.2)	−46.3	0.84	3.3
Construction	0.38 (1.0)	0.92 (2.0)	−67.1	0.60	1.8
Services	1.19 (4.6)		4.49	0.60	1.7
Trade	1.02 (3.6)		5.10	0.48	2.2
Large public corporations	1.12 (3.5)	0.30 (0.7)	−20.6	0.76	2.1

The endogenous variable is the annual growth rate of the nominal wage rate.
$\dot{p}$ = rate of growth of the price of households' final consumption,
u_5 = capacity utilization in the industry producing investment goods.

for instance [5]); the indicator in question is capacity utilization in the manufacturing industries, or, more specifically, in the industries producing investment goods. The main arguments in favour of such an indicator are

(*i*) the 'tension' to be measured is not a global one but refers in fact to skilled workers only, which are the only category for which actual tensions exist: this category is typically employed in the production of investment goods;

(*ii*) this first argument explains the leadership of such industries in the determination of wage rates, which has been observed by a number of authors (cf. [5] for references).

The final choice, between capacity utilization in the industries producing investment goods or in the whole manufacturing industry, was made on the grounds of the quality of the statistical fit. Table 9 presents the econometric results.

4. Annex: Main Characteristics of the Dynamic Simulation of DMS–2 over the Period 1962–1975

Three categories of results[17] are presented in this annex:

(1) A comparison of the dynamic simulations of DMS–2 with those of four other annual models over their sample periods (Table 10). For a correct understanding of the table, the following factors should be taken into account: (1) the periods are not identical, (2) the Hickman–Coen model is much smaller than the others, and (3) that the list of exogenous variables is different from one model to another.[18]

Table 10. Comparison of the dynamic simulations of five annual models over their sample periods (root mean square or average absolute errors in %).

Model (period)	CANDIDE (1955–1970)	Hickman–Coen (1951–1966)	Wharton Annual (1950–1969)	DMS–1 (1962–1972)	DMS–2 (1962–1975)
Gross output	0.8	2.1	1.6	0.9	1.1
Private consumption	1.0	1.6		0.8	1.5
GFCF equipment	4.9	8.2		2.7	4.2
GFCF business–construction	4.4			2.1	2.9
GFCF dwellings	5.5	12.6		2.2	5.5
Exports	1.5	3.3		2.5	3.1
Imports	2.2	3.4		2.9	4.5
Changes in inventories	60	67		18	24
Gross output deflator	0.8	2.7	2.9	0.7	2.7
Employment	0.5	1.6		0.6	0.5
Unemployment	8.7	22	26	21	13

Table 11. Statistical analysis of the ex-post dynamic simulation of DMS–2 for selected variables.

Variables	$U \times 10^2$	UM	US	UC	AAE	AAE (%)
Gross output (million 1970 F)	0.6	0.07	0.23	0.69	7667	1.1
Imports (million 1970 F)	1.8	0.28	0.11	0.61	3457	4.5
Private consumption (million 1970 F)	0.8	0.36	0.10	0.54	6011	1.5
GFCF equipment (million 1970 F)	3.3	0.01	0.10	0.89	2778	4.2
GFCF business–construction (million 1970 F)	1.9	0.30	0.01	0.70	1070	2.9
GFCF dwelling (million 1970 F)	3.0	0.33	0.30	0.37	2161	5.5
Changes in inventories (million 1970 F)	10.9	0.09	0.11	0.80	2900	24.1
Exports (million 1970 F)	2.8	0.24	0.53	0.23	4261	3.1
Rate of change of consumer price (%)	11.0	0.02	0.03	0.96	1.1	19.1
Rate of change of the gross output deflator (%)	12.9	0.05	0.12	0.83	1.4	25.3
Rate of change of average hourly wages (%)	7.0	0.04	0.42	0.55	1.3	13.0
Employment (thousands)	0.3	0.31	0.45	0.25	103	0.5
Unemployment (thousands)	8.2	0.46	0.18	0.36	69	12.6
Disposable income of households (million 1970 F)	1.2	0.44	0.10	0.46	13045	2.6
Degree of utilization of capacity (%)						
Intermediate goods	14.2	0.13	0.07	0.80	1.4	1.7
Investment goods	7.5	ϵ	0.05	0.95	1.0	1.2
Consumer goods	11.1	0.01	0.06	0.93	1.5	1.9
Profit rate (%)						
Intermediate goods	10.8	0.02	ϵ	0.98	1.3	30.5
Investment goods	6.0	0.16	0.01	0.83	0.9	15.6
Consumer goods	13.7	ϵ	0.07	0..93	1.6	22.4

U = Theil's inequality coefficient,
UM = partial coefficient of unequal central tendency,
US = partial coefficient of unequal variation,
UC = partial coefficient of unequal co-variation,
AAE = average absolute error,
AAE (%) = average absolute percentage error.

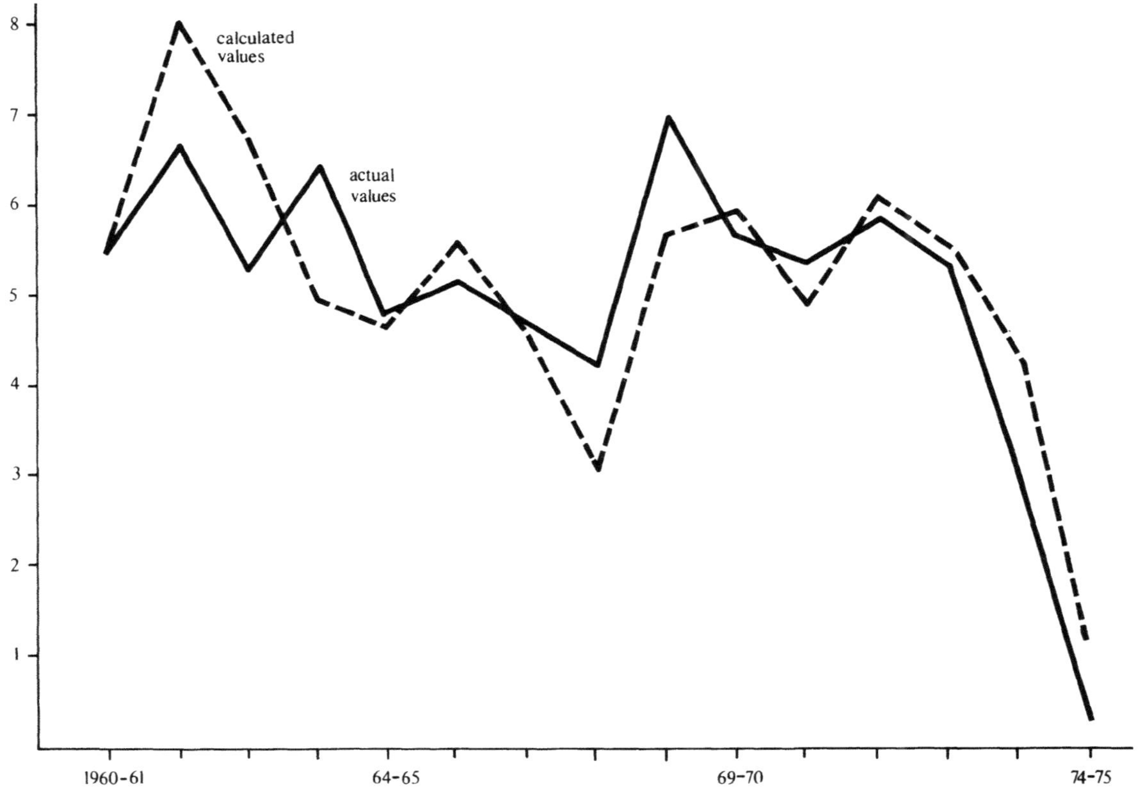

Fig. 4. Dynamic simulation of DMS–2 over the period 1962–1975: rate of cha ; of real gross output (%).

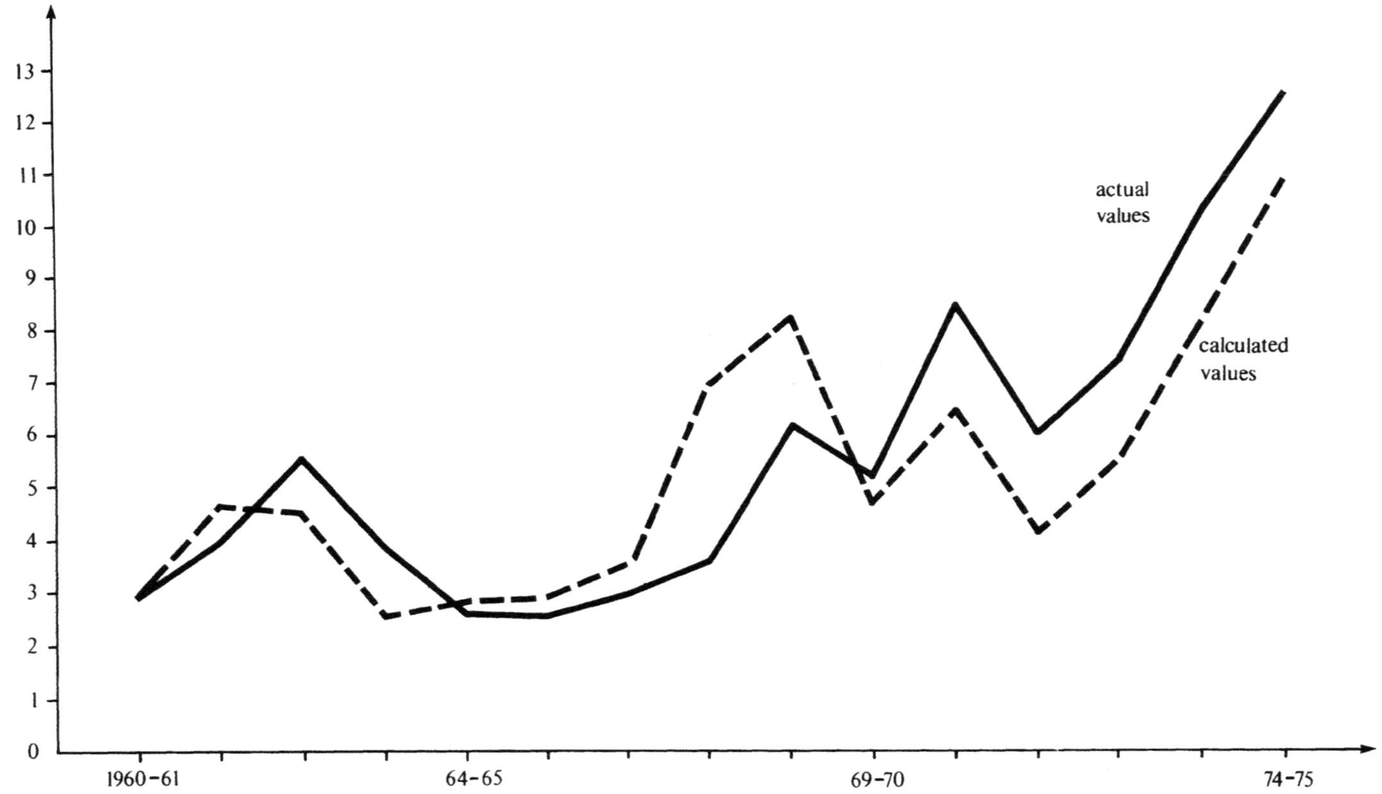

Fig. 5. Dynamic simulation of DMS–2 over the period 1962–1975: rate of change of the gross output deflator (%).

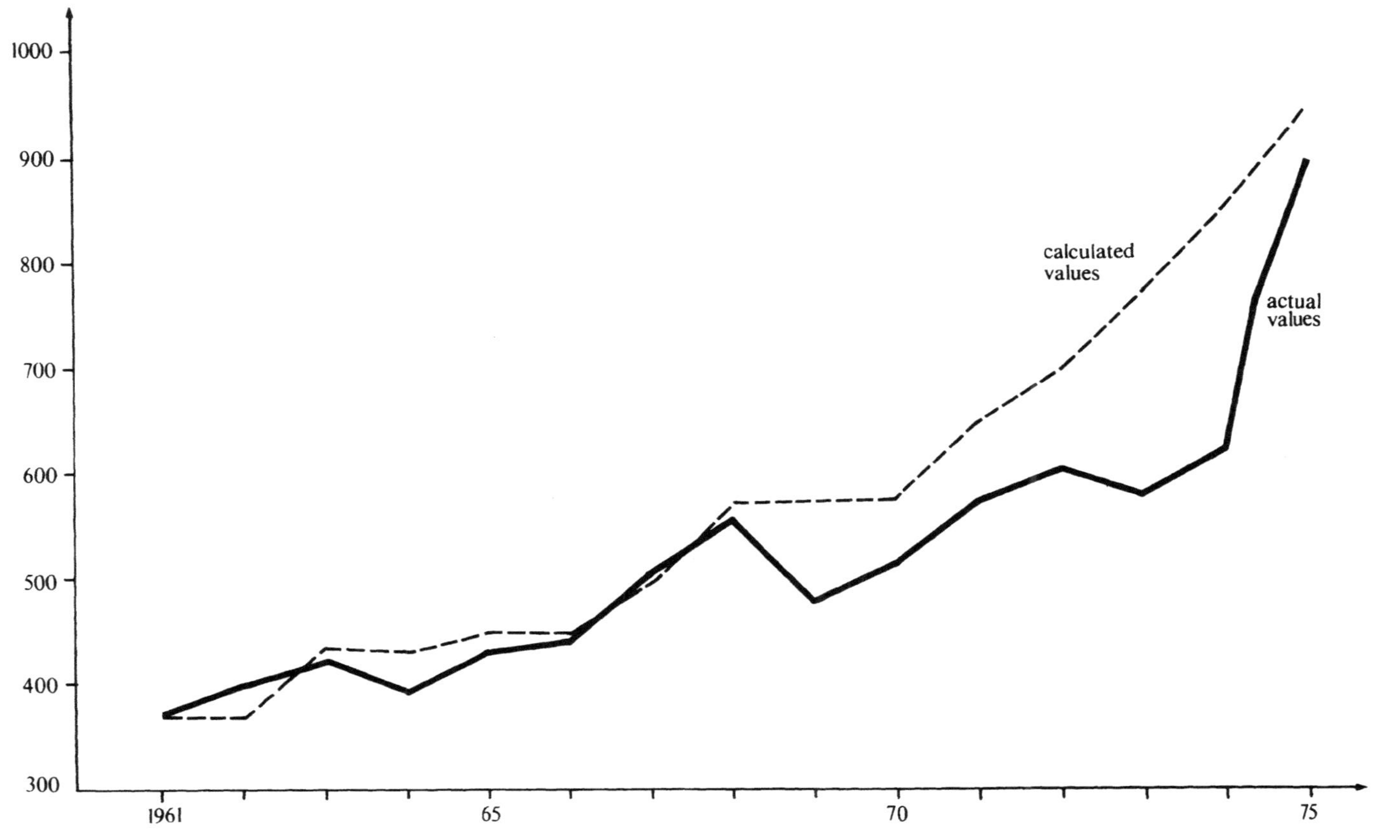

Fig. 6. Dynamic simulation of DMS–2 over the period 1962–1975: unemployment (thousands).

(2) A list of classical statistical indicators for some selected variables (Table 11).

(3) The diagrams of actual and calculated values for three variables: the rate of change of real gross output, the rate of change of the gross output deflator, and unemployment (Figures 4, 5 and 6).

References

1. Aglietta, M., Bussery, H., Courbis, R., and Seibel, C., 'Le modèle FIFI'. Les Collections de l'INSEE C22 (1973), C37–38 (1975).
2. Aglietta, M. and Courbis R. (1969), 'Un outil pour le plan: le modèle FIFI'. Économie et statistique, 1.
3. Artus, P. and Muet P.A. (1978), 'Une étude comparative des propriétés dynamiques de onze modèles américains et quatre modèles français'. Communication at the Journées sur la construction et l'utilisation de modèles macroéconomiques, Grenoble.
4. Benassy, J.P., Fouquet, D. and Malgrange, P. (1975), 'Estimation d'une fonction de production à générations de capital', Annales de l'INSEE, 19.
5. Boyer, R. and Mistral, J (1976), 'Formation de capital, prix relatifs, inflation'. Économie et statistique, 77.
6. Brillet, J.L. (1979), 'Mini-DMS version 2.0': presentation et premières résultats'. INSEE internal note 320/33.
7. Brillet J.L. (1979), 'Les multiplicateurs de Mini-DMS version 2.0'. INSEE internal note 320/44.
8. Charpin, J.M. (1976), 'Relance et inflation: une approche quantitative'. Économie et statistique, 77.
9. Charpin J.M., et al. (1978), 'Une projection de l'économie française à l'horizon 83'. Économie et statistique 100.
10. Fouquet, D., et al. (1976), 'DMS, modèle de prévision à moyen terme'. Économie et statistique, 79.
11. Fouquet, D., et al. (1977), 'Short and medium-term dynamics in the DMS–1 model of the French economy', in Systèmes dynamiques et modèles économiques. Colloques internationaux de CNRS, 259. Paris: Éditions du CNRS.
12. Fouquet, D., et al. (1976), 'DMS, French medium-term forecasting model'. Communication at the European Meeting of the Econometric Society, Helsinki.
13. Fouquet, D., et al. (1978), 'DMS, modèle dynamique multi-sectoriel'. Les Collections de l'INSEE, C64–65.
14. Guillaume, H. (1978), 'Analyse des multiplicateurs de politique économique de DMS'. Annales de l'INSEE, 32.
15. Guillaume, H. and Muet, P.A. (1979), 'Simulations et multiplicateurs dynamiques du modèle DMS'. Revue économique, 30: 2.
16. Houthakker, H.S. and Taylor, L.D. (1970), 'Consumer Demand in the United States'. Cambridge, MA: Harvard University Press.
17. McCracken, M.C. and Sonnen, C.A. (1972), 'A system for large econometric models: management estimation and simulation', in Proceedings of the Association for Computing Machinery: Annual Conference.
18. Muet, P.A. (1978), 'Croissance, profits et investissement: une étude empirique de l'investissement macroéconomique'. Thesis, University of Paris – I.
19. Muet, P.A. and Zagamé, P. (1976), 'Fonction d'investissement et retards échelonnés'. Annales de l'INSEE, 21.
20. Teillet, P. (1979), 'Un nouveau modèle de projection à moyen-terme: PROPAGE'. Courrier des Statistiques, 9.
21. Vallet, D. (1972), 'L'épargne à moyen terme: une approche économétrique'. Économie et statistique, 66.
22. Vallet, D. (1976), 'L'investissement en logement des ménages'. Annales de l'INSEE, 24.

23. 'Mini-DMS: rapport du groupe de travail sur l'étude des propriétes du modèle Mini-DMS'. ENSAE–INSEE–CEPREMAP internal note 320/3750 (1977).
24. Commissariat Général du Plan, 'Synthèse des travaux des commissions et comités consultés pour la révision du VIIe Plan 1978.
25. Ministère de l'Environnement et du Cadre de vie, Études et notes d'information, 20 (1978).

Endnotes

1. *Dynamique multi-sectoriel.*
2. Mainly by MM. J.M. Charpin, D. Fouquet, H. Guillaume, P.A. Muet (INSEE) and D. Vallet (CGP).
3. Under the direction of J.M. Charpin and with the participation of D. Bresson, J.L. Brillet, H. Chaillé, A. Claver, V. Genthon, Ph. Kaminski, J. Maurice, A. Orléan, E. Raoul, J. Rouchet, L. Tréca, H. Vigouroux, P. Villa.
4. The large public corporations are the eight major public enterprises comprising the energy, transport and communication industries.
5. This version is, in some respects, still provisional.
6. The projections at the second level (forty products) are made through the use of the PROPAGE model (INSEE), of which a short description can be found in [20], and at the third level by the BIPE (projection of approximately two hundred indicators in physical quantities).
7. However, for accounting reasons, complete generation and use of income accounts are described for the sub-sector of the industrial establishments of general government and private non-profit institutions serving households. Furthermore, a separate treatment is provided for large public corporations.
8. By aggregation of a more detailed classification.
9. The actual variable used in the model is real consumption per person.
10. The estimation has been made without taking into account the constraint $d/c = f/e = \lambda$.
11. A specific treatment is adopted for stocks of agricultural products.
12. But of opposite sign in these cases where a higher level of production is an indication of production surpluses (and not tensions on production capacity) and has a negative (and not positive) effect on imports.
13. The growth rate of capital productivity being in any case very low, capital-saving-embodied technical progress has been supposed to be nil.
14. Defined as $1 - W/\pi$, with W = real labour cost per person employed and π = labour productivity on equipment of vintage m_t^*.
15. Wage rates in agriculture, energy (large public corporations excluded), transport and communication (large public corporations excluded), and housing services are determined as linear functions of the average wage rate in the rest of the economy.
16. The indicator used was log (DENS/OENS), where DENS = registered unemployment and OENS = registered unfilled job vacancies.
17. As we are still in the process of testing and improving the model, these results are to be considered preliminary.
18. For example, DMS–2 contains almost no exogenous variables in nominal terms (except for foreign prices), which was not the case for DMS–1.

THE REGINA MODEL: A SHORT PRESENTATION AND SOME MAIN RESULTS

RAYMOND COURBIS and GÉRARD CORNILLEAU

Introduced in French planning for the IVth plan (related to years 1962–1965), regional planning was, until the VIth plan (related to 1971–1975), only a regionalisation of national figures, and so had no feedback on national planning. The purpose of the REGINA model proposed in 1971[1] was to avoid such a dichotomy and to analyse, interdependently, regional and national problems. REGINA is a large 'regional–national' model[2] which, because of its interdependent structure, enables the analysis not only of the impact of national development on regional development, but also of the impact of regional development (and regional policy) on national figures.

Built at the GAMA[3] from 1972 to 1975 for the French Planning Office (Commissariat Général du Plan), the REGINA model became operational in 1976 and then began to be used by the planning office and afterwards by other administrations.

Since the REGINA has been presented elsewhere in several papers,[4] we shall give only a brief description (section 1) before presenting some simulation results – on the impact of a change in location of manufacturing investment (section 2) and location of public demand (section 3) – analysing some multipliers of the model (section 4).

1. The REGINA Model: A Short Presentation

As indicated above, the REGINA model is an interdependent regional–national model. It analyses the French economy in five large regions (see Figure 1): (i) the *Parisian region,* the national capital area, a very developed, urbanised and congested area; (ii) the *Parisian basin,* the six regions surrounding Paris – a natural area for decentralisation for the Parisian region; (iii) *Northern and Eastern France,* an old industrial area under redevelopment; (iv) the *Mediterranean region;* (v) *Western and South-Western France,* a more agricultural, rural and less developed region. But, at the same time, each of these regions is divided between (i) rural zones; (ii) small urban zones (less than 60,000 inhabitants in 1968); and (iii) large urban zones; this enables the

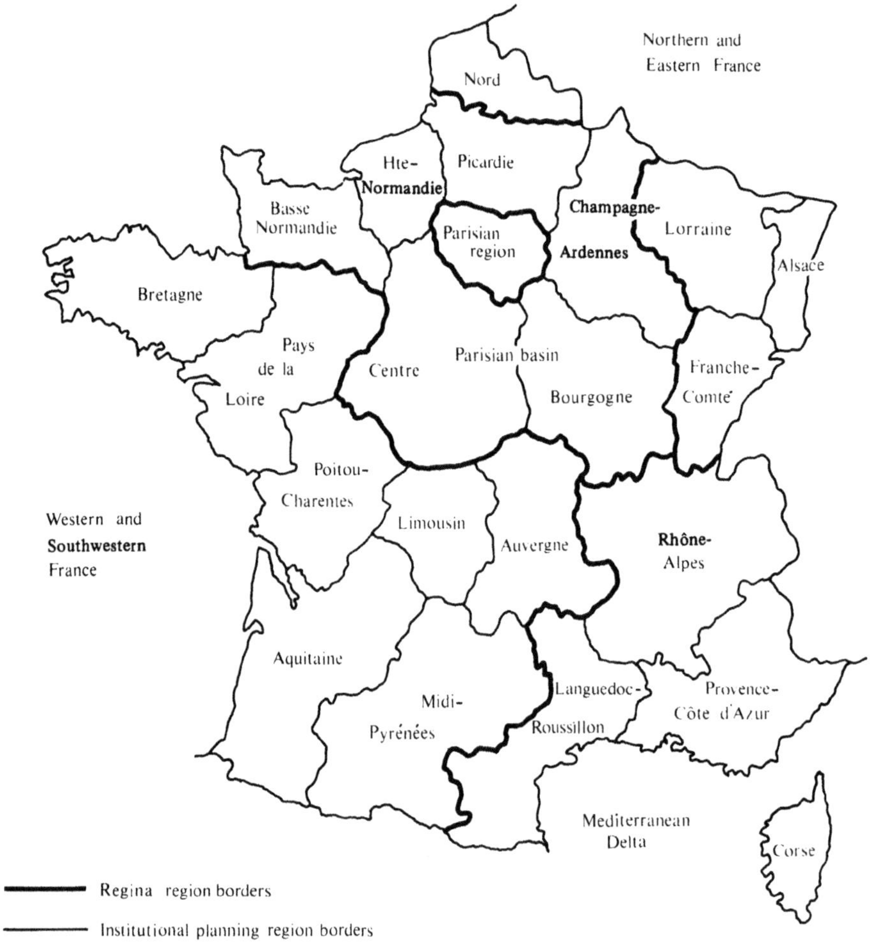

Fig. 1. The REGINA regions.

model to take into account the differences between rural and urban areas, and so to analyse the impact of national and regional development on urbanisation, and vice versa.

From an economic point of view, one of the main characteristics of the REGINA model is its recognition of the existence of multi-regional firms and the impact of their regional policy. Consequently, three groups of industries are distinguished, according to the nature of factors determining their location: (i) industries whose location is strictly determined by *geographical factors;* (ii) industries (mainly the major part of the tertiary sector) for which location is determined by *demand;* (iii) industries (mainly manufacturing) for which location depends on *location opportunities,* i.e. opportunities to invest in different regions.

The distinction between 'restricted location' industries and 'non-restricted location' industries is a central feature of the REGINA model. For the 'restricted location' industries, regional factors determine the regional production (dependent on regional effective demand for 'demand-located' industries) while production in 'non-restricted location' industries depends on national and interregional variables. More precisely, in this latter case, regional production is, in the medium term, determined by regional capital accumulation (which depends itself on the investments made in the region, i.e., on choices of location) – production depends therefore on supply factors. Thus for products in these industries, there is no equality between regional demand and regional production, so the medium-term equilibrium is achieved through external trade (with other regions or other countries).

So, regional output depends, for the demand-located sector, on existing effective demand, and, for the 'non-restricted location' sector, on capital accumulation (and investments) of this sector. But this latter has a more important effect, because production by 'non-restricted location' industries exerts a direct effect (via intermediate demand or demand for investment goods) or an indirect effect (via an influence on distributed income and hence on households' consumption) on the production in 'demand-located' industries.

Through the medium of regional investment, production by 'non-restricted location' industries depends on the national amount of investment in those industries, and so depends on national conditions (national total demand and financing possibilities). But, at the same time, because self-financing possibilities (important determinants of investment) are dependent upon national average costs and thus on regional costs and on national total demand resulting from an aggregation of regional demand, there is also a feedback from regional equilibrium on national investment in 'non-restricted location' industries. There is thus a strong interdependency between regional and national equilibria, as shown by figure 2. This interdependency is an important characteristic of the structure of the REGINA model.[5]

Since the supply conditions, and in particular the financing conditions, have an important impact on production in 'non-restricted location' industries (and thus on determination of regional – and national – equilibrium), the dynamics of regional wage determination (which influences unit costs and thus profitability and prices) are also central to the REGINA model. However, because labour mobility between regions is imperfect, there cannot be said to be a single labour market in which all wage rates are determined – as would be the case if the situations in the different labour markets were the same. An inflow of labour only partially compensates for growing labour market tightness. Consequently, determination of changes in wage rates is made separately and directly for each of the five Regina regions, and the relationships which are used for each of them are different. Regional Phillips curves are used but – and this is very important in the general framework of the REGINA model – there is a *leading effect* of the Parisian region

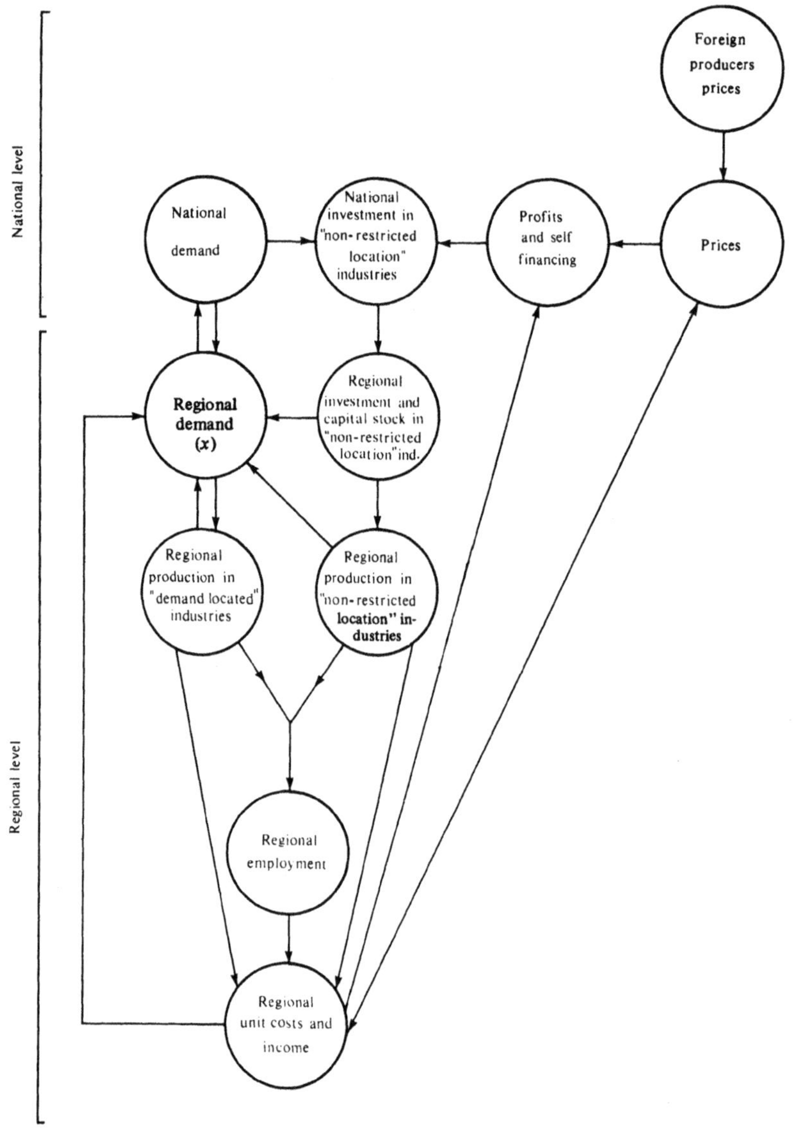

Fig. 2. Interdependency between ratio factors and regional equilibrium in the REGINA model. (*x*) Regional demand depends also upon price.

labour market: so increases in wage rates in the Parisian region (which depend on consumer price increases and labour market tightness) have a direct impact on wage rate increases for the other regions (these depend also – except in Eastern and Northern France – on regional labour market conditions).

So because of the leading effect of the Parisian region, but also because of the differentiation and non-linearity of the wage relationships, job creation in different regions does not have the same impact on increase in regional wage rates, and thus on average national wage rate increase – and consequently on average costs, prices and profits. So there is an impact of the regional distribution of the labour force and employment on investment and competiveness, and thus on national equilibrium, as will be apparent from the simulations we shall now present.

2. Impact on a Manufacturing Investment Transfer

We shall consider here the ten-year impact of a gradual modification, between 1970 and 1980, in the regional distribution of manufacturing investment. In practice, we shall assume that, over ten years, manufacturing investment in one of the five Regina regions increases by two percent of the national total (which leads over the ten years to the creation of some forty to fifty thousand jobs in manufacturing); on the other hand, we shall assume that the manufacturing investment share of the four other regions of the model is reduced, with an equivalent reduction in relative value.

This change in the distribution of manufacturing investment entails an ex-ante interregional transfer of production, but this has practically no effect on total manufacturing output, since we have assumed that the capital output ratio was the same for all regions with identical prices for equipment (these prices, in fact, vary from one region to another, so that there is at the same time a certain differentiation of the capital ratios, in monetary terms).

Since the model is nonlinear, the results of the simulations will depend on the reference trend chosen. Each variant thus must remain in the neighbourhood of three contrasted 'control solutions':

- the first assumption is that of fairly sustained growth between 1970 and 1980, corresponding to the aims of the VIIth Plan (600,000 unemployed in 1980);
- the second assumption is closer to the observed real trend (1,200,000 unemployed in 1980);
- the third assumption is that of much slower growth (1,800,000 unemployed in 1980).

Table 1 shows the results of a simulation for the five manufacturing distribution variants, in the light of these three assumptions on the initial trend.

First of all, it is clear that increased manufacturing investment in the Paris region would, in any event, affect national development very unfavourably, bringing about (1) a fall in national output in 1980 of 0.81 percent given the first assumption or 0.55 percent fiven the third assumption; (2) worsened inflation; (3) deterioration in the employment situation and increased unemployment, with from 77,000 to 120,000 more unemployed in 1980, depending on the assumptions; (4) deterioration of the trade balance, with an increase in deficit value terms in 1980 of 2910–3655 million francs) and (5)

Table 1. Impact of a transfer of manufacturing investment towards one region, with a two-point increase in that region and a concomitant equal relative decrease in other regions: effect after ten years (1980).

	Control solution 1 (national unemployment: 600,000)				
	PR	PB	NE	GD	WSW
National impact					
GDP in volume (Δ %)	−0.81	−0.04	+0.33	+0.21	−0.29
Manufacturing employment (Δ thousands)	−85.2	−0.6	+22.3	+17.5	−18.1
Total employment (Δ thousands)	−131.6	−4.6	+40.2	+31.7	−31.2
Unemployment (Δ thousands)	+120.5	+1.1	−35.2	−27.8	+25.6
Hourly wage rate (Δ %)	+2.08	−0.36	−0.59	−0.53	+0.72
GDP deflator (Δ %)	+1.27	−0.08	−0.49	−0.34	+0.76
Foreign trade balance in value (Δ in million francs)	−3655	−39	+1476	+1004	−2253
Public finance (Δ in million francs)	+4229	+428	−1588	−1529	+1868
Regional inequality: Δ (in points) of the ratio of private income per capita in Paris to private income per capita in other regions	+1.44	−0.56	+0.02	−0.11	−1.46
Impact on the region towards which investment is transferred					
GDP in volume (Δ %)	+1.89	+2.94	+2.97	+2.80	+3.70
Manufacturing employment (Δ thousands)	+39.6	+54.0	+51.4	+50.0	+58.4
Total employment (Δ thousands)	+63.3	+120.6	+76.4	+89.9	+166.3
Unemployment (Δ thousands)	−28.5	−59.8	−48.4	−51.6	−74.6
Hourly wage rate (Δ %)	+3.07	+4.52	−0.48	+0.68	+8.76

Regions: PR, Parisian region; PB, Parisian basin; NE, north and east; GD, Great Mediterranean Delta; WSW, west and south-west.

Table 1. Continued.

	Control solution 2 (national unemployment: 1,200,000)				
	PR	PB	NE	GD	WSW
National impact					
GDP in volume (Δ %)	−0.70	+0.08	+0.27	+0.16	−0.03
Manufacturing employment (Δ thousands)	−71.8	+11.9	+16.2	+11.8	+10.8
Total employment (Δ thousands)	−108.6	+14.5	+29.7	+22.4	+9.4
Unemployment (Δ thousands)	+99.2	−14.6	−25.9	−19.7	−9.7
Hourly wage rate (Δ %)	+1.80	−0.36	−0.50	−0.42	−0.01
GDP deflator (Δ %)	+1.17	−0.19	−0.41	−0.26	+0.10
Foreign trade balance in value (Δ in million francs)	−3243	+503	+1231	+750	−437
Public finance (Δ in million francs)	+3915	−413	−1342	−1267	+320
Regional inequality:					
Δ (in points) of the ratio of private income per capita in Paris to private income per capita in other regions	+1.00	−0.24	−0.02	−0.13	−0.56
Impact on the region towards which investment is transferred					
GDP in volume (Δ %)	+1.73	+2.38	+2.75	+2.52	+2.71
Manufacturing employment (Δ thousands)	+37.1	+52.5	+45.9	+44.7	+59.9
Total employment (Δ thousands)	+56.0	+87.6	+68.8	+77.5	+110.3
Unemployment (Δ thousands)	−26.8	−50.5	−42.9	−45.1	−59.7
Hourly wage rate (Δ %)	+2.20	+1.01	−0.42	+0.24	+2.48

Regions: PR, Parisian region; PB, Parisian basin; NE, north and east; GD, Great Mediterranean Delta; WSW, west and south-west.

Table 1. Continued.

	Control solution 3 (national unemployment: 1,800,000)				
	PR	PB	NE	GD	WSW
National impact					
GDP in volume (Δ %)	−0.55	+0.06	+0.21	+0.12	−0.01
Manufacturing employment (Δ thousands)	−57.1	+9.8	+10.6	+7.2	+11.9
Total employment (Δ thousands)	−70.8	+11.6	+19.9	+14.6	+11.6
Unemployment (Δ thousands)	+77.0	−11.5	−17.4	−12.8	−11.3
Hourly wage rate (Δ %)	+1.50	−0.28	−0.40	−0.32	−0.06
GDP deflator (Δ %)	+1.07	−0.16	−0.33	−0.20	+0.02
Foreign trade balance in value (Δ in million francs)	−2910	+402	+944	+543	−206
Public finance (Δ in million francs)	+3710	−378	−1102	−1020	+162
Regional inequality:					
Δ (in points) of the ratio of private income per capita in Paris to private income per capita in other regions	+0.74	−0.17	−0.05	−0.12	−0.36
Impact on the region towards which investment is transferred					
GDP in volume (Δ %)	+1.59	+2.09	+2.47	+2.23	+2.33
Manufacturing employment (Δ thousands)	+33.4	+45.6	+39.4	+38.5	+53.0
Total employment (Δ thousands)	+49.4	+71.9	+59.0	+65.6	+88.4
Unemployment (Δ thousands)	−25.2	−42.7	−36.6	−38.3	−50.0
Hourly wage rate (Δ %)	+1.69	+0.39	−0.35	+0.07	+1.24

Regions: PR, Parisian region, PB, Parisian basin; NE, north and east; GD, Great Mediterranean Delta; WSW, west and south-west.

increase in public finance (depending on the assumptions, financial needs for the administration will show an increase of 3710–4229 million francs). At the same time, income discrepancies between Paris and the provinces would widen.

The reason for this unfavourable inpact is simple. In the Paris region, an increase in manufacturing investment would entail increased output and employment, hence a more rapid rise in wages which would tend to spread to the provinces where, while the reduction in employment would certainly slow down wage rises, the effect of wage increases in the Paris region would nevertheless have to be taken into account. Overall, average wage rates for France as a whole would rise; costs would go up, and this would entail a loss of competitiveness that would hamper exports and increase imports and therefore slow down national growth, with the effects mentioned above. If, on the other hand, the share of industrial investment of a provincial region were to rise there would be both a general slowing effect on wage rises, because of the falling off in the Paris region (because of reduced manufacturing employment and increased unemployment in that region, and a corresponding quickening effect – confined to the region concerned – because of increased employment there. This would not happen, however, if manufacturing investment in northern and eastern France were to be increased, since there the rate of increase in wages does not depend on the labour market situation in the region (this may be due to the fact that a certain amount of transfrontier movement eliminates – or attenuates – possible tensions in the labour market).

If, overall, the first effect prevails, costs would rise more slowly, so there would be a downturn in inflation, accompanied by renewed expansion thanks to foreign trade; at the same time, the trade balance and public finance would show an improvement. This will occur especially if the manufacturing investment share of northern and eastern France were to increase and, to a lesser degree, in the case of a similar increase in the Mediterranean Delta.

If investment in the Parisian basin is increased, the two effects will more or less cancel each other out, and the effect on national development will be only slight. This effect will, however, be more favourable if growth is initially moderate (third assumption), and rather less favourable in the opposite event (first assumption).

Finally, for western and south-western France it will be the unfavourable effects that will prevail, especially in the context of strong national growth (first assumption). This is due both to the extreme sensitivity of wage rates in these regions to the creation of new job opportunities, and to the higher level of wage costs (while it is true that wage levels are lower, average industrial productivity is also much lower).

This leads us to three main conclusions. It is clearly better to:

(i) *slow manufacturing development in the Paris region, and decentralize manufacturing employment towards provincial regions:* such a policy would be advantageous both from the national development point of view (faster growth, less inflation and unemployment, inproved public finance and trade balance), and from that of reducing inequalities between regions (reduced income discrepancies).

(ii) *promote manufacturing investment in northern and eastern France* (where manufacturing development has hitherto been slow): reinforcement of manufacturing in this region would be particularly beneficial from the national point of view.

(iii) *find a less clear-cut solution in the case of western and south-western France:* in a context of sustained expansion (first assumption) the promotion of manufacturing in these regions would be unfavourable from the national point of view, but would reduce regional disparities to a maximum degree. From the national development viewpoint alone, therefore, such a policy should be avoided. Nevertheless, it was this policy that was followed in the 1960s, when the French economy was, in fact, rapidly expanding. In a context of slower growth (second and third assumptions) greater industrialization in the west and south-west would, however have only a slight effect on national development. (There would be some decrease in unemployment on the national scale, but this would be accompanied by a slight deterioration in the trade balance and public finance.) Manufacturing development in western and south-western France might thus be envisaged: nationally its impact would be slight,[6] but the effect on interregional income discrepancies would be favourable.

3. Effects of Regional Location of Public Investment

Here we consider the ten-year macroeconomic effects of a transfer of public investment to one of the five Regina regions, with simulation of a gradual transfer to one region of 2000 million francs of public investment at 1970 prices, spread over the period 1970–1980. It is assumed that investment in the other regions will be correspondingly reduced at the same time, proportionally to the investment's relative value, the ex-ante national total of public investment thus remaining unchanged. Table 2 summarizes the results of simulation of the five variants considered, for the three reference trends assumed.

As for the distribution of manufacturing investment, macroeconomic effects at the national level vary considerably, according to whether the transfer policy benefits the Paris region or the provinces. Development of public investment in the Paris region at the expense of the provinces upsets national economic equilibrium in the medium term, whereas the opposite policy brings about a clear improvement in this equilibrium.

It can be seen, however, that this effect, whether of deterioration or improvement, is of very minor importance as compared with that of a regional

Table 2. Impact of a 2,000 million franc transfer of public investment towards one region, with a concomitant equal relative decrease in other regions: effect after ten years (1980).

	Control solution 1 (national unemployment: 600,000)				
	PR	PB	NE	GD	WSW
National impact					
GDP in volume (Δ %)	−0.05	−0.01	+0.06	+0.04	−0.05
Manufacturing employment (Δ thousands)	−9.2	−0.3	+6.8	+6.6	−5.4
Total employment (Δ thousands)	−21.4	+2.5	+9.7	+9.4	−1.5
Unemployment (Δ thousands)	+20.8	−3.4	−8.3	−8.7	0.0
Hourly wage rate (Δ %)	+0.26	−0.09	−0.16	−0.15	+0.18
GDP deflator (Δ %)	+0.07	−0.01	−0.11	−0.08	+0.19
Foreign trade balance in value (Δ in million francs)	−262	−2	+336	+226	−439
Public finance (Δ in million francs)	+489	+66	−317	−427	+227
Regional inequality: Δ (in points) of the ratio of private income per capita in Paris to private income per capita in other regions	+0.29	−0.18	+0.04	+0.01	−0.31
Impact on the region towards which investment is transferred					
GDP in volume (Δ %)	+0.64	+0.76	+0.73	+0.69	+0.91
Manufacturing employment (Δ thousands)	−1.5	−0.1	+1.3	+1.0	−1.3
Total employment (Δ thousands)	+13.5	+36.9	+25.0	+29.5	+45.8
Unemployment (Δ thousands)	−6.2	−19.9	−15.7	−17.5	−22.8
Hourly wage rate (Δ %)	+0.47	+1.1	−0.09	+0.26	+1.96

Regions: PR, Parisian region; PB, Parisian basin; NE, north and east; GD, Great Mediterranean Delta; WSW, west and south-west.

Table 2. Continued.

	Control solution 2 (national unemployment: 1,200,000)				
	PR	PB	NE	GD	WSW
National impact					
GDP in volume (Δ %)	−0.04	+0.01	+0.05	+0.02	−0.02
Manufacturing employment (Δ thousands)	−8.3	+1.4	+5.7	+4.9	−1.5
Total employment (Δ thousands)	−19.6	+5.0	+7.8	+6.8	+3.8
Unemployment (Δ thousands)	+18.5	−5.3	−6.7	−6.4	−4.0
Hourly wage rate (Δ %)	+0.25	+0.08	−0.14	−0.12	−0.06
GDP deflator (Δ %)	+0.08	−0.02	−0.09	−0.05	+0.08
Foreign trade balance in value (Δ in million francs)	−228	+86	+293	+152	−160
Public finance (Δ in million francs)	+457	−52	−299	−377	+63
Regional inequality:					
Δ (in points) of the ratio of private income per capita in Paris to private income per capita in other regions	+0.22	−0.08	+0.01	−0.02	−0.17
Impact on the region towards which investment is transferred					
GDP in volume (Δ %)	+0.64	+0.68	+0.74	+0.68	+0.77
Manufacturing employment (Δ thousands)	−1.4	+0.4	+1.1	+0.8	−0.3
Total employment (Δ thousands)	+13.0	+31.2	+24.7	+28.8	+36.6
Unemployment (Δ thousands)	−6.9	−18.6	−15.4	−16.9	−20.6
Hourly wage rate (Δ %)	+0.35	+0.39	−0.1	+0.14	+0.85

Regions: PR, Parisian region; PB, Parisian basin; NE, north and east; GD, Great Mediterranean Delta; WSW, west and south-west.

Table 2. Continued.

	Control solution 3 (national unemployment: 1,800,000)				
	PR	PB	NE	GD	WSW
National impact					
GDP in volume (Δ %)	−0.03	+0.01	+0.04	0.0	−0.01
Manufacturing employment (Δ thousands)	−7.0	+1.2	+4.1	+3.0	−0.9
Total employment (Δ thousands)	−17.3	+4.8	+5.1	+3.9	+4.6
Unemployment (Δ thousands)	+17.0	−5.8	−4.3	−3.9	−4.8
Hourly wage rate (Δ %)	+0.22	−0.06	−0.12	−0.08	+0.03
GDP deflator (Δ %)	+0.06	−0.01	−0.08	−0.02	+0.06
Foreign trade balance in value (Δ in million francs)	−191	+71	+236	+86	−145
Public finance (Δ in million francs)	+475	−87	−228	−276	+50
Regional inequality:					
Δ (in points) of the ratio of private income per capita in Paris to private income per capita in other regions	+0.21	−0.07	0.0	−0.02	−0.13
Impact on the region towards which investment is transferred					
GDP in volume (Δ %)	+0.67	+0.69	+0.76	+0.67	+0.75
Manufacturing employment (Δ thousands)	−1.1	+0.3	+0.8	+0.5	−0.2
Total employment (Δ thousands)	+13.2	+29.7	+24.4	+26.9	+33.9
Unemployment (Δ thousands)	−6.5	−18.2	−15.0	−16.2	−19.8
Hourly wage rate (Δ %)	+0.27	+0.22	−0.09	+0.09	+0.53

Regions: PR, Parisian region; PB, Parisian basin; NE, north and east; GD, Great Mediterranean Delta; WSW, west and south-west.

transfer of manufacturing investment (see also, on this point, section 4). So, although the amount of public investment transferred is more or less twice that considered for industrial investment (two percent of the national total of manufacturing investment in 1980 accounts for some 1000 million francs at 1970 prices), the maximum variation observed ex post is some twenty thousand jobs for the country as a whole, whereas it may reach 130,000 jobs in the case of a transfer of manufacturing investment.

These different effects are related to the differences in the mechanisms set in motion: the increase of manufacturing investment supply in the beneficiary region stimulates regional activities as a whole. In contrast, for the regions in which the share of manufacturing investment goes down, restraints are increased. At regional level, the chain of events in figure 3 occurs.

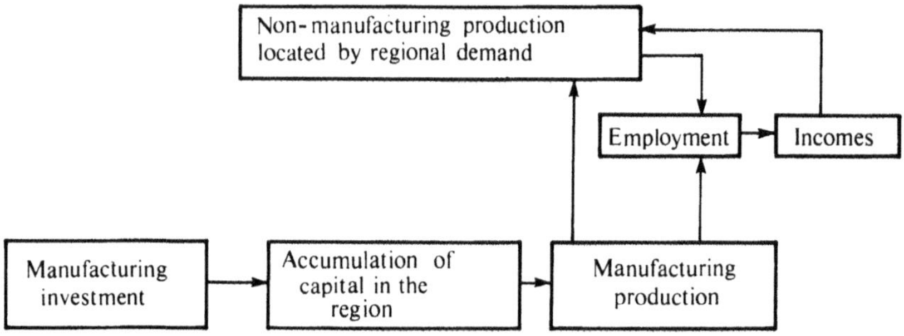

Fig. 3.

So there are substantial modifications to regional equilibria, especially to nationwide distribution of unemployment, which, as we have seen, plays a major role in determining trends in wage rates and production costs.

When there is a transfer of public demand, only the activities whose location depends on regional demand (in this case, ninety percent of construction activity, since it is public investment that is being transferred) are stimulated to any significant degree in the beneficiary region. Increased regional demand has no direct effect on manufacturing production in the region since this depends, *in the medium term,* on accumulation of capital in the region and not on regional demand, where a rise entails only an increase in numbers of manufacturing products brought from other regions or from abroad. At regional level, therefore, the main relationships are those shown in figure 4.

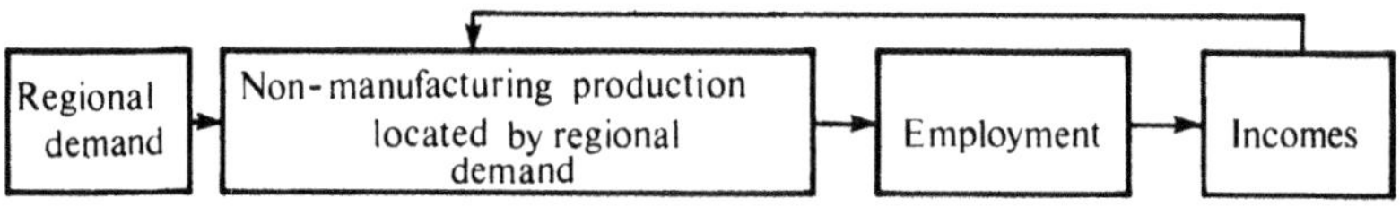

Fig. 4.

Thus, the impact on a regional economy of a transfer of public investment is only limited, and this explains why the effects at the national level are also minor.

In spite of these limitations, it is clear that *a policy of public investment transfer can be a useful tool for re-establishing regional equilibrium.* Even if the effects are less pronounced than those of a transfer of manufacturing investment, on a regional economy they will be far from negligible. They will depend, however, on regional structures: for instance, a gradual transfer of 2,000 million francs of public investment, in volume terms, would lead, in western and south-western France, to the creation, over ten years, of some 45,000 jobs, whereas an identical transfer towards northern and eastern France would result in only about 25,000 new jobs. This discrepancy is mainly accounted for by the different workings of the labour market in these two regions: in western and south-western France, labour market tension strongly influences the evolution of wage rates – the ex-post consequence of this is a substantial increase in real incomes in the region, which thus brings about an increase in demand there – but in northern and eastern France this does not occur, since there the evolution of wage rates does not depend on labour market tension.

The far less significant effect (13,000 new jobs in the region) of a transfer of public investment to the Paris region is explained, in turn, by the deterioration in the national situation it will bring about in the medium term.

4. Comparative Analysis of Multipliers

In order to compare the effects of regional policies on supply and demand, it is instructive to look at the multipliers associated with each policy. Table 3 shows two types of multipliers: (1) *'transfer' multipliers,* which measure the national effect of a change in the regional distribution of manufacturing

Table 3. National 'transfer' and regional multipliers: ratio of ex post variation in national or regional gross domestic product to ex ante value of the transfer (terminal year, control solution 2).

	Transfer to				
	Parisian region	Parisian basin	North and east	Great Mediterranean Delta	West and south-west
National multiplier					
Manufacturing investment	−6.90	+0.75	+2.67	+1.62	−0.32
Public investment	−0.23	+0.05	+0.27	+0.11	−0.09
Regional multiplier					
Manufacturing investment	+3.46	+5.08	+4.94	+4.89	+5.56
Public investment	+0.70	+0.80	+0.73	+0.72	+0.86

investment (supply variant) or in the regional distribution of public investment (demand variant); and (2) *regional multipliers*, which measure the effects in the beneficiary region of an ex-ante increase in *demand* (demand multiplier) or in *manufacturing supply* (supply multiplier).[7]

The values of these two sets of multipliers are closely linked, since the national effect of the policies considered depends upon their regional impact: if regional impact is pronounced, the balance between the regions will be considerably upset in relation to the reference solution, and the effects on national equilibrium substantial. Conversely, if the policy simulated entails significant changes in national equilibrium, this will have effects at the regional level.

Thus, if the distribution of manufacturing investment is modified in such a way as to be of advantage to the Paris region, we find that in the medium term the region's activity will be markedly stimulated (the regional multiplier is greater than 3). Because of the acceleration of inflation related to a *détente* in the Paris labour market (see section 2), there will be a substantial fall in national growth (the transfer multiplier is negative: −6.9). In the Paris region this ultimately limits the realisation of the growth potential brought about by an ex ante increase in manufacturing investment there: the regional multiplier, of the order of 3.5, is, in this case, distinctly lower than the regional multipliers calculated for the provincial regions, these latter being of the order of 5.

Furthermore, a comparison of supply and demand multipliers clearly shows the very substantial difference in impact that supply and demand policies may have:

– a policy which seeks to modify regional manufacturing supply will have far-reaching consequences for regional equilibrium, and therefore for national equilibrium, because of the stimulating effects of manufacturing activity on the regional economy as a whole;
– a policy concerned with regional demand will have much more limited effects on both regional and national equilibrium.

Regional activity can thus be much more effectively boosted by a policy on supply than by one concerned with demand. On the other hand, in the case of a supply-oriented policy, it is important to pay great attention to the national consequences, which will be far-reaching.

Endnotes

1. See R. Courbis and J.C. Prager, 'Analyse régionale et planification nationale: le projet de modèle REGINA d'analyse interdépendante', paper presented to the 1st Franco-Soviet Conference on the Use of Models in Planning, Paris, 11–15 October 1971, *Collections de l'INSEE* R12 (1973) 5–32.
2. REGINA means 'REGIonal–NAtional'.
3. Group for Applied Macroeconomic Analysis, a research centre (headed by Professor R. Courbis) of University of Paris-X Nanterre, associated with the French National Centre for Scientific Research (CNRS).

4. See R. Courbis, 'Le Modèle REGINA, modèle du développement national, régional et urbain de l'économie française', *Economie Appliquée* 28 (1975): 569–600, or: R. Courbis, 'The REGINA model: a regional–national model for French planning', *Regional Science and Urban Economics* 9 (1979): 117–139.
5. As indicated above, there is also a sub-regional (rural–urban) level and an interaction between regional (and national) equilibrium and sub-regional equilibrium. See Courbis, loc. cit. (1975, 1979).
6. This impact would, moreover, be favourable if the manufacturing employment transferred from only the Paris region to western and south-western France is taken into account.
7. The 'Keynesian demand multiplier' measures the extent of growth in overall production entailed by an ex ante increase in demand. The 'supply multiplier', on the other hand, measures that of higher production brought about by ex ante supplementary investment (acting as a factor of production). For a comparison of these two multipliers, see: R. Courbis, *Competitivité et croissance en économie concurrencée,* vol. 1 (Paris: Dunod, 1975), pp. 104–112, 138–149.

THE FORECASTING MODEL GRECON 79-D: SOME SPECIFICATION EXPERIMENTS

M.A. KOOYMAN

1. Introduction

In 1976 four staff members of the Econometric Institute of the University of Groningen started the work of constructing a model of the Dutch economy for the postwar period. The model had to serve the following two ends: (i) it was to give an adequate description of the Dutch economy, and (ii) it was to be supplemented with a procedure to predict the main economic variables one year ahead.

At that time only a few short-term forecasting models were operational: the Central Planning Bureau (CPB) was, as far as we know, using a mixture of its model 69-C, designed by Verdoorn et al. [11], and the model of Driehuis [5]. Model 69-C is based on prewar and postwar annual observations; the model of Driehuis is based on quarterly data for the postwar period. In recent years a lot of attention has been focussed on the design of models for the medium term. The VINTAF model, published by the CPB [3], is the outstanding example in the Netherlands.

The GRECON model has a few characteristics in which it differs from the other models mentioned: (i) it is of a limited size, with only eight behavioural and sixteen definitional equations; and (ii) the estimated coefficients are based on postwar annual data only – it is a short-term forecasting model.

From the start of our work on the GRECON model we set ourselves the restriction that the model should be small. The relevant considerations here are mainly of a statistical character. Bemer and van Miltenberg [1] simplified the CPB model 69-C drastically and in doing so they found that the prediction power of the model was improved. Furthermore we required that the two-stage least squares (TSLS) estimation method could be applied properly, meaning that the first stage could be executed using the set of predetermined variables as it stood. In an earlier publication [10] the author has shown that the use of a set of principal components or of a set of variables selected out of the whole set of predetermined variables leads to an additional source of uncertainty in the coefficients; different choices sometimes result in substantially different estimates. The GRECON 79-D model is based on data for the period 1952–1977. Consequently the first stage of the TSLS procedure demands that the model should contain less than 26 predetermined variables.

In section 3 it will be shown that the situation in which there are more predetermined variables than the number of observations is a special case of overfitting. It is argued there that overfitting should be avoided, for it implies misspecification of the model. Besides the wish to apply the TSLS procedure properly, we want to estimate the model with the full-information maximum-likelihood (FIML) method. As will be shown in section 3 the FIML procedure cannot be applied if the number of structural equations plus the number of predetermined variables exceeds the number of observations. This requirement in particular is very restrictive. Nevertheless we think that a model does not deserve the name simultaneous if it cannot, at least in principle, be estimated with a full-information method such as FIML.

The author [10] has shown for the CPB model 63-D, a predecessor of model 69-C, that the prewar and postwar periods do not possess the same structure, therefore the GRECON model is entirely based on postwar data. It is an annual model because quarterly data for the whole postwar period do not exist. Unlike Driehuis we have not constructed quarterly data from annual ones. Besides, a quarterly model would become too big to handle within the above constraints. Since GRECON 79-D is a short-term model, no account has been taken of relations which concern changing production capacity, and thus the model can more easily be kept of moderate size. More important in our view is that predicting one year ahead is still rather inaccurate, and we fear that a cumulation of prediction errors over a number of years will result in predictions without any practical use. At this stage of our project we would like to avoid those complications.

After stating the general principles upon which the GRECON model is based, section 2 contains more detailed information about the specification of the model as it stands. Section 3 explores in somewhat more detail the restrictions, set by the data, concerning the specification of a simultaneous model. Section 4 contains the predictions for 1979, with the estimated variances of the prediction errors. Section 5 proceeds with some results of specification analysis within the FIML framework. The criterion of the estimated variances of the reduced form disturbances is set forth, together with a number of still-available options, such as constraints originating from economic theory or from the demand for the parameters' significance. Appendix A contains the GRECON model 79-D, estimated with different methods like OLS, TSLS and FIML. In Appendix B the complete data set is presented.

2. The Specification of the GRECON Model 79-D

The specification of the GRECON model is based on that of earlier models of the CPB. Although the variables included in the relations differ, the number and characteristics of the equations has remained unchanged since the early sixties. These models contain behavioural equations for the following thirteen exogenous variables: consumption, investment, inventory changes, exports of commodities, imports of commodities, employment, unemployment, wage rate, consumption price, investment price, export price, prices of autonomous expenditure, and deposits. We started with the same set of endogenous variables, each of which ought to be explained with the help of a behavioural equation. The variables just stated are supplemented with a rather large set of variables from the national accounts. The option of lagging the variables is also available.

The specification procedure runs as follows (see also [8]). For each of the thirteen endogenous variables a set of acceptable explanatory variables is composed. These sets are determined by 'common sense'. The choice of the explanatory variables in each equation was made by trying to find the specification with the best fit. In that stage we use different stepwise procedures. Afterwards every explanatory variable was required to have an estimated coefficient of the right sign and to differ significantly from zero – the other explanatory variables were deleted. During the execution of these procedures we found that a few equations could not be estimated satisfactorily, so we decided to abandon the relations for the exports of commodities, the unemployment, the export price, the prices of autonomous expenditure and the deposits. All variables with regard to exports and autonomous expenditures are taken as exogenous. The labour market has been studied in a separate model, so in the GRECON model the rate of unemployment is treated as exogenous, while monetary variables, deposits included, were not found to play an important role in our model. Once the decision about the specification of the behavioural equations has been made, the definitional equations follow easily. Of course the specification procedure was not executed automatically; sometimes exceptions had to be made. For example, the investment function shows a poor fit, nevertheless we have maintained the relation in the model. The abovementioned procedure is repeated every year in order to incorporate the additional information contained in the latest issue of the national accounts.

One should realise that the specification has been executed within the context of the single-equation estimation method OLS. A simultaneous estimation method cannot be applied at this early stage because the whole model is not known yet. Once the first version of the model has been completed, specification experiments can be started using simultaneous estimation methods.

We will not discuss the specification of each equation separately as the model does not show important new characteristics. However, the specification of the definitional equations 9–13 do require some explanation. As an example equation 9 will be examined more carefully. All variables of the model are measured as relative first differences. The definitional equation 9, measured in volumes (indicated by bold italic) in fact reads as follows:[1]

$$\boldsymbol{v}' = \boldsymbol{c} + \boldsymbol{i}_m + \boldsymbol{i}_w + \boldsymbol{b} + \boldsymbol{x}_{ex}.$$

Expressed in first differences and dividing by $\boldsymbol{v}'_{-1}$ we arrive at

$$\frac{\Delta \boldsymbol{v}'}{\boldsymbol{v}'_{-1}} = \frac{\boldsymbol{c}_{-1}}{\boldsymbol{v}'_{-1}} \frac{\Delta \boldsymbol{c}}{\boldsymbol{c}_{-1}} + \frac{\boldsymbol{i}_{m-1}}{\boldsymbol{v}'_{-1}} \frac{\Delta \boldsymbol{i}_m}{\boldsymbol{i}_{m-1}} + \frac{\boldsymbol{i}_{w-1}}{\boldsymbol{v}'_{-1}} \frac{\Delta \boldsymbol{i}_w}{\boldsymbol{i}_{w-1}} + \frac{\boldsymbol{b}_{-1}}{\boldsymbol{v}'_{-1}} \frac{\Delta \boldsymbol{b}}{\boldsymbol{b}_{-1}} +$$

$$+ \frac{\boldsymbol{x}_{ex-1}}{\boldsymbol{v}'_{-1}} \frac{\Delta \boldsymbol{x}_{ex}}{\boldsymbol{x}_{ex-1}}$$

or

$$v' = g_1 c + g_2 i_m + g_3 i_w + g_4 b + g_5 x_{ex} \qquad \Sigma g_i = 1.$$

The weights g_i are different for each year. However, in the model they are taken fixed for the whole period and are estimated accordingly.

The GRECON model 79-D has been specified by means of the OLS estimation results. Afterwards the model has been estimated with TSLS and FIML. Two variants of the FIML method are presented in Appendix A; variant C uses the OLS results and variant D the TSLS estimated for the definitional equations 9–13. The differences between the four variants are not very remarkable in relation to the estimated standard deviations of the coefficients. Special attention has been given to the significance of the constants, for a significant constant must be interpreted as a significant trend movement in the absolute value of the dependent endogenous variable. The observation period does show cyclical movements, therefore trends should not be present. Fortunately it turns out that the constants are as a rule not significant.

3. Restrictions Implied by the Available Data Set: The Danger of Overfitting

This section discusses why the model is kept small, but before we can go into this matter, it is necessary to explain the FIML procedure in more detail. As a matter of fact the LISREL procedure (see Jöreskog and Sörbom [6]), of which FIML is a special case, is used. The approach in [6] shows very clearly why FIML cannot be applied if there is a lack of available data.

Jöreskog and Sörbom start, just as in the econometric approach, with two sets of observed variables, divided into G endogenous variables $y = (y_1, y_2, \ldots, y_G)'$ and K exogenous variables $x = (x_1, x_2, \ldots, x_K)'$. All variables are measured as deviations from their means. The sets of y and x variables satisfy factor analysis models with common factors $\eta = (\eta_1, \eta_2, \ldots, \eta_m)'$ and $\xi = (\xi_1, \xi_2, \ldots, \xi_n)'$ and unique factors $\epsilon = (\epsilon_1, \epsilon_2, \ldots, \epsilon_G)'$ and $\delta = (\delta_1, \delta_2, \ldots, \delta_K)'$. Furthermore a system of stochastic relationships between the factors is postulated. The whole system can be described as

$$B\eta = \Gamma\xi + \zeta, \quad y = \Lambda_y\eta + \epsilon, \quad x = \Lambda_x\xi + \delta. \tag{1}$$

The first equation of (1) can be interpreted as the structural part of the model and the remaining equations as the parts concerning errors of measurement. The authors derive the likelihood function under the assumption of multinormality of the y and x variables and by postulating the usual assumptions of factor analysis, i.e.,

$$E(\eta) = 0, \quad E(\xi) = 0, \quad E(\epsilon) = 0, \quad E(\delta) = 0$$

$$E(\eta\epsilon') = 0, \quad E(\xi\delta') = 0, \quad E(\epsilon\epsilon') = \theta_\epsilon^2, \quad E(\delta\delta') = \theta_\delta^2,$$

$$E(\epsilon\delta') = 0.$$

where θ_ϵ and θ_δ are diagonal matrices, and the usual assumptions of regression analysis, i.e.,

$$E(\zeta) = 0, \quad E\xi\zeta' = 0.$$

It is obvious that the LISREL program is able to deal with the standard econometric estimation problem with no errors of measurement in y and x and with non-stochastic x variables. One has to impose the following restrictions:

$$\Lambda_y = I_G \quad (m = G) \quad \text{and} \quad \epsilon = 0,$$

$$\Lambda_x = I_K \quad (n = K) \quad \text{and} \quad \delta = 0.$$

In so doing, (1) boils down to

$$By = \Gamma x + \zeta. \tag{2}$$

Model (2) does not contain definitional equations: these equations are eliminated by substitution into the behavioural equations. What remains is a set of G behavioural equations. The relevant variables of the model consist of the remaining G endogenous variables and the total number K of exogenous variables.

Because of the assumption of multinormality and by taking the variables as deviations from their means, all the information the sample can provide about the parameters out of the likelihood function is contained in the covariance matrix of y and x variables. This sample covariance matrix is of order $(G+K)$. A covariance matrix must have full rank, otherwise the variables are not independent. However, the covariance matrix of the $G+K$ variables cannot be of rank $G+K$ unless the number of observations T is at least equal to $G+K$. If the number of observations is too small, one must conclude that $G+K-T=p$ variables can be expressed as exact linear combinations of the other T variables. Those p variables appear in fact in the form of definitional equations and consequently the original model is mis-specified. It is obvious that the situation of undersized samples ($K > T$), which prevents the execution of the first stage of TSLS, can be seen of as a particular case of overfitting.

The restriction $T \geqslant G + K$ was already mentioned by Koopmans et al. [9]. FIML cannot be executed unless this restriction is met. Our model with $G = 8, K = 17$ and $T = 26$ is small enough to be fitted with FIML.

4. The Prediction Procedure: Results for 1979

Predicting with an econometric model requires (i) a set of estimates of the coefficients of the model and (ii) estimates of the exogenous variables for the year to be predicted. In practice there is a complicating factor present. At the time the predictions for 1979 are made, the data for 1978 are not available. The national accounts for 1978 are issued in September 1979. As a consequence of this lag of about nine months, it is impossible to include 1978 in the sample period, so in fact a prediction two years ahead of the sample period has to be made. Nevertheless we incorporated some information about 1978 by using preliminary results to estimate the lagged variables.

Once the coefficients and the values of the predetermined variables are given, they can be substituted in the predictor

$$y^p_{1979} = \hat{B}^{-1} \hat{\Gamma} x_{1979}$$

A simultaneous model can be estimated by different methods. In the appendix four different results are presented, i.e., the OLS, TSLS and two FIML estimates. The definitional equations 9–13 are not exact identities: equations 9 and 13 are identities if the variables are measured in absolute values, but this property is destroyed when the transformation to relative first differences is made. Equations 10, 11 and 12 are approximations even when the variables are measured in absolute values. However, it is not possible to estimate equations 9–13 together with the behavioural equations with FIML, because of the restriction $T \geqslant G + K$, so the coefficients are taken as fixed. Variant C contains the TSLS estimates, variant D those of OLS. In Section 2 it is shown that equation 9 has time-variant coefficients, so for prediction purposes it is obvious that the most recent weights, i.e. those for 1977, should be used. The following values of the predetermined variables are substituted:

p_m	3.5,	L_0	7.0
p_{m-1}	−0.9,	v'_{-1}	3.0,
n'_{-2}	0.108,	a_{-1}	0.4,
i_w	2.5,	p_{c-1}	4.5,
b	3.5,	l_{-1}	7.5,
x_{ex}	4.5,	y^d_{g-1}	2.5,
p_b	2.5,	B^n_{g-1}	10.0,
B^n_g	10.0,	Δw	0.3.

These values for the exogenous variables are as a rule obtained from a CPB publication [4]. The lagged variables originate from preliminary data for

Table 1. Predictions for 1979.

Variable	TSLS prediction	FIML variant C		FIML variant D		Standard deviation in sample period 1952–1977
		Prediction	$\hat{\sigma}_\eta$	Prediction	$\hat{\sigma}_\eta$	
c	2.98	3.05	1.58	3.02	1.57	2.23
i_m	1.79	1.50	6.51	1.43	6.53	10.32
m	1.82	1.13	3.37	2.04	3.45	7.88
n'	−0.58	−0.54	0.79	−0.43	0.81	1.48
p_c	3.01	3.84	3.00	4.02	3.03	3.29
p_i	3.14	3.33	1.73	3.42	1.74	3.53
l	6.21	6.89	2.49	7.10	2.53	3.53
a	0.61	0.67	0.62	0.63	0.62	1.52
v'	3.06	3.07	1.1*	3.05	1.1*	3.29

Note: $\hat{\sigma}_\eta$ is the estimated standard deviation of the reduced-form disturbance (see also the appendix). * indicates an approximation.

1978 published by the CBS [2]. The variable n'_{-2} is known from the national accounts for 1977 and Δw is determined with the help of another model. Table 1 contains the 1979 predictions for three different estimates of the coefficients of the model: (i) TSLS, (ii) FIML variant C, and (iii) FIML variant D. In all the cases the 1977 weights are substituted in equation 9.

In our view predictions should be accompanied with an indication of their uncertainty. In [8] the procedure is exposed fully, but it can be summarized as follows. The prediction error is

$$y^p_{t+1} - y_{t+1} = (\hat{B}^{-1}\hat{\Gamma} - B^{-1}\Gamma)x_{t+1} - B^{-1}\zeta$$

If the estimators $\hat{B}$ and $\hat{\Gamma}$ are independent of ζ the variance of the prediction error consists of the sum of the variances of the 'systematic' part $(\hat{B}^{-1}\hat{\Gamma} - B^{-1}\Gamma)x_{t+1}$ and of the reduced-form disturbances $B^{-1}\zeta$. For the 1978 version of the GRECON model we found (see [8, table 5.3.1]) that the variance of the 'systematic' part can be neglected compared to the variance of the reduced-form disturbances. This is a very convenient circumstance, for the LISREL procedure includes only the calculation of the variances of the reduced-form disturbances. In appendix A these variances are indicated with $\hat{\sigma}^2_\eta$; in table 1 the matching standard deviations are presented.

Table 1 shows that the different estimation methods produce approximately the same results. In relation to the values of their standard deviations, the differences can be neglected. If one looks at the relation between the prediction and its standard deviation, only two predictions differ significantly (i.e., by more than twice the standard deviation) from zero, the wage rate l and the total output v'. In particular the prediction of the investments is of bad quality. If would be a stimulating question to ask whether the GRECON model has any predictive power at all. Until now the predictive power of a model has been studied by relating the predictions made with the actual outcomes, but there is no direct relation between this criterion and the demand for statistical significance of the predictions. Nevertheless a reduction

Table 2. Predictions and actual outcomes for 1977 and 1978.

Variable	1977			1978		
	GRECON	Actual outcome	CPB	GRECON	Actual outcome*	CPB
c	2.9	4.3	3.5	4.1	3.5	3
i_m	1.4	15.5	8	−0.9	6.2	3
m	5.6	2.5	6	1.5	1.9	3
n'	0.3	0.1	0.6	−1.2	n.a.	0.5
p_c	7.5	7.3	6.5	5.2	4.5	4.5
p_i	7.5	6.5	6	5.2	n.a.	5
l	9.8	7.8	7.5	9.6	7.5	7
a	0.2	0.5	0.15	0.3	0.4	−0.5
v'	4.1	3.1	4.5	3.8	3.0	2.5

*Preliminary results.
n.a. = not available.

of those standard deviations is as such attractive; in the next section this point will be elaborated.

This section is concluded with a survey of the GRECON predictions made until now, with a comparison with the actual outcomes and the predictions published by the CPB. The GRECON predictions were published about a month earlier than those of the CPB. As is seen from table 2, the quality of the predictions of GRECON and the CPB is about the same.

5. Some Specification Results within the LISREL Procedure

At this point the LISREL procedure must be explained more fully. We follow the manual [7], using for the LISREL computer program the fitting function

$$F = \ln|\Sigma| + \mathrm{tr}\,(S\Sigma^{-1}) - \ln|S| - (G+K)$$

where Σ = the population covariance matrix of y and x; it is a function of all the parameters of the model, i.e. the βs, γs and the elements of ψ, the covariance matrix of ζs.
S = the sample covariance matrix of y and x.

If the distribution of y and x is multinormal, the minimization of F with respect to all the unknown parameters yields maximum-likelihood estimates which are efficient in large samples. At the minimum of F, the information matrix is computed and used to obtain standard errors for all the estimated parameters. When the maximum-likelihood estimates of the parameters have been obtained, the goodness of fit of the whole model can be tested, under multinormality and in large samples, by the likelihood ratio technique. Let H_0 be the null hypothesis of the model under the given specification about the parameters. The alternative hypothesis H_1 is that Σ is any positive definite matrix. Then minus twice the logarithm of the likelihood ratio is equal to $(T/2)F_0$, where F_0 is the minimum value of F, and T is the sample size. If the model holds, this is distributed, in large samples, as χ^2 with

$$d = \tfrac{1}{2}(G+K)(G+K+1)-p$$

degrees of freedom, where p is the total number of estimated βs, γs and ψs under H_0. This overall measure of goodness of fit is presented in the appendix for the variants C and D. Of course the requirement of a large sample is not met; however this is a common feature of most models in econometrics. The LISREL program proceeds with some testing devices. Let H_0 be any specified hypothesis, concerning the parametric structure of the general model, which is more restrictive than an alternative hypothesis H_1. Let F_0 be the minimum of F under H_0 and let F_1 be the minimum of F under H_1. Then $F_1 < F_0$ and, in large samples, minus twice the logarithm of the likelihood ratio becomes $(T/2)(F_0 - F_1)$. Under H_0 this is distributed approximately as χ^2 with degrees of freedom equal to $s_1 - s_0$, the difference in number of independent parameters estimated under H_1 and H_0. Thus the removal of a variable from a behavioural equation leads to an increase of one in the number of degrees of freedom of the χ^2 statistic. The effect for the fit of the whole model can be judged by looking at the increase of the χ^2 statistic, which has 1 degree of freedom. The effects of introducing new explanatory variables can be studied in a similar way.

Though the research is still exploratory, Jöreskog and Sörbom suggest the following use of the χ^2 measure of goodness of fit. If a value of χ^2 which is large compared with the number of degrees of freedom is obtained, the fit may be examined and assessed by an inspection of the covariance residuals, i.e. the discrepancies between the observed S and the fitted Σ and of the magnitudes of the first derivatives of F with respect to the a priori fixed parameters. Often such an inspection will suggest ways of relaxing the model somewhat by introducing more parameters. The new model usually yields a smaller χ^2. A large drop in χ^2, compared to the difference in degrees of freedom, indicates that the changes made in the model represent a real improvement.

Now that the LISREL procedure is sufficiently introduced, we proceed with the exposition of our specification experiments. Section 2 explains how the GRECON model has been specified. The R^2 of each behavioural equation separately is an important criterion in that stage. However, the aim is to build a forecasting model, so while a good fit of the structural equations may give some guarantee there is more to it than this. Forecasts are computed with the help of the reduced form of the model, so it is obviously important to specify the model in such a way that the error variances of the reduced form are minimized. In the appendix the estimated variances of the reduced-form residuals are presented. The first-order derivatives of the fitting function F with respect to those parameters which are fixed at zero – the excluded variables – are now studied in order to find a reduction in the error variances of the reduced-form residuals. It is obvious

Table 3. Results of specification experiments along line 2.

Equation	79-D, Variant *C*		s_{yy}	Run 8		Run 15		Run 16	
	s_{uu}	$\hat{\sigma}^2_\eta$		s_{uu}	$\hat{\sigma}^2_\eta$	s_{uu}	$\hat{\sigma}^2_\eta$	s_{uu}	$\hat{\sigma}^2_\eta$
1. c	2.10	2.49	4.99	2.10	2.52	2.11	2.46	1.82	2.36
2. i_m	39.59	42.38	106.57	42.37	42.37	42.31	42.31	42.39	42.39
3. m	6.02	11.33	62.13	9.17	10.04	15.66	12.39	14.80	11.28
4. n'	0.49	0.62	2.20	1.00	0.55	0.91	0.54	0.85	0.49
5. p_c	2.85	8.99	10.82	2.09	9.17	2.26	7.51	2.39	7.07
6. p_i	2.54	2.99	12.46	2.51	3.00	2.51	2.92	2.57	2.84
7. l	3.02	6.22	12.44	3.18	6.35	3.05	5.76	2.98	5.39
8. a	0.48	0.38	2.32	0.66	0.25	0.63	0.26	0.69	0.27
Value of χ^2 (d.f.)	χ^2 (109) = 411.1			χ^2 (109) = 374.6		χ^2 (108) = 369.0		χ^2 (107) = 359.2	
Additions (+) and exclusions (−) in relation to previous column*				$+\gamma_{4\ 4}$ $+\gamma_{5\ 8}$ $+\beta_{8\ 2}$ $-\beta_{2\ 21}$ $-\beta_{3\ 15}$ $-\beta_{4\ 18}$		$+\gamma_{5\ 1}$ $+\gamma_{5\ 2}$ $+\gamma_{5\ 4}$ $-\beta_{3\ 4}$ $-\gamma_{4\ 4}$		$+\gamma_{1\ 15}$	
Non-significant coefficients (t value)	$\beta_{3\ 15}$ ($t = 1.4$) $\beta_{2\ 21}$ ($t = -1.1$)			none		$\beta_{5\ 16}$ ($t = 1.9$) $\gamma_{5\ 1}$ ($t = 1.9$)		$\beta_{5\ 16}$ ($t = 1.8$)	

Table 3. Continued.

Equation	Run 17		Run 24		Run 32		Smallest and largest values obtained in the experiments	
	s_{uu}	$\hat{\sigma}^2_\eta$	s_{uu}	$\hat{\sigma}^2_\eta$	s_{uu}	$\hat{\sigma}^2_\eta$	s_{uu}	$\hat{\sigma}^2_\eta$
1. c	1.82	2.32	1.76	2.07	1.75	1.89	1.73–2.11	1.89–2.71
2. i_m	42.38	42.38	43.57	43.57	42.77	42.77	39.79–43.73	39.79–43.73
3. m	15.40	11.41	14.15	12.65	11.68	10.87	7.62–16.45	10.04–13.41
4. n'	0.89	0.50	0.82	0.56	0.58	0.38	0.58–1.28	0.38–0.60
5. p_c	0.93	6.62	2.30	5.22	1.93	4.71	1.71–3.00	4.42–9.37
6. p_i	2.54	2.81	2.61	2.20	2.42	2.05	2.35–2.77	2.07–3.01
7. l	2.93	5.10	2.80	5.00	2.86	4.81	2.79–3.40	4.75–6.38
8. a	0.67	0.27	0.94	0.30	0.81	0.27	0.62–0.96	0.25–0.34
Value of χ^2 (d.f.)	χ^2 (108) = 361.1		χ^2 (104) = 342.0		χ^2 (103) = 330.4			
Additions (+) and exclusions (−) in relation to previous column*	$-\beta_{5\ 16}$		$+\gamma_{5\ 6}$ $+\gamma_{6\ 15}$ $+\gamma_{8\ 5}$ $+\gamma_{8\ 6}$		$+\gamma_{4\ 6}$ $+\gamma_{3\ 6}$ $-\gamma_{8\ 6}$			
Non-significant coefficients (t value)	None		None		None			

*The symbol γ indicates predetermined variables, β endogenous variables. The first index refers to the number of the equation, the second to the variable. The latter numbers indicate, when used with β: 9, v'; 10, p_v'; 11, y^d_g; 12, Y^d_g; 13, L_T; 14, L; 15, $p_m - p_v'$; 16, $(v' - a)_{-1/2}$; 17, $(v' - a)_{-1}$; 18, Δp_c; 19, $p_{c-1/2}$; 20, $l_{-1/2}$; 21, $v'_{-1/2}$; 22, $y^d_{g-1/2}$; 23, $p_{m-1/2}$; 24, $B^n_{g-1/2}$ and when used with γ: 1, p_m; 2, p_{m-1}; 3, n'_{-2}; 4, i_w; 5, b; 6, x_{ex}; 7, p_b; 8, B^n_g; 9, L_0; 10, v'_{-1}; 11, a_{-1}; 12, p_{c-1}; 13, l_{-1}; 14, y^d_{g-1}; 15, B^n_{g-1}; 16, constant, 17, Δw.

Table 4. Results of specification experiments along line 1.

Equation	79-D, variant C		s_{yy}	Run 2		Run 3		Run 4		Run 5		Run 6	
	s_{uu}	$\hat{\sigma}^2_\eta$		s_{uu}	$\hat{\sigma}^2_\eta$	s_{uu}	$\hat{\sigma}^2_\eta$	s_{uu}	$\hat{\sigma}^2_\eta$	s_{uu}	$\hat{\sigma}^2_\eta$	s_{uu}	$\hat{\sigma}^2_\eta$
1. c	2.10	2.49	4.99	2.10	2.40	2.10	2.30	1.87	2.30	1.87	2.29	1.94	2.30
2. i_m	39.59	42.38	106.57	39.39	41.44	40.29	42.03	39.52	42.19	39.45	42.25	40.09	42.28
3. m	6.02	11.33	62.13	5.15	11.07	27.48	14.69	16.59	12.63	12.84	11.82	10.66	10.31
4. n'	0.49	0.62	2.20	0.70	0.72	1.29	0.68	1.00	0.62	0.87	0.57	1.61	0.55
5. p_c	2.85	8.99	10.82	3.74	8.24	3.17	8.02	3.49	7.91	3.45	7.86	11.20	7.75
6. p_i	2.54	2.99	12.46	2.56	3.00	2.51	2.73	2.61	2.64	2.30	2.37	2.34	2.39
7. l	3.02	6.22	12.44	2.93	5.81	3.04	5.55	2.93	5.43	2.95	5.44	2.89	5.62
8. a	0.48	0.38	2.32	0.48	0.39	0.71	0.26	0.86	0.27	0.88	0.27	0.82	0.26
Value of χ^2 (d.f.)	χ^2 (109) = 411.1			χ^2 (108) = 405.0		χ^2 (107) = 386.2		χ^2 (106) = 376.0		χ^2 (105) = 372.4		χ^2 (104) = 355.7	
Additions (+) and exclusions (—) in relation to previous column*				$+\gamma_{5\ 2}\ (p_{m-1})$		$+\beta_{8\ 2}\ (i_m)$		$+\gamma_{1\ 15}\ (B^n_{g-1})$		$+\gamma_{6\ 4}\ (i_w)$		$+\gamma_{5\ 12}\ (p_{c-1})$	
Non-significant coefficients (t value)	$\beta_{3\ 15}$ ($t = 1.4$ $\beta_{2\ 21}$ ($t = -1.1$)			$\beta_{3\ 15}$ ($t = 1.5$) $\beta_{2\ 21}$ ($t = -0.8$) $\beta_{4\ 18}$ ($t = -1.6$) $\beta_{5\ 16}$ ($t = -0.3$)		$\beta_{3\ 15}$ ($t = -0.6$) $\beta_{2\ 21}$ ($t = -0.6$) $\beta_{4\ 18}$ ($t = 1.5$) $\beta_{5\ 16}$ ($t = 1.3$) $\beta_{3\ 4}$ ($t = 0.9$)		$\beta_{3\ 15}$ ($t = 0.3$) $\beta_{2\ 21}$ ($t = -1.1$) $\beta_{4\ 18}$ ($t = 0.6$) $\beta_{5\ 16}$ ($t = 0.8$) $\beta_{3\ 4}$ ($t = 0.3$) $\beta_{8\ 21}$ ($t = -1.5$)		$\beta_{3\ 15}$ ($t = 0.5$) $\beta_{2\ 21}$ ($t = -1.2$) $\beta_{4\ 18}$ ($t = 0.0$) $\beta_{5\ 16}$ ($t = 0.7$) $\beta_{3\ 4}$ ($t = -0.2$) $\beta_{8\ 21}$ ($t = -1.4$)		$\beta_{3\ 15}$ ($t = 0.2$) $\beta_{2\ 21}$ ($t = -0.9$) $\beta_{4\ 18}$ ($t = 1.0$) $\beta_{5\ 16}$ sign. $\beta_{3\ 4}$ ($t = -0.9$) $\beta_{8\ 21}$ ($t = -1.8$) $\beta_{5\ 7}$ ($t = 0.6$)	

*See table 3.

that different options are still open. For example one can think of combinations of the following criteria

(1) A. introduction of the next additional variable is done in the equation for which the ratio $\hat{\sigma}_\eta^2/s_{yy}$ has the greatest value,
B. instead of $\hat{\sigma}_\eta^2/s_{yy}$ the ratio s_{uu}/s_{yy}, which presents the fit of the structural equation, is used;

(2) A. restrictions originating from economic reasoning are maintained,
B. these restrictions are not maintained;

(3) A. additional coefficients must show a t value greater than 2,
B. non-significant additional coefficients can be maintained;

(4) A. all coefficients must be significantly different from zero,
B. non-significant coefficients can be maintained.

We present a set of experiments along the line 1A, 2A, 3A and the line 1A, 2B, 4A. Of course we do not advocate following the second line of approach – it is presented to give an impression of the effects on the ratio $\hat{\sigma}_\eta^2/s_{yy}$ of rather different approaches. The results of the second line of approach are stated in table 3. Table 4 contains the results of the first strategy.

5.1. Discussion of the Results

The final runs of both tables show, when compared with 79-D variant *C*, that the variances of the reduced-form residuals have been lowered. (The only exception is equation 2 in table 3.) Remarkable however is that the fit of the individual equations, indicated with s_{uu}, has not always been improved. Table 3 shows in run 32 that four out of eight equations have a poorer fit. Table 4 contains even five out of eight with a poorer fit, with equation 5 being especially bad ($s_{uu} > s_{yy}$). Sometimes the s_{uu} values belonging to 79-D variant *C* have never been improved at all during the experiments (see the last column of table 3, the equations 3 and 8, and in table 4 the equations 3, 4, 5 and 8). We can conclude from these results that there is no reason to rely on the fit of the individual structural equation when the aim is to achieve small prediction errors. Specification experiences as explained above may turn out to be very fruitful after the first version of the specification of the model has been compiled.

The introduction of an additional variable can lead to quite different results: (i) both s_{uu} and $\hat{\sigma}_\eta^2$ in the relevant equation are lowered (table 3, run 16, equation 1); about the effects on the other equations nothing can be said in advance: (ii) s_{uu} may become larger and $\hat{\sigma}_\eta^2$ smaller (table 4, run 6, equation 5), (iii) s_{uu} may become smaller and $\hat{\sigma}_\eta^2$ larger (table 3, run 24, equation 3), or (iv) both s_{uu} and $\hat{\sigma}_\eta^2$ may become larger.

The investment equation cannot be improved, because the first-order derivatives are small, so we must conclude that the variables of the model are not able to explain investment behaviour sufficiently. This fact can be seen as an indication to call investment an exogenous variable. The absence of fairly large first-order derivatives sometimes forced us to abandon the principle stated under 1A. Later, however, we returned to this criterion.

Table 3 shows that the improvement of equation 5 (p_c) requires a lot of additional variables. Furthermore it is remarkable that these would almost always be predetermined variables. Perhaps this is a drawback of the procedure for it could mean that one is specifying the reduced form instead of the structural form.

It is obvious from the list of additions from table 3 that the procedure used is not very attractive. For example the introduction of investments in housing construction into the consumption price equation cannot be interpreted as a contribution to economic science. Also the significant positive coefficient of B^n_{g-1} in the consumption function is rather strange. Besides, the approach along line 1 renders much faster reasonable results and shows further possibilities of improvement more directly. This is obvious, because a large number of additions can be excluded a priori. However, as a rule those restrictions must be paid for with a smaller decrease in the $\hat{\sigma}^2_\eta$s than otherwise might occur. Perhaps the line 1A, 2A, 3B, 4B is the least restrictive and consequently the most promising one, but further research will be needed to answer the remaining questions. It must be kept in mind that the results are related to this specific model and data set: conclusions concerning the approach explained in this paper should not be generalized too easily from these results, as further evidence with other models is needed.

6. Appendix: The GRECON model 79-D

The results of the following estimation procedures are considered:

A. ordinary least squares (OLS),
B. two-stage least squares (TSLS),
C. full-information maximum likelihood (FIML) – in the definitional equations 9–13 the TSLS coefficients are used as fixed parameters;
D. the same as C with OLS coefficients in equations 9–13.

Symbols without special indication refer to relative changes. Absolute quantities are indicated by bold italic. Capital symbols refer, as a rule, to values, lowercase symbols to volumes and prices. The estimated standard deviations are mentioned within brackets; coefficients not significant at a probability level of about 5% (t values $\leqslant 2$) are in italics. The sample variance of the left-hand variable is indicated by s_{yy} and the estimated variance of the residuals by s_{uu}. For C and D the estimated variances of the reduced-form residuals (indicated by $\hat{\sigma}^2_\eta$) are also stated. The overall measure of goodness of fit for C is χ^2 (109) = 411.1, and for D, χ^2 (109) = 411.6; the significance levels for C and D are equal to 0.0%.

6.1. Behavioural Equations

1. Private consumption

	Equation	s_{yy}	s_{uu}	$\hat{\sigma}_\eta^2$
A	$c = 0.63\, y^d_{g-1/2} + 1.36$	4.99	2.03	–
	$(0.11) \quad (0.66)$			
B	$c = 0.63\, y^d_{g-1/2} + 1.35$	4.99	2.03	–
	$(0.10) \quad (0.64)$			
C	$c = 0.61\, y^d_{g-1/2} + 1.55$	4.99	2.10	2.49
	$(0.11) \quad (0.67)$			
D	$c = 0.64\, y^d_{g-1/2} + 1.37$	4.99	2.09	2.47
	$(0.11) \quad (0.69)$			

2. Gross investment of enterprises (Excluding Residential Construction)

	Equation	s_{yy}	s_{uu}	$\hat{\sigma}_\eta^2$
A	$i_m = -8.37\, \Delta w + 0.84\, v'_{-1/2} + 1.14$	106.57	39.85	–
	$(2.51) \quad (0.70) \quad (4.55)$			
B	$i_m = -9.05\, \Delta w + 0.57\, v'_{-1/2} + 2.78$	106.57	40.10	–
	$(2.39) \quad (0.68) \quad (4.37)$			
C	$i_m = -9.19\, \Delta w + 0.65\, v'_{-1/2} + 2.29$	106.57	39.59	42.38
	$(2.05) \quad (0.61) \quad (3.98)$			
D	$i_m = -8.77\, \Delta w + 0.72\, v'_{-1/2} + 1.88$	106.57	39.85	42.66
	$(2.10) \quad (0.61) \quad (4.00)$			

3. Import of commodities

	Equation	s_{yy}	s_{uu}	$\hat{\sigma}_\eta^2$
A	$m = 2.94\, n' + 1.19\, v' - 0.37\,(p_m - p_{v'}) + 0.04$	62.13	5.89	–
	$(0.46) \quad (0.20) \quad (0.14) \quad (1.28)$			
B	$m = 3.12\, n' + 1.15\, v' - 0.36\,(p_m - p_{v'}) + 0.29$	62.13	5.94	–
	$(0.45) \quad (0.20) \quad (0.13) \quad (1.24)$			
C	$m = 2.01\, n' + 1.80\, v' - 0.14\,(p_m - p_{v'}) - 3.29$	62.13	6.02	11.33
	$(0.64) \quad (0.31) \quad (0.11) \quad (1.83)$			
D	$m = 2.55\, n' + 1.49\, v' - 0.19\,(p_m - p_{v'}) - 1.42$	62.13	5.23	11.90
	$(0.61) \quad (0.28) \quad (0.10) \quad (1.65)$			

4. Inventory change

	Equation	s_{yy}	s_{uu}	$\hat{\sigma}_\eta^2$
A	$n' = 0.20\, v' + 0.08\,(p_m - p_{v'}) + 0.18\, \Delta p_c -$			
	$(0.05) \quad (0.04) \quad (0.05)$			
	$-0.34\, n'_{-2} - 0.91$	2.20	0.47	–
	$(0.10) \quad (0.34)$			
B	$n' = 0.21\, v' + 0.08\,(p_m - p_{v'}) + 0.18\, \Delta p_c -$			
	$(0.05) \quad (0.04) \quad (0.04)$			
	$-0.33\, n'_{-2} - 0.96$	2.20	0.47	–
	$(0.09) \quad (0.31)$			

		s_{yy}	s_{uu}	$\hat{\sigma}^2_\eta$
C	$n' = 0.24\, v' + 0.08\,(p_m - p_{v'}) + 0.13\, \Delta p_c -$			
	(0.06) (0.03) (0.05)			
	$- 0.41\, n'_{-2} - 1.15$	2.20	0.49	0.62
	(0.08) (0.41)			
D	$n' = 0.21\, v' + 0.08\,(p_m - p_{v'}) + 0.16\, \Delta p_c -$			
	(0.06) (0.03) (0.05)			
	$- 0.40\, n'_{-2} - 0.94$	2.20	0.47	0.66
	(0.08) (0.38)			

5. Consumption price

A	$p_c = 0.85\, l - 0.63\,(v' - a)_{-1/2} - 0.75$	10.82	3.05	–
	(0.11) (0.23) (1.27)			
B	$p_c = 0.86\, l - 0.71\,(v' - a)_{-1/2} - 0.54$	10.82	3.07	–
	(0.11) (0.23) (1.24)			
C	$p_c = 0.74\, l - 0.59\,(v' - a)_{-1/2} + 0.21$	10.82	2.85	8.99
	(0.13) (0.22) (1.18)			
D	$p_c = 0.70\, l - 0.56\,(v' - a)_{-1/2} + 0.45$	10.82	2.92	9.21
	(0.14) (0.22) (1.24)			

6. Investment price

A	$p_i = 0.30\, l + 0.40\, p_{m-1/2} + 0.74$	12.46	2.50	–
	(0.11) (0.06) (1.05)			
B	$p_i = 0.29\, l + 0.40\, p_{m-1/2} + 0.82$	12.46	2.50	–
	(0.11) (0.06) (1.03)			
C	$p_i = 0.27\, l + 0.43\, p_{m-1/2} + 0.91$	12.46	2.54	2.99
	(0.11) (0.05) (1.05)			
D	$p_i = 0.28\, l + 0.43\, p_{m-1/2} + 0.87$	12.46	2.54	3.02
	(0.11) (0.05) (1.07)			

7. Wage rate

A	$l = 0.88\, p_{c-1/2} + 1.14\,(v' - a)_{-1/2} +$			
	(0.12) (0.21)			
	$+ 0.14\, B^n_{g-1/2} - 1.04$	12.44	2.60	–
	(0.03) (1.34)			
B	$l = 0.87\, p_{c-1/2} + 1.27\,(v' - a)_{-1/2} +$			
	(0.11) (0.20)			
	$+ 0.14\, B^n_{g-1/2} - 1.66$	12.44	2.66	–
	(0.03) (1.30)			
C	$l = 0.76\, p_{c-1/2} + 1.09\,(v' - a)_{-1/2} +$			
	(0.13) (0.19)			

		s_{yy}	s_{uu}	$\hat{\sigma}^2_\eta$
	$+\,0.13\,B^n_{g\,-1/2} \;-\, 0.30$	12.44	3.02	6.22
	(0.02) (1.27)			
D	$l = 0.71\,p_{c\,-1/2} + 1.04\,(v' - a)_{-1/2} +$			
	(0.14) (0.19)			
	$+\,0.14\,B^n_{g\,-1/2} + 0.07$	12.44	3.18	6.42
	(0.02) (1.33)			

8. Private employment

A	$a = 0.42\,v'_{-1/2} - 0.21\,l_{-1/2} + 0.80$	2.32	0.47	–
	(0.05) (0.05) (0.58)			
B	$a = 0.42\,v'_{-1/2} - 0.21\,l_{-1/2} + 0.78$	2.32	0.47	–
	(0.05) (0.04) (0.55)			
C	$a = 0.43\,v'_{-1/2} - 0.25\,l_{-1/2} + 1.16$	2.32	0.48	0.38
	(0.05) (0.04) (0.55)			
D	$a = 0.42\,v'_{-1/2} - 0.26\,l_{-1/2} + 1.26$	2.32	0.49	0.39
	(0.05) (0.05) (0.56)			

6.2. Definitional Equations

9. Total output

A	$v' = 0.60\,c + 0.10\,i_m + 0.04\,i_w + 0.29\,b +$			
	(0.07) (0.02) (0.01) (0.03)			
	$+\,0.09\,x_{ex} - 0.58$	10.83	0.34	–
	(0.02) (0.37)			
B	$v' = 0.54\,c + 0.11\,i_m + 0.04\,i_w + 0.26\,b + 0.08\,x_{ex}$	10.83	0.39	–
	(0.06) (0.02) (0.01) (0.02) (0.02)			
1977 weights	0.45 0.09 0.04 0.34 0.06			

10. Total output price

A	$p_{v'} = 0.49\,p_c + 0.18\,p_i + 0.33\,p_b + 0.24$	14.21	0.49	–
	(0.06) (0.06) (0.03) (0.30)			
B	$p_{v'} = 0.53\,p_c + 0.17\,p_i + 0.32\,p_b + 0.07$	14.21	0.51	–
	(0.06) (0.06) (0.03) (0.29)			

11. Disposable income of households (volume)

A	$y^d_g = 0.97\,Y^d_g - 1.01\,p_c + 0.19$	10.28	0.01	–
	(0.01) (0.01) (0.06)			
B	$y^d_g = 0.96\,Y^d_g - 1.01\,p_c + 0.21$	10.28	0.01	–
	(0.01) (0.01) (0.06)			

12. Disposable income of households

		s_{yy}	s_{uu}	$\hat{\sigma}^2_\eta$
A	$Y^d_g = 0.94\,L_T - 0.12\,B^n_g + 0.84$ (0.09) (0.02) (1.01)	13.55	2.25	–
B	$Y^d_g = 1.01\,L_T - 0.12\,B^n_g$ (0.03) (0.02)	13.55	2.32	–

13. Total wage bill

A	$L_T = 0.79\,L + 0.20\,L_0 + 0.02$ (0.00) (0.00) (0.02)	14.13	0.00	–
B	$L_T = 0.80\,L + 0.20\,L_0$ (0.00) (0.00)	14.13	0.00	–

14. $L = a + l$

15. $(p_m - p_{v'}) = p_m - p_{v'}$

16. $(v' - a)_{-1/2} = \frac{1}{2}v' - \frac{1}{2}a + \frac{1}{2}(v' - a)_{-1}$

17. $(v' - a)_{-1} = v'_{-1} - a_{-1}$

18. $\Delta p_c = p_c - p_{c-1}$

19. $p_{c-1/2} = \frac{1}{2}p_c + \frac{1}{2}p_{c-1}$

20. $l_{-1/2} = \frac{1}{2}l + \frac{1}{2}l_{-1}$

21. $v'_{-1/2} = \frac{1}{2}v' + \frac{1}{2}v'_{-1}$

22. $y^d_{g-1/2} = \frac{1}{2}y^d_g + \frac{1}{2}y^d_{g-1}$

23. $p_{m-1/2} = \frac{1}{2}p_m + \frac{1}{2}p_{m-1}$

24. $B^n_{g-1/2} = \frac{1}{2}B^n_g + \frac{1}{2}B^n_{g-1}$

6.3. List of Symbols

6.3.1. Endogenous Variables

c Consumption of households (volume)

i_m Gross investment of enterprises, excluding residential construction (volume)

m Import of commodities, c.i.f. (volume)

n' Inventory change (volume), expressed as a percentage of total output

Table 5. Annual observations of the endogenous variables of the GRECON model 79-D

Year	c	i_m	m	n'	p_c	p_i	l	a	v'	p_v'	y_g^d	Y_g^d	L_T	L	p_m-p_v'
1950	–	–	–	3.496	–	–	–	–	–	–	–	–	–	–	–
1951	–	–	–	−1.104	12.221	–	10.511	1.596	0.531	–	0.023	–	–	–	–
1952	0.624	−9.647	−10.556	−4.227	0.000	9.574	5.681	−1.571	1.858	1.786	3.353	3.353	3.816	4.025	−3.221
1953	5.443	12.790	18.281	0.253	−0.989	−2.913	4.077	2.310	10.668	−3.465	10.282	9.191	6.718	6.482	−5.689
1954	6.573	21.917	24.015	3.493	4.001	1.000	8.967	3.818	8.501	2.707	10.949	15.389	13.787	13.140	−4.583
1955	7.528	22.648	8.689	1.085	0.960	3.961	8.948	3.084	11.095	0.613	14.070	15.166	12.467	12.309	0.406
1956	7.516	9.458	13.934	0.140	0.951	6.666	8.775	2.493	6.644	3.915	5.755	6.761	11.442	11.476	−0.852
1957	0.806	0.418	2.881	0.306	5.662	6.249	11.775	0.524	2.231	4.968	0.565	6.259	12.437	12.372	−0.063
1958	0.336	−16.352	−5.885	−1.670	2.528	2.379	4.403	−0.856	−1.005	0.584	2.580	5.173	3.774	3.495	−6.156
1959	4.398	13.481	13.498	0.390	0.999	−0.999	2.369	1.953	7.190	0.402	2.766	3.793	4.134	4.375	−3.359
1960	6.058	17.144	16.899	2.319	1.981	1.009	8.145	3.352	10.246	−0.123	8.807	10.962	11.516	11.779	0.123
1961	5.412	8.155	7.540	−0.365	1.943	0.999	7.236	2.352	4.977	0.980	3.901	5.919	9.808	9.744	−3.041
1962	6.137	5.423	5.740	−0.802	1.903	0.991	5.872	3.064	5.594	1.989	6.003	8.020	9.877	9.127	−2.982
1963	7.146	−9.966	9.567	−0.256	4.365	5.066	8.963	3.264	7.569	2.465	6.231	10.868	11.543	11.428	−0.894
1964	5.873	17.306	15.943	1.868	7.000	5.999	14.947	2.775	9.231	5.934	9.330	16.983	19.339	18.134	−3.713
1965	7.817	2.459	5.635	−0.989	3.738	3.774	11.144	1.575	8.194	2.506	7.549	11.570	13.302	12.897	−1.488
1966	3.179	10.137	6.009	−0.447	5.405	4.545	10.973	1.076	4.507	4.299	2.514	8.056	12.515	12.165	−3.191
1967	5.439	6.188	6.489	−0.254	3.419	1.739	8.767	−0.407	6.363	2.046	5.336	8.937	9.143	8.318	−2.948
1968	6.590	10.529	12.722	−0.122	2.479	1.710	8.872	1.572	9.093	1.829	6.961	9.613	10.286	10.586	−4.656
1969	7.897	−1.196	15.453	1.544	6.452	5.041	13.434	2.352	7.699	5.189	7.043	13.950	15.858	16.105	−2.079
1970	7.664	15.650	15.739	0.189	4.159	7.272	13.224	1.784	10.064	5.072	7.379	11.845	14.592	15.240	0.883
1971	2.991	0.775	5.990	−0.676	8.001	8.999	13.133	0.654	5.326	6.981	4.464	12.822	14.567	13.877	−2.787
1972	3.234	−7.888	5.224	−0.488	8.333	7.340	12.589	−1.387	4.427	6.035	4.178	12.859	12.021	11.024	−5.691
1973	3.864	10.693	12.663	1.205	9.402	5.129	15.589	0.299	7.040	7.720	5.113	14.996	15.552	15.936	−0.918
1974	2.691	−0.340	−0.995	0.509	9.374	10.569	15.670	0.119	1.726	16.400	3.425	13.121	16.208	15.808	14.847
1975	3.400	−7.535	−5.292	−2.305	11.485	11.138	12.812	−0.864	−0.797	8.612	0.414	11.947	12.823	11.835	−2.585
1976	3.777	−3.686	9.762	1.362	9.000	8.000	10.868	−0.451	5.865	7.974	4.783	14.213	10.993	10.368	−0.306
1977	4.262	15.476	2.461	0.108	7.339	6.481	7.831	0.453	3.059	5.661	1.931	9.412	8.764	8.322	−2.736

The variables L and $p_m - p_v'$ are obtained by differencing L and p_m/p_v' respectively, therefore equations 14 and 15 do not hold exactly.

Table 6. Annual observations of the exogenous variables and some other variables of the GRECON model 79-D.

Year	p_m	i_w	b	x_{ex}	p_b	B_g^n	L_0	Δw		
1950	–	–	–	–	–	–	–	–	–	–
1951	22.935	–	–	–	–	8.424	–	–	–	–
1952	−1.493	1.687	8.025	10.823	0.000	21.295	2.884	1.566	1.217	−1.049
1953	−8.957	24.126	12.562	28.734	−8.258	−5.338	7.780	−1.191	5.825	3.483
1954	−2.000	3.179	13.653	−6.365	−2.000	−2.945	16.667	−1.084	6.341	8.167
1955	1.020	−1.155	9.897	8.266	2.041	−8.263	13.148	−0.786	6.142	4.514
1956	3.030	26.390	3.459	4.499	2.000	40.816	11.299	−0.439	5.910	7.771
1957	4.902	13.733	5.396	−3.523	2.942	42.029	12.717	0.329	2.874	4.050
1958	−5.607	−5.594	9.715	−10.503	−3.809	−12.104	4.968	1.407	0.773	1.698
1959	−2.970	4.229	11.876	−0.353	0.000	6.765	3.115	−0.672	2.493	−0.152
1960	0.000	−1.653	14.763	11.330	−1.000	10.799	10.394	−0.856	5.905	5.138
1961	−2.091	1.146	1.737	7.741	−1.010	14.992	10.086	−0.437	4.618	6.671
1962	−1.053	0.252	7.459	3.519	−1.019	1.207	13.109	−0.057	2.509	2.565
1963	1.549	35.359	6.632	8.589	2.054	4.565	12.021	−0.020	3.821	2.453
1964	2.000	31.651	12.901	0.881	2.000	29.004	24.327	−0.104	5.735	5.189
1965	0.980	12.176	8.852	−1.815	1.961	8.515	14.896	0.094	6.399	6.282
1966	0.971	7.035	6.591	−0.839	0.000	16.210	13.866	0.251	4.956	6.517
1967	−0.962	12.089	7.738	5.604	−0.962	14.974	12.284	1.142	5.096	3.395
1968	−2.913	9.424	14.724	5.993	−0.970	4.490	9.182	−0.288	7.100	6.796
1969	3.003	−2.967	16.686	−0.080	−1.961	17.075	14.939	−0.496	6.314	7.404
1970	6.000	1.775	14.596	6.967	3.349	10.331	12.158	−0.200	6.680	5.224
1971	4.000	8.721	11.370	3.296	2.000	15.664	17.229	0.328	6.389	8.135
1972	0.000	14.706	12.470	−7.155	0.981	8.857	15.763	1.128	5.269	4.643
1973	6.731	2.020	13.670	−5.782	6.795	26.159	14.168	0.036	3.303	5.896
1974	35.135	−12.490	3.024	1.901	28.182	15.465	17.673	0.604	4.189	0.711
1975	4.667	−7.485	−4.656	5.959	4.836	−12.673	16.373	1.475	3.862	7.668
1976	7.643	2.540	12.737	1.384	6.000	−2.338	13.152	0.408	3.207	0.056
1977	2.769	15.872	−1.651	−0.688	2.830	−3.099	10.252	−0.182	4.476	6.358

The variable $(v' - a)$ is obtained by differencing v'/a and is therefore not exactly equal to $v' - a$.

p_c Consumption price index (1975 = 100)
p_i Investment price index (1975 = 100)
l Average gross wages, private sector
a Number of dependent employees in private enterprises (× 1000 man-year)
v' Total output less inventory changes and services (volume)
$p_{v'}$ Price index of total output (1975 = 100)
y_g^d Disposable income of households (volume)
Y_g^d Disposable income of households
L_T Total wage bill
L Wage bill of private sector

6.3.2. Exogenous Variables

p_m Import price index (1970 = 100)
i_w Gross investment in residential construction (volume)
b Export of commodities, f.o.b. (volume)
x_{ex} Consumption of goods and services by the government (volume)
p_b Export price index (1975 = 100)
B_g^n Direct taxes of households minus income transfers (net)
L_0 Wage bill of government
w Rate of unemployment

Annual observations are given in Tables 5 and 6.

References

1. Bemer, R. and van Miltenburg, A.J.M. (1974), 'Enkele experimenten met het jaarmodel 1969', onderzoekverslag 1 (Delft University of Technology).
2. Centraal Bureau voor de Statistiek, Het Jaar 1978 in Cijfers. The Hague: Centraal Bureau voor de Statistiek, January 1979.
3. Central Planning Bureau, 'Een macro model voor de Nederlandse economie op middellange termijn (VINTAF-II)', Occasional paper 12 (The Hague, 1977).
4. Centraal Planbureau, Macro Economische Verkenning 1979. The Hague: Staatsuitgeverij, September 1978.
5. Driehuis, W. (1972), Fluctuations and Growth in a Near Full-Employment Economy. Rotterdam: Rotterdam University Press.
6. Jöreskog, K.G. and Sörbom, D. (1977), 'Statistical models and methods for analysis of longitudinal data', in D.J. Aigner and A.S. Golberger, eds., Latent Variables in Socio-Economic Models. Amsterdam: North-Holland Publishing, pp. 285–325.
7. Jöreskog, K.G. and Sörbom, D. (1978), 'LISREL IV, a general computer program for estimation of linear structural equation systems by maximum likelihood methods' (University of Uppsala).
8. Ketellapper, R.H., Bos, B., Kooyman, M.A. and Voorhoeve, W. (1977), 'A simultaneous econometric model for the Dutch economy'. Statistica Neerlandica 31, 4, 141–159.
9. Koopmans, T.C., Rubin, H. and Leipnik, R.B. (1950), 'Measuring the equation systems of dynamic economics', in T.C. Koopmans, ed., Statistical Inference in Dynamic Economic Models, Cowles Commission Monograph 10. New York: John Wiley and Sons, pp. 53–237.

10. Kooyman, M.A. (1976), Dummy Variables in Economics. Rotterdam: Tilburg University Press.
11. Verdoorn, P.J., Post, J.J. and Goslinga, S.S. (1970), The 1969 Re-estimation of the Annual Model, Model 69-C. The Hague: Central Planning Bureau.

Endnote

1. For the meaning of the symbols see the appendix.

THE METRIC MODEL: PRESENTATION, SIMULATION AND MULTIPLIERS

PATRICK ARTUS and MICHEL VOLLE

The METRIC model was created jointly by the INSEE and the Direction de la Prévision. Begun in 1975, it has been in operation since Autumn 1977, with its maintenance assured by the Quarterly Accounts Division of the INSEE, which also produces the national quarterly accounts. This partly accidental administrative situation has had important technical consequences: experience has shown in effect that the physical proximity between the 'quarterly' accountants and those responsible for the model is an important factor in its quality, as it favours the innumerable exchanges of information necessary for a proper understanding of the statistical possibilities and characteristics of the series.

METRIC serves in various capacities: it satisfies the needs of short-term analysis and economic budgets; it permits a rapid response to demands for variants and the carrying out of economic studies in depth.

(a) *The needs of short-term analysis.* Four times a year, the INSEE publishes a 'short-term analysis note' summarizing the present economic situation and the prospects for the following six months. For the preparation of each note, METRIC provides quarterly macroeconomic forecasts for a time span of three years, enabling us both to insert the short-term prospects within a complete, coherent framework and to situate them against the 'background' of medium-term prospects.

(b) *The needs of economic budgets.* The Forecasting Office twice a year produces budgets, concerning the year in progress and on the one to come; each year a 'variants operation', the aim of which is to clarify the conditions and consequences of alternative options in economic policy, is drawn up. METRIC is utilized for this work, which enables us to situate it in a wider time span and to specify the evolutions, by giving their quarterly profile.

(c) *Economic studies in depth.* In 1978, two studies in depth were published, one on inflation,[1] the other on the crisis.[2] In the latter study, the historical exogenous factors were modified to reconstruct the evolution of the French economy in the absence of the impact on oil prices.

(d) *Rapid responses to demands.* The METRIC team is able to reply within 48 hours to demands for simple variations made by the most diverse administrations and ministeries.

On the technical level, METRIC is a medium-sized model (275 exogenous variables, 500 equations); it belongs to the class of demand models of neo-Keynesian inspiration. It contains a financial sector permitting the transmission of the financial situation to the real field. Its principal statistical characteristics are its incorporation of the essential part of information derived from short-term surveys (opinions on the level of stocks and liquidity problems, margins of unemployed productive capacities, and so on). Moreover, its quarterly periodicity permits the study of short-term dynamics, mainly by taking into account lag structures (prices–wages, investment–production, consumption–incomes). The analysis of economic policy is notably favoured by the large number of exogenous variables related to the economic behaviour of the state.

METRIC is at present being reestimated with the base year of the SECN,[3] 1971; during this reestimation, essential points, to which we shall return later in this note, are being perfected.

After a rapid description of the METRIC model, we shall present its development prospects, and then take a brief look at studies of simulation and multipliers which have been carried out on the model.

1. Presentation of the METRIC Model

Elsewhere[4] can be found a complete description of the model: here we shall only take a brief look at the structure and at the most important equations, those sufficient to understand the results of the tests which have been carried out.

1.1. Structure of the Model

A schema of the model is presented in figure 1. Economic agents (households, firms, administrations, foreign countries) make a demand for goods and services, which leads to production. This, in its turn, requires the presence of factors of production (manpower, capital). The lesser or greater utilization of these provokes 'tensions', which act on the labour market or on the production system. These tensions intervene in the majority of behaviours: they affect demand itself (the greater the utilization of production capacities is, the more is invested and the less is exported), price and wage fixing (the tighter the labour market is, the more quickly the real wage rate will grow), production factors, and so on. Once we know the prices, wages and production factors, it is possible to move on to the calculation of incomes, then pass on to transfers, taking the fiscal and social policy of the administration into account. The incomes of households and the production expenses of

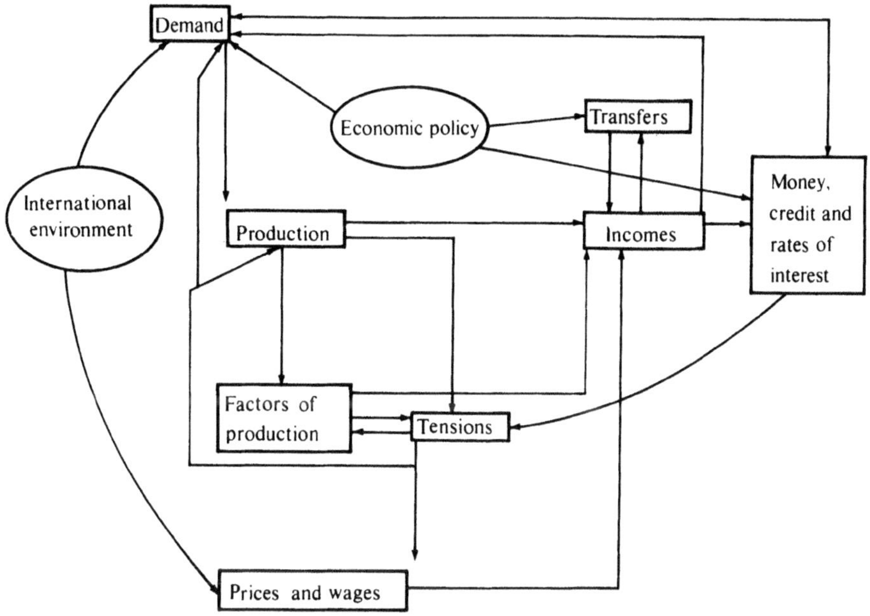

Fig. 1. Schema of the METRIC model.

firms determine their demand for money. This is part of their usage, while their demand for credit adds to their resources. The level of credit demand intervenes, together with monetary policy, in the fixing of the rate of interest. The rates of interest, as well as the lesser or greater liquidity problem (which is the last 'tension' of the model), intervene in the fixing of demand, of production factors and wages, the firms modifying their total expenses as their financial situation changes.

The general structure is finally completed by the dependence of demand on incomes after transfers.

With regard to a simple neo-Keynesian schema, one can see that the structural originalities concern:

- the central role played by tensions (labour market, production capacities, liquidity problems),
- financial integration, essentially through rates of interest, liquidity problems of firms and financial relations with foreign countries.

The implementation of this global structure itself contains some original characteristics. Let us look at some of them:

- the utilization and explanation of short-term surveys (opinions on stocks, capacity margins, price forecasting, liquidity problems) – this integration of surveys inside national accounts variables enriches the short-term significance of the model;

– the richness of the model's dynamics, and the care taken in the estimation of lags, which are extremely numerous for a quarterly model;
– the disintegration of the model into six branches, giving it a relatively large dimension: almost 500 equations, 275 exogenous variables;
– the detail in the representation of transfer operations, which enables us to simulate in this area the effects of extremely refined economic policies;
– the detailed modelling of the inventory investment in industrial products, which will be described below;
– the explanation of the large components of the balance of payments and of the rate of exchange.

After this general survey we shall give the most important equations of the model, following the structure presented above.

1.2. Demand

Demand consists of:

– the demand of government agencies, a variable exogenous to the model,
– housing demand,
– household consumption,
– exports,
– fixed investment by firms.

1.2.1. Housing. The essential variable is the number of housing starts (MCH), which the retained equation links to the permanent income of households (RP), to housing stock (KL), to the rate of interest of housing credit (TXL), to the anticipated growth of their price (PFL^a), to the price ratio of housing and consumption (PFL/PCM) and to the extension of the length of housing credit (DUR).

$$\begin{aligned}\frac{MCH}{KL_{-1}} &= 0.0012 + 0.011 \log(RP) - 0.013 \log(KL_{-1}) \\ &\quad - 1.310^{-6}\, TXL + 0.00054\, PFL^a \\ &\quad - 0.039 \log(PFL/PCM) + 0.039\, \Delta(1/DUR).\end{aligned}$$

1.2.2. Consumption. The economic consumption of households (CE) is linked to an average of their salary (MMRS) and non-salary (MMRNS) incomes, to the loss in the purchasing power of their liquid assets (PAL), to the variations of tensions of the labour market (ΔLDO) and to the difference between recent inflation and average inflation (AP).

$$\begin{aligned}\Delta CE &= 3424 - 0.57\, CE_{-1} + 0.28\, MMRNS + 0.46\, MMRS \\ &\quad - 0.19\, PAL - 654\, \Delta LDO + 519\, AP.\end{aligned}$$

1.2.3. Exports. The exports of industrial products (EXI) depend on foreign demand (DM), on the competitivity of French products (COMP), and on the ratio of international demand and production capacity (PDI); the different variables are in fact all lagged.

$$\log(\text{EXI}) = 1.18 \log(\text{DM}) - 1.16 \log(\text{PDI}) + 0.85 \log(\text{COMP}) + 10.03.$$

1.2.4. Fixed Investment. The equation for fixed investment is extremely complicated. Fixed investment in equipment (INV) depends on a double lag on the value added of firms (VA) and on the optimal coefficient of capital (V), which itself depends on a time trend and on the relative cost of production factors. This double lag is weighted by cash flow difficulties (TRES) and capacity margins (CAPA); because of its still experimental character, the equation will not be reproduced here.

1.3. Desired Inventories, Building Stock of Industrial Products, and Production

The schema for desired inventories, for the desired building stock of industrial products and for production is shown in Figure 2. The anticipated demand (D^a), the price of products placed in stock (imported raw materials, PMPI), liquidity problems (TRES), the after-tax profit margin rate of companies (TM) and their anticipation of production costs (API) determine their desired level of inventories (NSD):

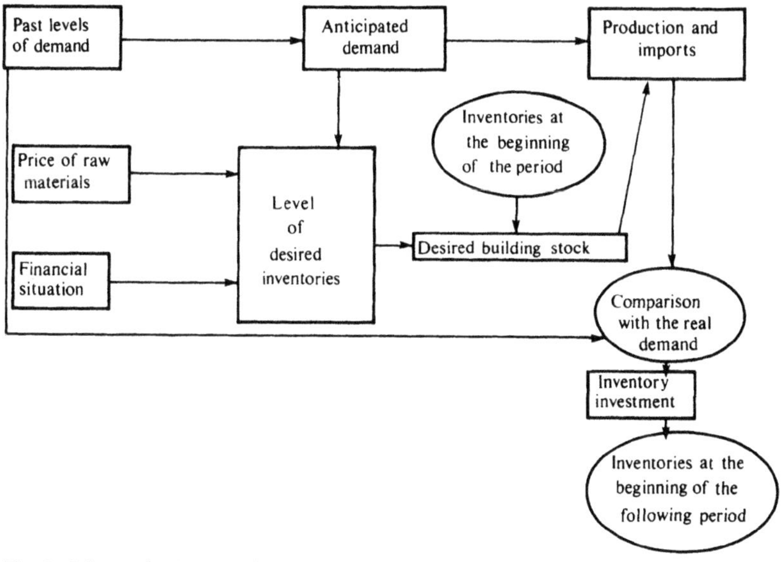

Fig. 2. Schema for inventories, stocks and production.

$$NSD = -10780 - 2474\,API - 88926\,\frac{PMPI}{\Sigma_i PMPI} + 71.9\,PMPI$$
$$+ 25.7\,PMPI_{-1} - 20.6\,PMPI_{-2} - 69.8\,PMPI_{-3}$$
$$- 718\,TRES - 513\,TRES_{-1} - 308\,TRES_{-2}$$
$$- 205\,TRES_{-3} + 0.37 \times 10^6\,TM + 1.84\,D^a.$$

The price of raw materials intervenes twice:

- in the form of the ratio to its tendency, to show that if the price rises abruptly one would wish to keep fewer stocks of raw materials,
- in the form of a lag, to represent the effect of speculative stock building.

Once the desired inventories are known, the comparison with the inventories held at the beginning of the period gives the desired inventory investment (DSD). The total: production (XI) + imports (IM) is then calculated by:

$$XI + IM = 0.10\,DSD + 0.88\,D^a$$

The division between production and imports finally depends on the rate of capacity utilization in France and abroad, on the competitivity of French goods and on a time trend representing the opening of borders.

1.4. Employment and Hours Worked

The basic employment formulation represents the process of adaptation to a desired employment level, itself based on the anticipated production and productivity tendency for non-industrial sectors and on the desired inventory investment and anticipated demand for industry. This formulation is enriched by the presence of tension terms and, in the sector of services and utilities alone, by that of the duration of work (divided by its trend). Thus, for industry, employment (EFI) is linked to its desired level (EFI*) and to the indicator of tensions in the labour market (LDO):

$$\log(EFI) = 0.7 + 0.09 \log(EFI^*) - 0.01\,LDO$$
$$+ 0.85 \log(EFI_{-1}).$$

The divergence from its trend ($\overline{HI}$) of the length of the work week (HI) depends on the variations of production (ΔXI), on tension terms, and, in the branch of services alone, on the evolution of employment. For industry, we have:

$$HI - \overline{HI} = 1.5 + 0.04\,\Delta XI_{-1} - 52.4\,LDO + 0.83\,(HI - \overline{HI})_{-1}.$$

1.5. Tensions

1.5.1. In the Labour Market. The indicator of tensions is the logarithm of the ratio of unemployment (DENS) to job vacancies (OENS). The two elements of the ratio are separately represented by the model. DENS depends on the difference between employment (EF) and potential active population (PAC), and on the fluctuation of the activity rates, which is assumed to depend on the recent evolution of employment (in fact it is the population available seeking employment, PDRE, which is represented in the model, and the relation between PDRE and DENS depends on an exogenous coefficient).

$$\begin{aligned}\text{PDRE} = {} & 15643 + 82.7\,T + 36.1\,T_1 + 0.157\,\text{PAC} - 0.27\,\text{EF} \\ & - 0.87\,\Delta\text{EF} - 0.16\,\Delta\text{EF}_{-1} + 0.36\,\text{PDRE}_{-1}\end{aligned}$$

where T and T_1 are time trends.

Job vacancies depend on the length of the work week, on the anticipated value added of firms and on their liquidity problems.

1.5.2. Of Production Capacity. The capacity margins available in industry (CAPA) depend on the gap between the industry's production (XI) and its production capacity, $\overline{\text{XI}}$ (calculated from the investment equation) as well as on the tension indicator in the labour market (LDO):

$$\text{CAPA} = 0.25 + 0.55 \log(\overline{\text{XI}}) - 0.56 \log(\text{XI}) + 0.02\,\text{LDO}.$$

1.5.3. Of the Liquidity Problems of Firms. The liquidity problems of firms (TRES) depend on a trend, on firms' investment rate (TINV), on the rate of interest (TXCT), on a lag of the ratio of firms' liquid assets to their total expenses (MLIQ), on a variable representing credit rationing (RES), and on their financial expenses divided by their added value (CHAR).

$$\begin{aligned}\text{TRES} = {} & 77 - 0.42\,T + 0.0026\,\text{CHAR} + 0.015\,\text{TXCT} \\ & + 49.6\,\text{TINV}_{-1} + 0.0005\,\text{RES} - 190\,\text{MLIQ}.\end{aligned}$$

1.6. Prices and Wage Rates

1.6.1. Wage Rates. The growth rate of nominal wage rates (TS) depends on lags over five quarters (since 1968) in the growth rate of the price of households' consumption (TP), and on a lag in the indicator of tension in the labour market (MMLOD). In non-industrial sectors, it also depends on the SMIC (legal minimum salary) and on the wage rate in large public companies.

1.6.2. Prices. The price structure of METRIC is complex. For each product there is a production price, and utilization prices for each kind of utilization of the product. The utilization price equations are relatively simple. They link the explained price with the production price, the import price and a tension term representing the pressure of the demand for the product.

The production price equations are more complicated. In industry, the price of production (PXI) is adapted to a desired price (PXI*) following a process

$$\frac{PXI}{PXI_{-1}} = \left(\frac{PXI^*}{PXI_{-1}}\right)^a$$

in which a is variable: it depends on the growth of the demand for industrial products ($\dot{D}$) and somewhat on a price freeze variable (BLOC):

$$a = 0.196 + 3.4\dot{D} - 0.09\,BLOC.$$

The desired price results from the application of a desired margin rate (TM*) to the unit cost of production, CU (intermediary consumption, wages and unitary welfare contributions):

$$PXI^* = (1 + TM^*)\,CU.$$

The desired margin rate depends on the rate of investment (TINV):

$$TM^* = 0.24 + 0.78\,TINV.$$

1.7. Incomes and Transfers

The incomes and transfers sector of METRIC contains around a hundred equations. We shall not introduce them here, as they are not essential for an understanding of the multipliers constructed by METRIC. Let us say only that all taxes, all welfare contributions, interest paid and received, the incomes and investments of unincorporated private businesses, the majority of insurance components, the value added of households, all welfare allowances, relief, etc., are also the concern of equations in METRIC.

1.8. Financial Sector

The structure of the financial sector is illustrated in Figure 3.

Households and firms make a demand for money; households also buy stocks and bonds: these are partly made up of public bonds, others are issued by firms. According to their money demand (for firms), and to their expenses and incomes, economic agents make demands for financing. This money demand is partly satisfied by the issue of shares (for companies); the rest is a demand for credit. This demand for credit is partly satisfied by the CDC[5] or by other financial institutions; the remainder is directed at banks, which, according to (1) the demand they receive, (2) monetary policy (interest rate on the monetary market, special reserves rate, and so on), and (3) their financial situation (which depends on their share in the collection of liquid assets and on monetary policy), fix their interest rate for bank credit. We are going to present only two of the most important equations: the demand for liquid assets from firms and the fixing of the interest rate by banks.

The purchasing power of the companies' liquid assets (LIQEN/P) depends on the anticipated inflation (P^a), on their total expenses, CHARP (wages, welfare contributions, taxes, intermediary consumption, and so on), and on a variable representing credit rationing (RESP):

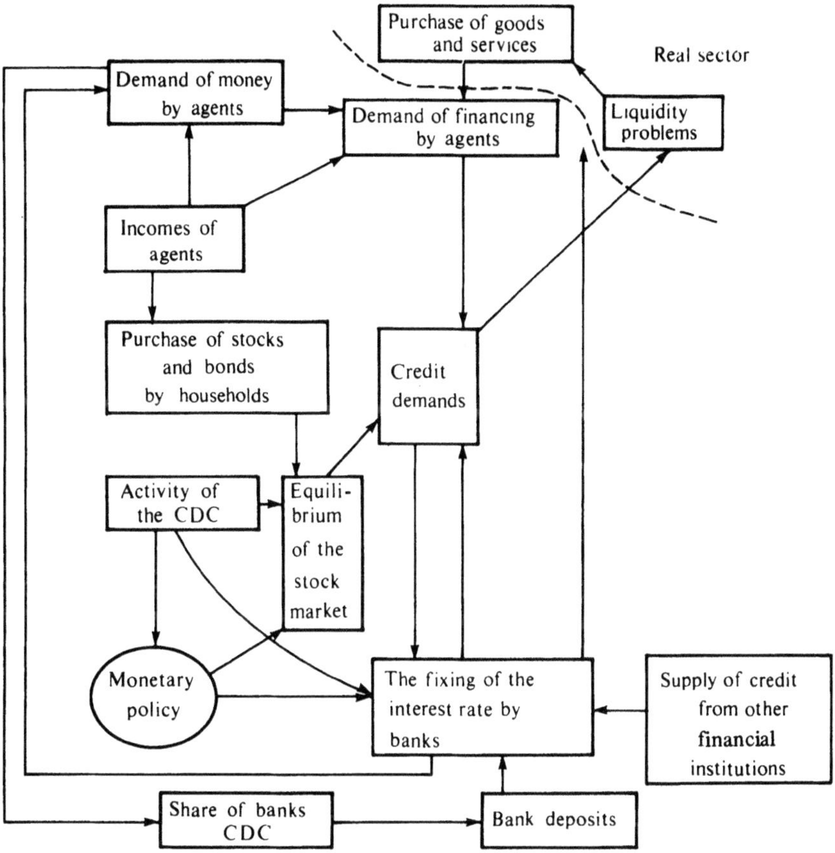

Fig. 3. The financial sector.

$$\text{LIQEN/P} = -3915 - 6.4\,\dot{\text{P}}^a + 0.24\,\text{CHARP} - 0.66\,\text{RESP} + 0.56\,(\text{LIQEN/P})_{-1}$$

The interest rate fixed by banks (TXCT) depends on the interest rate on the monetary market (TXAJJ), alone and weighted by the ratio of refinancing to bank credit, on the credit demand variation divided by the current gross domestic product (ΔC/PIBV), and on a representative variable of credit rationing (RESTR):

$$\text{TXCT} = \text{TXAJJ} \times \frac{\text{REFIN}}{\text{CREDB}} + 125.5 - 0.014\,\text{RESTR} + 3094\,\frac{\Delta\text{C}}{\text{PIBV}} + 0.29\,\text{TXAJJ} + 0.19\,\text{TXAJJ}_{-1} + 0.10\,\text{TXAJJ}_{-2}\,.$$

1.9. Balance of Payments and Rate of Exchange

The rate of exchange depends on the exchange market in which are involved the amount of the current balance (SOL), the capital flows of the private and banking sectors (MC), the long-term public capital flows (MCP), and the variations of official reserves (DOD):

$$DOD = SOL + MC + MCP.$$

The monetary authorities intervene:

- by fixing the amount of intervention on the market with reserves (DOD),
- by fixing the interest rate on the monetary market (R).

These two variables, DOD and R, are the subject of econometric equations which clarify the reactions of the authorities: the private capital flows depend on the anticipated difference in profitability between investments in France and those abroad. This difference brings into play the anticipated evolution of the exchange rate, which is constructed from the observed evolution and the export–import ratio of the trade balance.

The equation of private capital flows (MC) is:

$$\frac{MC}{CEX} = 0.02 - 0.65\,\dot{S} + 0.00011\,(\Delta R - \Delta\overline{RE}) + 0.388\,\Delta(TC - TC_{OECD})$$

where

CEX	:	value of foreign trade, normalizing the equation;
$\dot{S}$	:	growth rate of the exchange rate;
RE	:	foreign interest rate;
TC	:	export–import ratio of the trade balance;
TC_{OECD}	:	the same for the OECD countries.

The capital flows are finally shared among the various agents (households, banks and firms) and inserted in the financial flows described above.

2. Prospects and Evolution of the Model

The version of the METRIC model which has just been briefly described was based on the national quarterly accounts in base year 62. At present, the model is in the process of being reestimated and tested with the aid of the new national quarterly accounts in base year 71. This reestimation is an occasion for improving and complementing the present version of the model.

2.1. Improvements

In the reestimated model hiring and investment behaviour of the industrial sector is unified around a production function of the 'putty–clay' type. The estimation of the investment equation provides the optimal equipment and employment coefficients. We can then work out the optimal manpower employed to the full use of its capacities, then move on to the desired manpower, and finally to the real manpower by an adjustment to the desired manpower, the speed of which depends on the liquidity problems of companies. In base year 62 this unification came up against difficulties that were both statistical and econometric.

The explanation of industrial exports is improved by a simultaneous estimation of the volume of these exports (from the formulation of exports demanded) and their price (from the inversion of an equation of supplied exports). The effects of competitivity and the profitability of exports will be refined.

The coherence of the households account will be improved by increasing the links, at the level of specification and estimation, between their expenditure, financial investment and debt decisions.

2.2. Extensions of the Model

The complete accounts – real and financial – of all the agents (households, companies, public administrations, foreign countries, private administrations, credit institutions) will be explained. The disintegration of the model is increased by the distinction between agriculture and the agricultural and food industries, and by the division of services into 'transports and telecommunications' and 'other services'. However, at the beginning, the model will still include only one industrial sector. Subdivisions of this, which complicate the model, are envisaged for later.

2.3. Interchangeable Behaviour

The last stage of the model's evolution – or of a simplified version of it – is the possibility of changing fundamental behaviour. In a number of cases, the choice of a set of specifications in a model depends more on the theoretical a prioris of its authors than on the results of econometric study. Therefore it is useful, in the construction of the model, to provide for several alternative specifications in a certain number of key areas, enabling us to work out variants, not only by modifying economic policy or the international environment, but also by changing the description of the agents' behaviour; the dependence on variational results with regard to the choice of specifications can then be evaluated.

3. Simulations

During the implementation of successive versions of METRIC a large number of simulations were undertaken, as follows

A. Simulations over the sample period:
- some groups of equations alone;
- the whole model;

– the model of some variables exogenized;
– static simulation.

B. Simulations two and four quarters ahead:
– over the sample period, a large number of simulations two quarters ahead;
– simulations four quarters ahead.

C. Simulations outside the sample period.

Group A simulations verified whether the model correctly reproduced the past. They also helped to identify the least precise parts of the model and those whose precision suffers most from the simultaneity of the whole. Group B simulations give an idea of the precision which may be expected during the practical utilization of the model forecasting several quarters ahead. Group C simulations serve to identify the equations whose specification is unsatisfying or fragile. As soon as one uses the model outside the sample period the results given by these equations are generally far from reality.

We shall give here the numerical results of the simulation of the whole model over its sample period, as well as the conclusions drawn from all the other simulations which we have just mentioned.

3.1. Simulations over the Sample Period

We were able to estimate only from 1971 to 1975, for statistical reasons, certain equations of the financial sector essentially concerning the stock market. The dynamic simulation therefore covers the period of the first quarter of 1971 to the fourth quarter of 1975, or twenty quarterly periods. We also made a simulation by removing the crisis year 1975. In the annex are graphs presenting the dynamic simulation of the principal variables.

The most important divergences between simulation and reality are:
– the overestimation of households' consumption at the end of 1974;
– the insufficient reduction of employment in 1975;
– the too strong drop in the interest rate at the beginning of 1972;
– the permanent overestimation of fixed investment since the end of 1973.

The precision of the simulation is measured by the root mean square error divided by the mean of the variable (RMSE (%)) and defined by:

$$\text{RMSE}\,(\%) = \frac{1}{\bar{y}}\sqrt{\frac{1}{N}\sum_i (y_i - \hat{y}_i)^2}\,,$$

where y_i : the real value of a variable for quarter i,
$\hat{y}_i$: simulated value,
N : number of quarters, and
$\bar{y}$: mean of the variable.

The root mean square errors on these simulations are shown in Table 1. We

Table 1. Root mean square errors (RMSE (%)) for simulations over the sample period.

Variable	RMSE (%), 71–75	RMSE (%), 71–74
Households' consumption	0.7	0.6
Industrial exports	2.3	2.1
Firms' fixed investment	2.8	2.4
Industrial imports	3.3	3.3
Industrial production	1.4	1.3
Inventory investment	32.5	30.9
Level of industrial inventories	1.8	1.4
Gross domestic product	1.1	0.8
Employment	0.2	0.1
Length of working week	0.2	0.2
Unemployment	7.1	4.9
Job vacancies	10.6	8.6
Capacity margins	5.0	3.4
Liquidity problems	11.3	12.6
Price of industrial production	1.0	1.0
Comsumer price index	0.6	0.6
Wage rate in industrial sectors	1.0	1.2
Liquid assets of households	1.6	1.2
Firms' liquid assets	2.8	2.9
Bank credit	2.0	2.0
Short-term interest rate	6.1	6.2

can see that the exclusion of the crisis year 1975 improves the results, but not in important proportions. The most marked improvements concern the fixed investment, the inventories and the labour market. In fact the examination of the simulations shows that the end of 1974 is rather poorly simulated, especially for consumption and investment: over both periods the variables showing the most important mistakes are the fixed investment, industrial imports and interest rates. The error in this last variable is due to the difficulty of correctly simulating the balance of the stock market. Certain mistakes are connected: the lack of precision on liquidity problems leads to a mediocre reproduction of job vacancies.

The average mistake made on inventory investment is important as an absolute value, but the sum of mistakes over several periods tends to cancel itself out in such a way that the simulations of the stock level and industrial production are not seriously upset.

Finally prices, salaries, manpower, length of the working week and households' consumption are correctly reproduced. For the first two variables this result is satisfying considering the complexity of the system of price equations and the interactions between price and wage rate equations.

It is now possible to sum up what the other simulations have taught us.

3.2. Other Simulations

3.2.1. Exogenization of Blocks of Equations. We have been able to determine that the endogenization of the financial sector and of fixed investment did not markedly upset the simulations of the whole model. There doubtless exists a feedback effect of the following kind: if the FBCF calculated by the real sector is too high, the interest rate will itself be too high as the demand for credit will be strong, and the FBCF will be reduced in the second period. The sectors which simultaneity harms most are:

- households' consumption, where incomes and prices intervene;
- firms' fixed investment, where prices, salary costs and added value come into play.

Table 2 gives some calculated values illustrating these results.

Table 2. Comparison of model results with exogenization of the financial sector.

Variable	Whole model (RMSE (%))	Financial sector exogenized (RMSE (%))	Block alone (RMSE (%))
Households' consumption	0.7	0.8	0.5
Firms' fixed investment	2.8	2.5	1.4
Price of industrial production	1.0	1.3	1.3
Employment	0.2	0.2	0.2
Wage rate in industrial sectors	1.0	1.2	0.9

3.2.2. Static Simulation. In a static simulation, the lagged variables take on their real value, and not their simulated value, so there is not, as in dynamic simulations, an accumulation of mistakes form one period to another. We can therefore determine in what measure the existence of lags is harmful to the precision of the simulation by comparing the RMSE (%) of static and dynamic simulations. As one might expect, the variables most susceptible to mistakes on the lagged variables are those whose explicative equation brings about long lags: consumption (lags on incomes and prices), investment (lags on the gross domestic product and the relative cost of factors), desired inventories (lag on demand), and wage rate (lag on prices). Table 3 gives the most characteristic results.

Table 3. Percentage root mean square errors for static and dynamic simulations.

Variable	Dynamic simulation	Static simulation
Households' consumption	0.7	0.4
Firms' fixed investment	2.8	1.4
Desired inventories	4.4	2.4
Wage rate in industrial sectors	1.0	0.7

3.2.3. Simulations Two and Four Quarters Ahead. About ten dynamic simulations over two and four quarters were carried out over the sample period (1971–1975). The mean of the RMSE (%) of these simulations gives an idea of the model's precision in practical forecasting work over two or four quarters. In the majority of cases, the means of RMSE (%) over two and four quarters are inferior to the values calculated in dynamic simulations over 1971–1975. The two years which give the most mediocre results are without doubt 1972 and 1974. In 1972, we underestimate domestic activity and over-estimate imports: this mistaken division of supply partly arises from over-estimating the tensions on the labour market. We also underestimate the fall of activity in the fourth quarter of 1974. (The simulated fall of gross domestic product for this quarter is 2.3% in the long dynamic simulation, against 3.9% in reality). Table 4 summarizes the results obtained for RMSE.

Table 4. Percentage root mean square errors for dynamic simulations and simulations two and four quarters ahead.

Variable	Dynamic simulation (1971–1975)	Simulations two quarters ahead	Simulations four quarters ahead
Households' consumption	0.7	0.4	0.7
Firms' fixed investment	2.8	2.1	2.5
Gross domestic product	1.1	0.2	0.4
Industrial imports	3.3	1.8	2.3
Employment	0.2	0.2	0.2
Wage rate in industrial sectors	1.0	0.4	0.8
Unemployment	7.1	2.5	2.9
Consumer price index	0.6	0.2	0.4
Liquidity problems (interest rate)	10.9	8.3	8.5

3.2.4. Simulations Outside the Sample Period. The model is of course frequently used during forecasting work to carry out simulations outside the sample period. It is therefore interesting to make an initial summary of the experience of the model's utilization and the weak points which we have found in it. The variables which pose a problem when we use the model in forecasting are the following.

- *Job vacancies.* Spontaneously the model generates more job vacancies than there are. We do not know precisely if that is due to a deficient functioning of the corresponding equation, or to a statistical rupture due to a change in methods used by the ANPE (the national employment agency).
- *The desired stocks of industrial products.* It was necessary to reduce the demand coefficient in the equation of desired inventories. It seems that since the crisis, businessmen have had a more rigourous management of stocks and have wished to reduce their stock level for the same demand.
- *Fixed investment.* The effect of acceleration is sometimes too violent, and during sudden reversals of activity investment movements are exaggerated.
- Finally, it was necessary to stop at a certain date the majority of time trends which were found in various equations (division of supply, the share of banks in the collection of liquid assets). The maintenance of these trends would have led the explained variables into highly improbable zones.

4. Multipliers

During the implementation of each version of METRIC, the effects of modifying all the important exogenous variables (about 70 of them) were studied. We shall limit ourselves here to three essential and traditional multipliers: the multiplier of public expenditures, the raising of the interest rate on the monetary market, and the change in the exchange rate of the franc.

4.1. The Reference Simulation

The reference simulation covers the period 1972–1977, but it differs from the real economic evolution of this period. When one runs multipliers from the real evolution, the important fluctuations of 1974–1975–1976 seriously upset their values. In particular, the considerable easing on production capacities which occurred in 1975 upset the division of supply and the export possibilities. It is therefore necessary to calculate the multipliers from a relatively smooth reference simulation. To do this, from the period 1972–1977 the movements of exogenous variables at the origin of the crisis (oil prices, raw materials, foreign demand, and so on) were removed, as well as the measures of economic policy which responded to the crisis situation (the economy-boosting plan of 1975, the Barre plan) and the changes in behaviour of economic agents caused by the crisis (behaviour of companies' stocking). We then obtain, for this period, a quite regular reference simulation, whose principal characteristics are summarized in table 5.

Table 5. Annual growth rates and absolute values for variables in the reference simulation. (millions of 1963 francs)

Variable	1973	1974	1975	1976	1977
Households' consumption (%)	6.7	6.4	4.5	4.8	5.2
Gross domestic product (%)	6.9	4.0	3.2	3.9	3.4
Wage rate (%)	13.6	15.2	15.8	15.8	14.4
Consumer price index (%)	5.7	7.9	9.1	9.4	8.7
Rate of utilization of capacity (absolute %)	87.2	85.8	83.9	82.7	80.8
Unemployment (absolute '000)	4477	5900	6037	7299	8908

It is from this simulation that all the multiplier calculations will be carried out. We are therefore dealing with entirely new multipliers in the case of METRIC. Notice that in this account the rate of utilization of capacity still falls, but much less so than in the historical evolution. This drop can, however, lead to a higher multiplier at the end of the period.

4.2. Multiplier of Public Expenditure

It is possible with METRIC to study the effect of a rise in public expenditure with all the possible forms of financing this rise may have: monetary financing, state loan, putting local administration into debt, raising various kinds of taxes, and so on. We shall limit ourselves here to two cases:

- monetary financing, that is to say, with the treasury borrowing from the Bank of France;
- financing by a state loan, issued to the public.

In every case, we shall study the effects of *a sustained rise of 1000 million francs at 1963 prices per quarter of the investment of administrations in public works* taking effect in the first quarter of 1972: remember that in METRIC, a disintegrated model, the choice of product in which supplementary public expenditure is brought to bear matters (the public works is the product which gives the largest multiplier, as the increase in imports is weakest). This rise represents 0.66% of the initial gross domestic product (first quarter of 1972). The rate of exchange of the franc will be held constant in all the multipliers which follow (METRIC also enables us to make flexible exchange multipliers). Finally all the exogenous variables expressed in current francs (wage rates in administrations, wage rates of large public enterprises, and so on) are indexed on the differences of prices with the reference simulation.

4.2.1. Rise in Public Expenditure with Monetary Financing. Every quarter, the treasury runs into debt to the Bank of France for the amount necessary to finance ex post, that is to say by taking into consideration supplementary fiscal returns, the 1000 million 1963 francs of supplementary expenditure. The evolution of the general balance in constant 1963 francs is shown in table 6. We can see that the multiplier does not reach the maximum level: after three years its value is 2.02, after four years 2.21, and after six years 2.77. This result clearly differs from those obtained with METRIC in which a maximum of about 2 was reached after four years. The reasons for these differences are doubtless:

- the fact that the reference simulation differs from historic reality, and in particular presents a regular drop in the rate of utilization of capacity instead of a very choppy evolution;
- the care taken for the first time in indexing all the current exogenous variables.

We find, however, all the known characteristics of the public expenditure multiplier of METRIC:

- initial destocking to satisfy a part of the abrupt rise in demand, followed by stock building which compensates for the initial drop in stocks and which, moreover, results in a rise in demand, and therefore of the desired inventories;
- permanently increasing share of imports in the rise in supply – this share rises from 10% in the first quarter to 20% after 3 years and is then stabilized at this level; the increase is due to the changes in inventories, which

Table 6. Simulation of monetary financing of 1000 million francs (1963 prices) of additional public expenditure per quarter from the first quarter of 1972: differences from the reference simulation (million 1963 francs).

Variable	1972.1	1972.2	1972.3	1972.4	1973.4	1974.4	1975.4	1976.4	1977.4
Gross domestic product	+900	+1140	+1260	+1380	+1630	+2020	+2210	+2460	+2770
	(+0.6%)	(+0.8%)	(+0.8%)	(+0.9%)	(+1.0%)	(+1.2%)	(+1.2%)	(+1.3%)	(+1.4%)
Imports	+103	+203	+269	+321	+413	+539	+577	+608	+729
Households' consumption	+66	+132	+217	+310	+780	+1310	+1820	+2290	+2780
Fixed investment	+206	+310	+379	+445	+594	+734	+742	+874	+1041
Residential construction	–	+1	+3	+5	+27	+71	+125	+179	+229
Exports	−142	−206	−250	−283	−428	−610	−771	−953	−1174
Inventory investment	−127	+106	+180	+224	+70	+54	−129	−322	−377

Table 7. Evolution of production factors and tensions under the monetary financing simulation: differences from the reference simulation.

Variable	1972.1	1972.2	1972.3	1972.4	1973.4	1974.4	1975.4	1976.4	1977.4
Employment in non-agricultural sectors, in thousands (%)	+10 (+0.1)	+24 (+0.2)	+40 (+0.3)	+54 (+0.4)	+98 (+0.7)	+130 (+1.0)	+153 (+1.1)	+167 (+1.2)	+177 (+1.3)
Length of the working week in non-agricultural sectors (%)	–	–	–	–	+0.1	+0.1	+0.1	+0.1	+0.1
Unemployment (thousands)	−6	−12	−18	−24	−43	−56	−63	−66	−70
Capacity margins (%)	−0.2	−0.4	−0.4	−0.5	−0.6	−0.6	−0.5	−0.4	−0.4
Liquidity problems (%)	−0.6	−0.7	−0.6	−0.6	−0.1	−0.3	−0.1	−0.9	−0.8
Productivity in non-agricultural sectors (%)	+0.5	+0.6	+0.5	+0.5	+0.2	+0.1	–	–	–

Table 8. Evolution of prices, salaries and incomes under the monetary financing simulation: percentage differences from the reference simulation.

Variable	1972.1	1972.2	1972.3	1972.4	1973.4	1974.4	1975.4	1976.4	1977.4
Consumer price index	–	–	–	−0.1	–	+0.2	+0.6	+1.1	+1.6
Wage rate	–	–	+0.1	+0.1	+0.5	+1.1	+1.9	+2.8	+3.8
Real wage rate	–	–	+0.1	+0.2	+0.5	+0.9	+1.3	+1.7	+2.2
Disposable income	+0.1	+0.1	+0.2	+0.3	+0.7	+1.3	+2.1	+2.8	+3.7
Profits	+1.0	+1.0	+0.9	+0.8	+0.5	+0.6	+0.9	+1.1	+1.8
Gross domestic product deflator	−0.1	−0.1	−0.2	−0.2	–	+0.3	+0.9	+1.5	+2.1
Unit wage cost	−0.5	−0.6	−0.4	−0.4	−0.3	+1.0	+1.9	+2.8	+3.8

have a strong content in imports, and to the rise in internal prices which damages the competitivity of French products;

- the reduction of capacity margins and the rise in prices reduce exports – after three years, foreign trade has declined in volume by 1150 million 1963 francs, after six years by 1903 million 1963 francs, against a rise in demand by administrations of 1000 million 1963 francs.

The evolution of production factors and tensions is shown in Table 7. The most remarkable point is the rigidity of manpower. Its elasticity to gross domestic product is 0.4 at the end of the first year, 0.8 after three years, and is almost 1 after six years. During the first three years this results in productivity gains, which, as we shall see, play an important role in the evolution of prices.

Capacity margins in industry are at first strongly reduced, then ease up because of the rise in fixed investment. During the first three years, the liquidity problems of companies are reduced, especially because of the rigidity of manpower which diminishes, as we shall see, the salary cost per unit produced. Afterwards the rise in manpower, the rise in prices and the increased incurring of debts tend to increase liquidity problems. After four years the number of unemployed workers is reduced by 63,000 (only 41% of the rise in manpower because of the flexibility of activity rates). We shall see below that the trade deficit of the fourth year is about 6000 million francs. To diminish by one unit the number of unemployed costs 95,000 francs in balance of trade. The modifications made to prices, salaries and incomes are given in Table 8.

The initial rise in productivity, which we explained above, enables the rise in public expenditure to have no inflationary effect for the first two years. However the real wage rate increases from the start, because of the increased tensions in the labour market (fall in unemployment and stronger anticipations of production bringing about a rise in vacancies). As soon as the productivity gains disappear, the rise in salaries brings about rises in prices. From the third year inflation rises by about 0.5% per year. The rise in salaries and employment also makes the purchasing power gains of the corporate profit disappear from the third year on, which is one of the elements of the increased liquidity problems.

The modified financing needs and capacities are given in Table 9. From the second year, the demand for financing of companies is increased by the rise in investment and salary expenses. The decline of the balance of trade is continuous. However, it represents no more than 16% of the GDP rise in value after six years against 37% the first year and 41% in the second.

The lowering of the demand for financing of administrations fluctuates, essentially because of lag between incomes and taxes. In particular, the profit of the first year is markedly improved, so the company tax of the second year increases. After three years, the increase in fiscal returns and

Table 9. Evolution of financing needs and capacities under the monetary financing simulation: differences from the reference simulation (million francs).

Variable	1972	1973	1974	1975	1976	1977
Households' capacity of financing (1963 francs)	+105	+15	+36	+54	+522	+436
Firms' need of financing (1963 francs)	−3020	+942	+598	+1988	+3871	+4485
Administrations' need of financing (1963 francs)	−2105	−3610	−4975	−6246	−7392	−9239
Financial institutions' need of financing (1963 francs)	+5130	+2371	+4002	+3845	+3388	+6556
Trade balance (1963 francs)	−100	−312	−411	−467	−655	−1366
Public investment (current francs)	5840	6380	6840	7640	8720	9440
Gross domestic product (current francs)	5670	8760	14870	24150	37880	56020

social contributions covers 41% of the rise in administrative expenses; after five years, 60%. The financing capacity of financial institutions rises at the end of the period because of the rise in the interest rate.

The modifications undergone by the principal financial variables are given in table 10. The demand of financing (bonds and credit) of firms is a direct result of their financing need and of the increase in their liquid assets (1972 example: liquid assets = +1070; financing need = −3020; so financing demand = −1950). At the beginning the fall in financing need allows a fall in the demand for credit, which reduces interest rates. Then the need of financing increases as well as does the amount of liquid assets (which are linked to costs): the credit level of companies increases, and this exerts an upward pressure on interest rates.

The purchase of stocks and bonds by households rises initially because of the increase in their incomes; this enables companies to issue more stocks. Afterwards, the interest rates rise and households must increase their personal contribution to the buying of housing and durable goods: they therefore reduce their shareholdings, and companies issue smaller numbers of bonds.

After describing in detail the public expenditure multiplier with monetary financing, we are going to study this same multiplier with loan financing, dealing only with those points in which there are marked differences between the two multipliers.

4.2.2. Rise in Public Expenditure with State Loan Financing. We shall see two versions of state loan financing:

- one in which ex ante, the state issues each quarter a loan equal to the sum of the supplementary expenses (table 11);
- one in which ex post, the state issues a loan equal to the difference between supplementary expenses and supplementary resources, i.e. taxes and social contributions (table 12).

Table 10. Modifications in principal financial variables under the monetary financing simulation.

Variable	1972.1	1972.2	1972.3	1972.4	1973.4	1974.4	1975.4	1976.4	1977.4
Short-term interest rate (%)	−0.2	−0.1	−0.1	−0.1	–	+0.1	+0.1	+0.3	+0.3
Interest rate on bonds (%)	–	–	−0.1	−0.1	–	–	–	+0.1	+0.2
Households' liquid assets (million francs)	+10	+80	+160	+1280	+750	+2050	+4970	+10070	+18100
Firms' liquid assets (million francs)	+348	+634	+687	+1070	+1720	+2950	+3580	+5520	+7820
Demand for credit by firms (million francs)	−1101	−1949	−2540	−2930	−740	+300	+4630	+11870	+22410
Stocks and bonds issued by firms (million francs)	+346	+317	+201	+116	−78	−249	−318	−809	−1476
Demand for financing by firms (million francs)	−755	−1286	−1676	−1950	−359	+862	+4077	+19896	+16694

Table 11. Simulation of ex ante state loan financing of 1000 million francs (1963 prices) of additional public expenditure per quarter from the first quarter of 1972: comparison with the reference simulation for principal variables.

Variable	1972.1	1972.2	1972.3	1972.4	1973.4	1974.4	1975.4	1976.4	1977.4
Short-term interest rate (%)	+0.1	+0.1	+0.1	+0.1	+0.3	+0.4	+0.4	+0.7	+0.6
Interest rate on bonds (%)	–	–	+0.1	+0.1	+0.2	+0.2	+0.2	+0.3	+0.4
Bonds issued by firms	–1526	–1682	–1680	–1596	–1824	–2167	–2019	–3419	–3331
Demand for credit by firms	+727	+1804	+2980	+4150	+12290	+19600	+28480	+44870	+61430
Demand for financing by firms	–799	–1404	–1908	–2334	–1688	–2079	–1522	+3586	+7865
Liquidity problems (%)	+0.1	+0.2	+0.5	+0.5	+1.4	+1.7	+2.0	+2.8	+3.0
Fixed investment (million 1963 francs)	+140	+204	+240	+269	+302	+321	+273	+292	+314
Inventory investment (million 1963 francs)	–148	+32	+58	+62	–131	–161	–276	–446	–507
Households' consumption (million 1963 francs)	+53	+114	+192	+280	+680	+1080	+1470	+1770	+2040
Gross domestic product (million 1963 francs)	+870	+1070	+1140	+1220	+1360	+1630	+1760	+2090	+2020
Consumer price index (%)	–	–	–0.1	–0.1	–	+0.2	+0.4	+0.7	+1.1
Gross domestic product deflator (%)	–0.1	–0.1	–0.1	–0.2	–	+0.2	+0.6	+1.0	+1.4
Wage rate (%)	–	–	–	+0.1	+0.4	+0.8	+1.3	+1.9	+2.5
Real wage rate (%)	–	–	+0.1	+0.2	+0.4	+0.6	+0.9	+1.2	+1.4
Trade balance (million 1963 francs)*				–1686	–2613	–3379	–3358	–4782	–5356
Need for financing of administrations (million francs)*				5216	2636	4327	3780	3805	9066
Unemployment (thousands)	–5	–12	–17	–21	–37	–45	–49	–50	–50
Employment (thousands)	+9	+22	+36	+48	+84	+106	+119	+127	+128

*Cumulative figures for whole years.

Table 12. Simulation of ex post state loan financing of 1000 million francs (1963 prices) of additional public expenditure per quarter from the first quarter of 1972: comparison with the reference simulation for principal variables.

Variable	1972.1	1972.2	1972.3	1972.4	1973.4	1974.4	1975.4	1976.4	1977.4
Short-term interest rate (%)	+0.1	+0.1	+0.1	+0.1	+0.2	+0.3	+0.3	+0.5	+0.5
Interest rate on bonds (%)	–	–	–	–	+0.1	+0.1	+0.1	+0.2	+0.3
Bonds issued by firms	–1327	–1470	–1480	–1417	–737	–1497	–1064	–1835	–3708
Demand of credit by firms	+537	+1405	+2390	+3390	+7250	+12490	+18450	+28980	+47880
Demand of financing by firms	–790	–1392	–1887	–2304	–1363	–1202	+460	+5689	+11072
Liquidity problems (%)	+0.1	+0.1	+0.3	+0.4	+0.6	+1.0	+1.1	+2.0	+2.5
Fixed investment (million 1963 francs)	+142	+208	+246	+278	+362	+407	+384	+456	+478
Inventory investment (million 1963 francs)	–146	+40	+71	+79	–28	–68	–273	–348	–500
Households' consumption (million 1963 francs)	+54	+116	+195	+280	+700	+1150	+1580	+1970	+2310
Gross domestic product (million 1963 francs)	+880	+1080	+1150	+1240	+1470	+1770	+1930	+2160	+2280
Consumer price index (%)	–	–	–0.1	–0.1	–	+0.2	+0.5	+0.8	+1.3
Gross domestic product deflator (%)	–0.1	–0.1	–0.1	–0.1	–	+0.2	+0.6	+1.1	+1.6
Wage rate (%)	–	–	–	+0.1	+0.4	+0.9	+1.5	+2.2	+3.0
Real wage rate (%)	–	–	+0.1	+0.8	+0.4	+0.7	+1.0	+1.4	+1.7
Trade balance (million 1963 francs)*				–1730	–2931	–3983	–4890	–6022	–6886
Need of financing administrations (million francs)*				5210	2559	4184	4128	3746	7575
Unemployment (thousands)	–5	–11	–17	–21	–39	–49	–54	–56	–57
Employment (thousands)	+9	+22	+37	+49	+88	+114	+131	+143	+147

*Cumulative figures for whole years.

When the state finances the rise in public expenditure by a loan, the possibilities left to companies for the issue of shares are reduced, since the demand for shares by households and the CDC initially shows little change. While reducing their total demand for financing, companies are forced to have greater recourse to credit. The demand for bank credit increases; banks must be more frequently refinanced, and they raise their rate of interest on bank credits. The rise in rates has repercussions, as we shall see in detail, on all companies' expenses. What results is of course a reduction of the multiplier in relation to monetary financing (see table 13).

Table 13. Values of the public expenditure multiplier for different types of financing.

	After 1 year	After 2 years	After 3 years	After 5 years	After 6 years
Monetary financing	1.38	1.63	2.02	2.46	2.77
Ex ante state loan	1.22	1.36	1.63	2.09	2.02
Ex post state loan	1.24	1.47	1.77	2.16	2.28

The reduction of the multiplier is very marked. It is, of course, weaker when the loan financing is done ex post. In the single case of the ex ante loan, we observe a maximum of the multiplier (2.09 the fifth year), followed by a decrease. In the other two cases, the multiplier does not stop increasing.

We shall now move on to the second kind of multiplier: the rise of the interest rate in the money market.

4.3. Rise in the Interest Rate in the Money Market

We increase over the period 1972–1977 the interest rate on the money market by 1% in relation to its real value. Tables 14, 15 and 16 give the principal effects of this rise, which is reflected by banks in their interest rate. In the short term, the rise in interest rates increases the personal contribution of households and reduces their purchase of shares and, therefore, companies' opportunities to issue such shares. We then observe the curious phenomenon that their credit demand increases, although their financing demand diminishes since their total expenses diminish, as we shall later see. From the third year, the rise in the interest rate on bonds attracts investments on the stock market and companies can issue more shares. Their credit demand is therefore reduced, which exerts a downward pressure on the interest rate.

This inversion phenomenon of the effect on the stock market is quite violent. We are at present in the process of working again on the household account in order to see if this phenomenon is steady.

The rise in interest rates leads to increased liquidity problems. These two rises have repercussions on all the expense components of companies: investment, hiring, inventory investment, and the fixing of the wage rate. However the fall in exploitation costs is not sufficient to maintain the profit. The apparent elasticity of investment to the rate of interest seems high. After

Table 14. Money market interest rate increase of 1% from 1972 to 1977: effects on the financial sector.

Variable	1972.1	1972.2	1972.3	1972.4	1973.4	1974.4	1975.4	1976.4	1977.4
Short-term interest rate (%)	+0.4	+0.5	+0.6	+0.7	+0.6	+0.4	+0.3	+0.3	+0.3
Interest rate on bonds (%)	+0.1	+0.1	+0.2	+0.3	+0.4	+0.3	+0.3	+0.2	+0.2
Households' liquid assets,	−80	−230	−480	−800	−2550	−5050	−8630	−13360	−19500
million francs (%)	(0.0)	(0.0)	(−0.1)	(−0.2)	(−0.4)	(−0.7)	(−1.1)	(−1.4)	(−1.8)
Firms' liquid assets,	−8	−26	−53	−90	−300	−550	−940	−1530	−2380
million francs (%)	(0.0)	(0.0)	(−0.1)	(−0.1)	(−0.3)	(−0.4)	(−0.6)	(−0.9)	(−1.2)
Demand of credit by firms (million francs)	+347	+1039	+1730	+2260	+2150	−290	−4220	−8910	−15020
Stocks and bonds issued by firms (million francs)	−411	−822	−907	−832	−307	+274	+346	+637	+625
Demand of financing by firms (million francs)	−64	−194	−410	−712	−2568	−6118	−9158	−12285	−16430

Table 15. Money market interest rate increase of 1% from 1972 to 1977: effect on companies' expenses.

Variable	1972.1	1972.2	1972.3	1972.4	1973.4	1974.4	1975.4	1976.4	1977.4
Liquidity problems (%)	+1.0	+1.7	+2.2	+2.5	+2.4	+1.7	+1.4	+0.9	+1.0
Firms' fixed investment (%)	−0.2	−0.4	−0.6	−0.8	−1.4	−1.5	−1.4	−1.5	−1.5
Inventory investment (million 1963 francs)	−35	−124	−229	−328	−379	−164	+16	+95	+139
Employment (%)	0	0	−0.1	−0.1	−0.2	−0.3	−0.3	−0.3	−0.3
Length of working week (%)	–	–	–	–	–	–	–	–	–
W [illegible]te (%)	0	0	0	−0.1	−0.3	−0.6	−0.9	−1.3	−1.6
Real wage rate (%)	0	0	0	−0.1	−0.2	−0.4	−0.5	−0.7	−0.8
Financing needs	−53	−116	−184	−262	−500	−633	−748	−736	−957
Profit (%)	−0.1	−0.2	−0.4	−0.5	−0.6	−0.5	−0.6	−0.9	−1.0

Table 16. Money market interest rate increase of 1% from 1972 to 1977: effects on demand, activity and prices.

Variable	1972.1	1972.2	1972.3	1972.4	1973.4	1974.4	1975.4	1976.4	1977.4
Households' consumption (%)	–	–	–0.1	–0.1	–0.2	–0.3	–0.4	–0.5	–0.6
Exports, constant francs (%)	+0.1	+0.2	+0.3	+0.3	+0.6	+0.7	+0.8	+1.0	+1.2
Imports, constant francs (%)	–0.1	–0.3	–0.5	–0.6	–0.8	–0.7	–0.5	–0.4	–0.5
Trade balance*				+801	+2000	+2367	+2372	+2541	+3018
Gross domestic product (%)	–	–0.1	–0.1	–0.2	–0.3	–0.3	–0.3	–0.3	–0.2
Productivity (%)	–	–0.1	–	–0.1	–0.1	–	–	–	+0.1
Consumer price index (%)	–	–	–	–	–0.1	–0.2	–0.4	–0.6	–0.8
Gross domestic product deflator (%)	–	–	–	–	–0.1	–0.3	–0.5	–0.8	–1.0
Unemployment (thousands)	+1	+2	+4	+5	+13	+17	+17	+16	+16
Need of financing of administrations*				+178	+557	+792	+412	–282	–135

*Cumulative figures for whole years.

Table 17. Simulation of a 10% undervaluation of the franc from 1972 to 1977: percentage effects on foreign trade.

Variable	1972.1	1972.2	1972.3	1972.4	1973.4	1974.4	1975.4	1976.4	1977.4
Exports (constant francs)	+2.8	+3.5	+3.5	+3.3	+2.3	+1.5	+0.9	+0.3	–0.1
Price of exports	+5.2	+6.8	+7.5	+7.9	+8.6	+8.7	+9.1	+9.3	+9.6
Exports (current francs)	+8.1	+10.5	+11.3	+11.5	+11.1	+10.3	+10.1	+19.6	+9.5
Imports (constant francs)	–0.5	+0.4	+0.8	+0.3	–0.4	+0.3	+0.6	+0.7	+0.6
Price of imports	+11.1	+11.1	+11.1	+11.1	+11.1	+11.1	+11.1	+11.1	+11.1
Imports (current francs)	+10.5	+11.5	+12.0	+11.4	+10.7	+11.4	+11.8	+11.9	+11.8

Table 18. Simulation of a 10% undervaluation of the franc from 1972 to 1977: effects on demand and activity.

Variable	1972.1	1972.2	1972.3	1972.4	1973.4	1974.4	1975.4	1976.4	1977.4
Households' consumption	−0.3	−0.2	−0.1	−0.2	−0.1	+0.3	+0.7	+1.0	+1.2
Liquidity problems (%)	+1.3	+0.8	+0.7	+0.9	+1.8	+1.2	+1.8	+2.8	+3.0
Fixed investment (%)	+0.9	+2.2	+3.0	+2.9	+2.0	+2.3	+2.0	+2.6	+2.4
Inventory investment (million 1963 francs)	−228	+200	+494	+159	−340	+126	+284	+254	+109
Gross domestic product (%)	+0.4	+1.0	+1.3	+1.1	+0.6	+0.9	+1.0	+1.2	+1.2

Table 19. Simulation of a 10% undervaluation of the franc from 1972 to 1977: percentage effects on prices and salaries.

Variable	1972.1	1972.2	1972.3	1972.4	1973.4	1974.4	1975.4	1976.4	1977.4
Consumer price index (%)	+0.5	+0.8	+1.0	+1.3	+2.3	+3.2	+4.1	+4.9	+5.7
Wage rate (%)	+0.3	+0.4	+0.7	+1.1	+2.5	+3.7	+5.0	+6.1	+7.3
Real wage rate (%)	−0.2	−0.4	−0.3	−0.2	+0.2	+0.5	+0.9	+1.1	+1.5

three years it is 1.5 against the rate of interest on the money market, and 5 against the rate of interest on bonds.

The increase in liquidity problems reduces the desired inventories and companies reduce actual inventories; the interest rate then falls, as we saw above. The expenses of companies being reduced, moreover, liquidity problems decrease and some stock building takes place.

We can see that, after three years, the apparent elasticity of the GDP to the interest rate on the money market is 0.3. From the second year, this 1% rise in the interest rate reduces inflation by about 0.2% per year. The improvement of the balance of trade is about 2500 million francs a year from the third year, but this is obtained at the cost of a rise of 17,000 in the number of seekers of employment (or an improvement of 147,000 francs per supplementary unemployed worker). The figure was weaker in the case of the public expenditure multiplier (95,000 francs): the movement of interest rates is especially influential on investment and inventory investment, whose content in imports is very great.

4.4. Change in the Exchange Rate of the Franc

We assume that the exchange rate of the franc in relation to all other currencies drops in the first quarter of 1972 to 10% below its real value, and that it remains constantly over the whole period inferior by 10% to its historical value (because of the sense of the exchange rate in METRIC, this fall leads to a rise of 11.1% in the price of imports in francs).

The export price behaviour represented in METRIC (see Table 17) leads exporters to raise their prices in francs by 70% of the amount of the devaluation (it is the average behaviour of the export margin that we have estimated). The result is that the advantage in competitivity rapidly weakens and the growth of constant price exports remains moderate. The rise in activity reduces even further these exports and leads to a rise in constant price imports despite a share of supply more favourable to the gross domestic product.

The fluctuations of activity (table 18) are due essentially to those of inventory investment: in the short term, there is speculative and precautionary stock building because of the price rise in francs of products in stock. There follows negative inventory investment to reduce the financial burden of stocks that have become more costly. Finally there is stock building to follow demand.

In the medium term devaluation is slightly favourable to activity, the effects incurred by the initial rise of exports being superior to those of the rise in prices which reduce the real salary rate and provoke a reconstitution of real balances by households.

While the prices of imports increase by 11.1% after six years internal prices have only risen by 5.7% (table 19). We can observe however that the latter continue to rise rapidly, but their level will only catch up with that of foreign prices after a very long time.

To summarize the devaluation effects, according to METRIC, it is sufficient to recall the two following results:

- in spite of the rise in prices, there is a durable increase in activity;
- this growth of activity leads to an important trade deficit from the fourth year: over the first three years, we can observe a traditional J curve.

Endnotes

1. 'L'explication de l'inflation par le modèle METRIC', *Cahiers du Séminaire Malinvaud.*
2. 'La crise vue par METRIC', *Revue économique.*
3. 'Système élargi de Comptabilité nationale'.
4. *Annales de l'INSEE* 26–27 (1977).
5. Caisse des dépôts et consignations.

5. Annex: Dynamic Simulation, 1971–1975

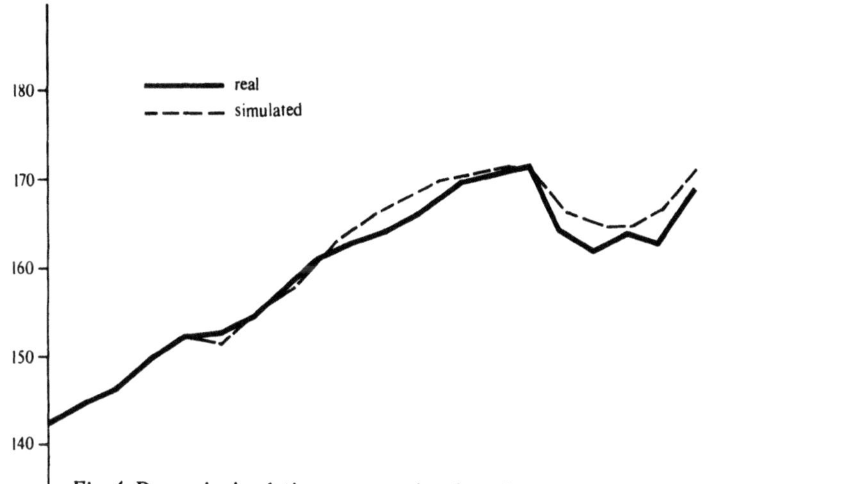

Fig. 4. Dynamic simulation: gross national product.

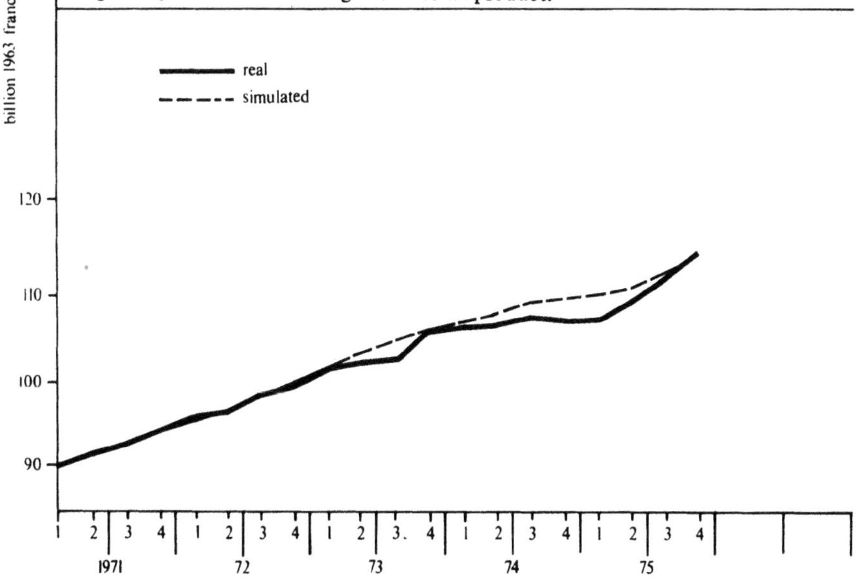

Fig. 5. Dynamic simulation: households' consumption.

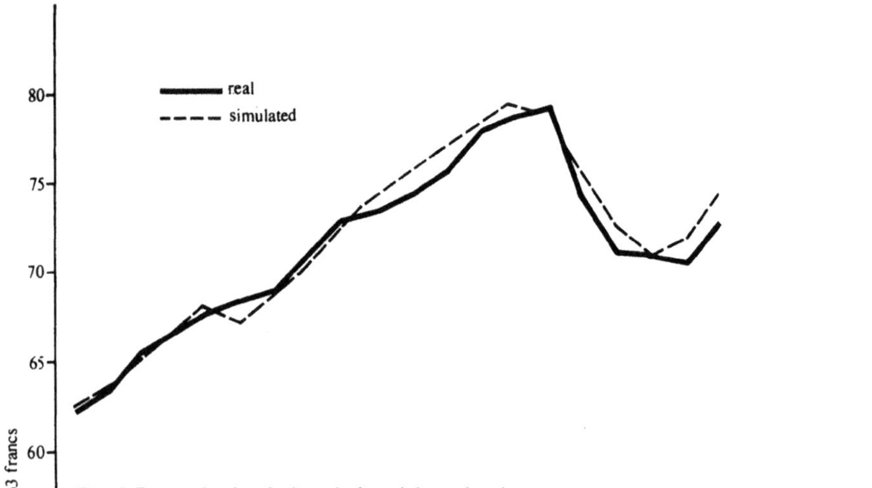

Fig. 6. Dynamic simulation: industrial production.

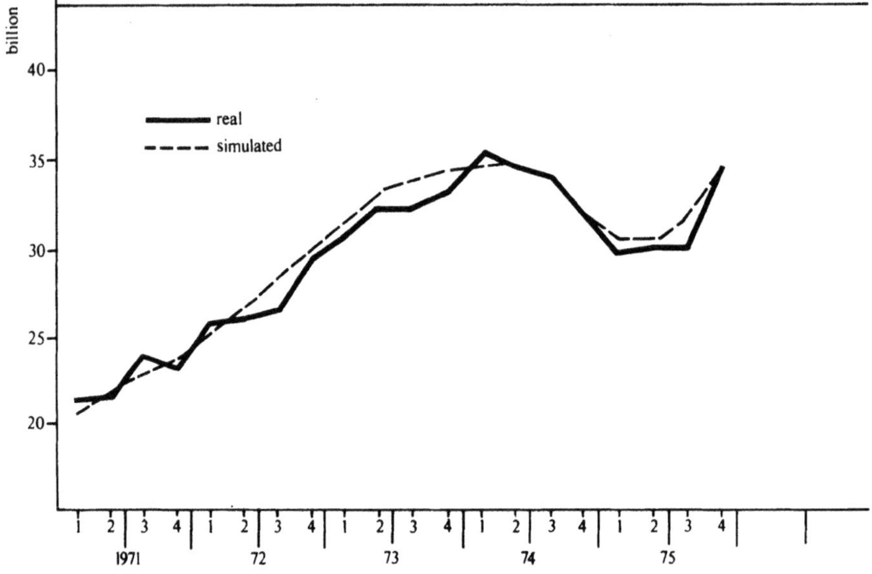

Fig. 7. Dynamic simulation: industrial imports.

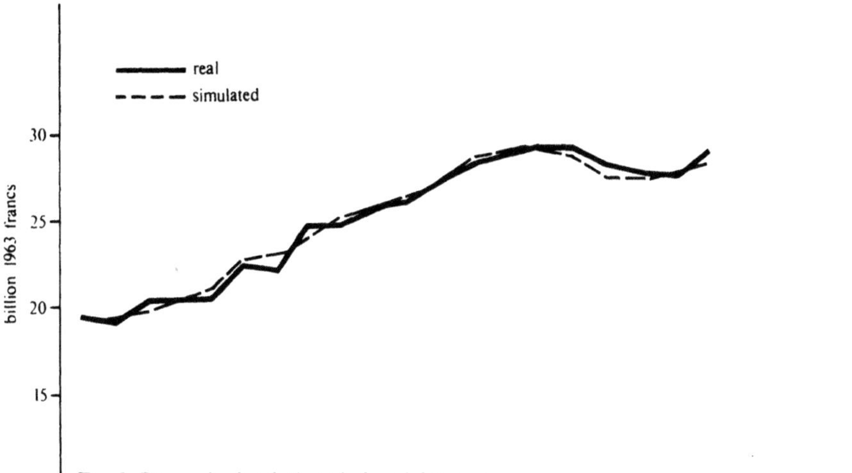

Fig. 8. Dynamic simulation: industrial exports.

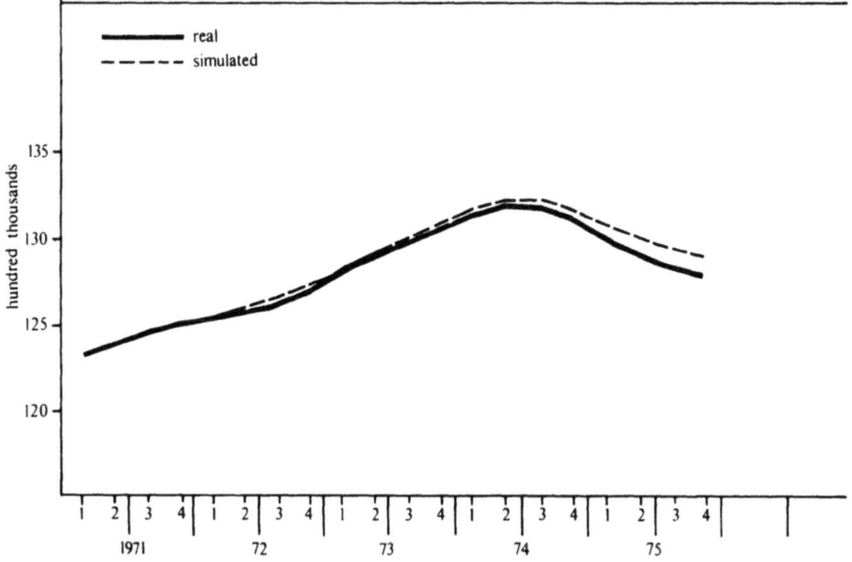

Fig. 9. Dynamic simulation: non-agricultural employment.

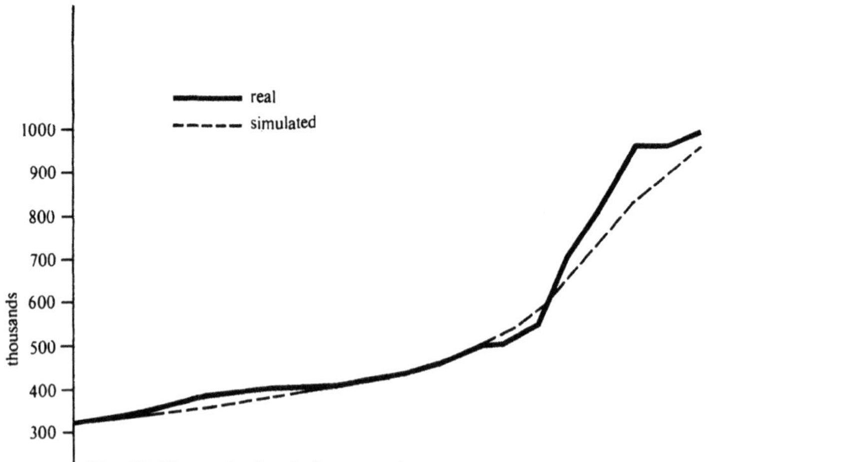

Fig. 10. Dynamic simulation: employment.

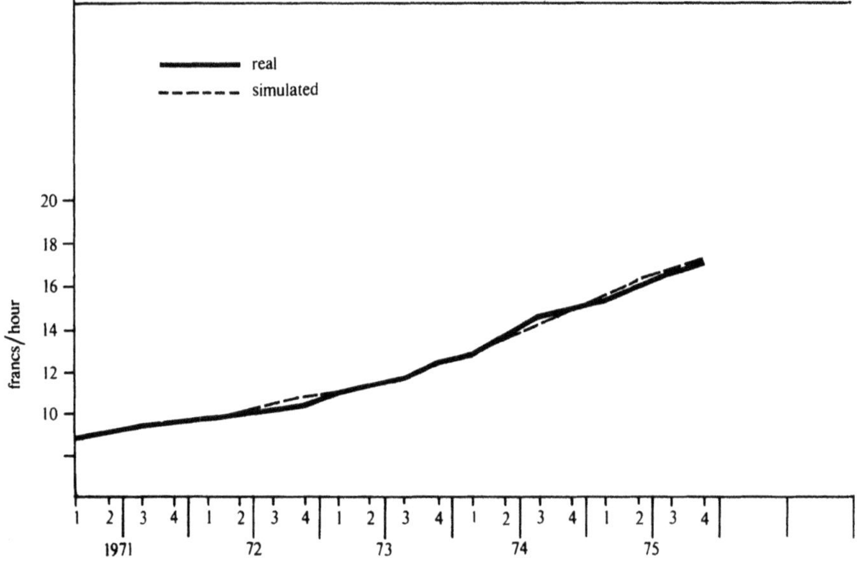

Fig. 11. Dynamic simulation: wage rates in industry.

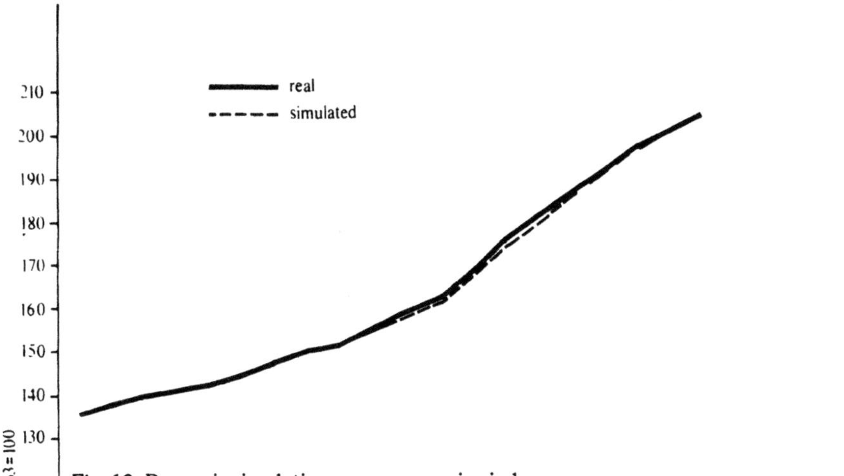

Fig. 12. Dynamic simulation: consumer price index.

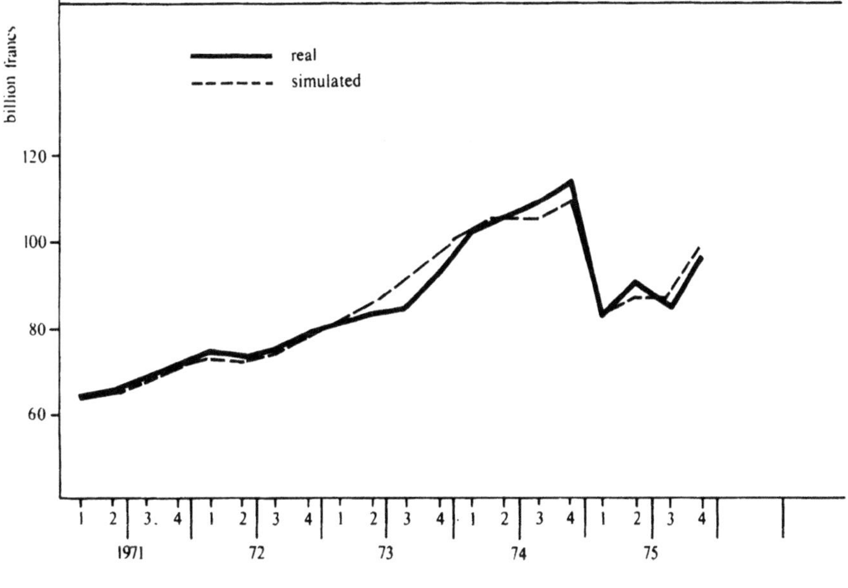

Fig. 13. Dynamic simulation: firms' profits.

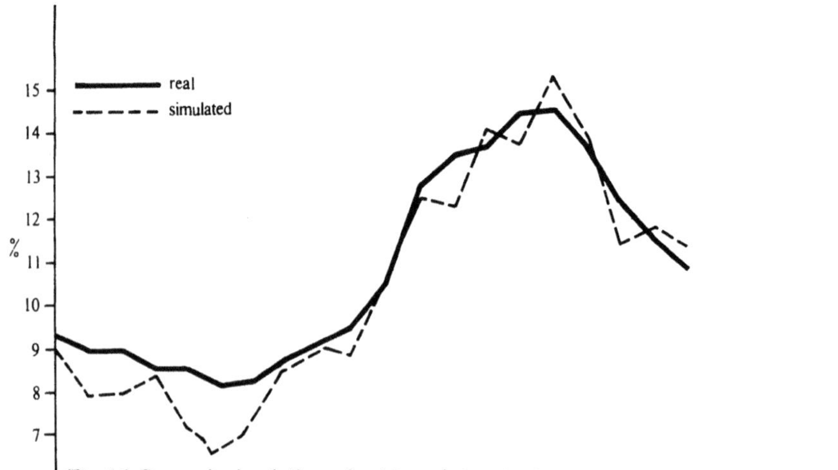

Fig. 14. Dynamic simulation: short-term interest rate.

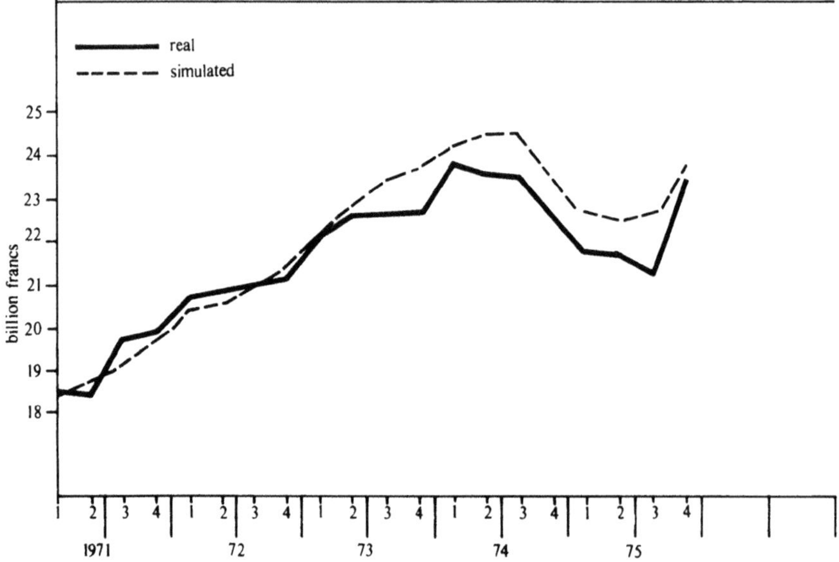

Fig. 15. Dynamic simulation: fixed investment.

THE VINTAF-II MODEL FOR THE DUTCH ECONOMY

TH. VAN DE KLUNDERT

1. Introduction

During the late sixties and the early seventies a serious employment problem emerged in the Dutch economy. The percentage of unemployed rose, while at the same time the number of people unfit to work increased substantially. With a normal increase in labour supply there would have been a large gap between demand for and supply of labour with regard to the private sector of the economy. This is illustrated in figure 1. A lower demand for labour may of course be the result of a lower demand for final products. As a result of the world recession the rise in production slowed down after 1973, but the structural development with regard to employment set in motion much earlier did not disappear. In fact, there was a remarkable fall in marginal labour intensity of production in enterprises showing as early as in 1964. The relation between employment and production is given in figure 2. The change in the relation would even be more striking if employment would have been measured in terms of man-hours instead of man-years.

To deal with the problem of structural unemployment H. den Hartog and H.S. Tjan [4, 5] implemented a 'clay-clay' vintage model for the Dutch economy. Both authors belong to the staff of the Central Planning Bureau. The model emphasizes the neo-classical relation between labour demand and real labour cost, the latter measured as nominal wages per employee deflated by the (revenue) price of production. Real labour costs increased substantially in the sixties and early seventies. As a result of this the share of labour in gross production of enterprises went up from 73% in 1956 to 82% in the top year 1970.

The 'clay-clay' model was discussed intensively in the Netherlands. As a result of that discussion it seemed worthwhile to construct a more complete model of the economy around the vintage block. This led to the Vintaf model as presented in H. den Hartog, et al [6]. Important variables of the vintage sub-model like real labour cost and investment by enterprises are endogenous in the larger model. Actual employment is explained by potential employment calculated from the vintage sub-model and the state of effective demand

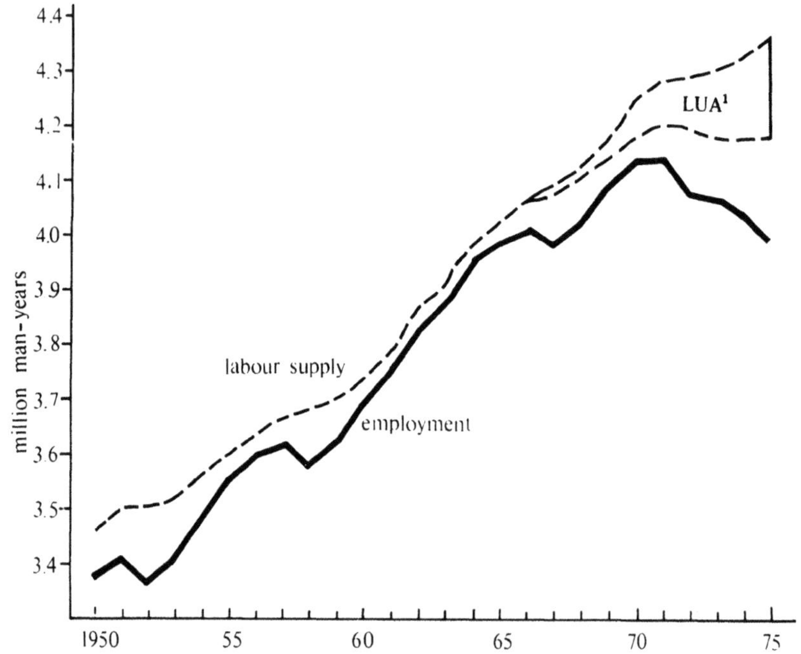

[1] Reduction of labour supply since the labour unfitness act (LUA)

Fig. 1. Employment and labour supply in enterprises 1950–1975.

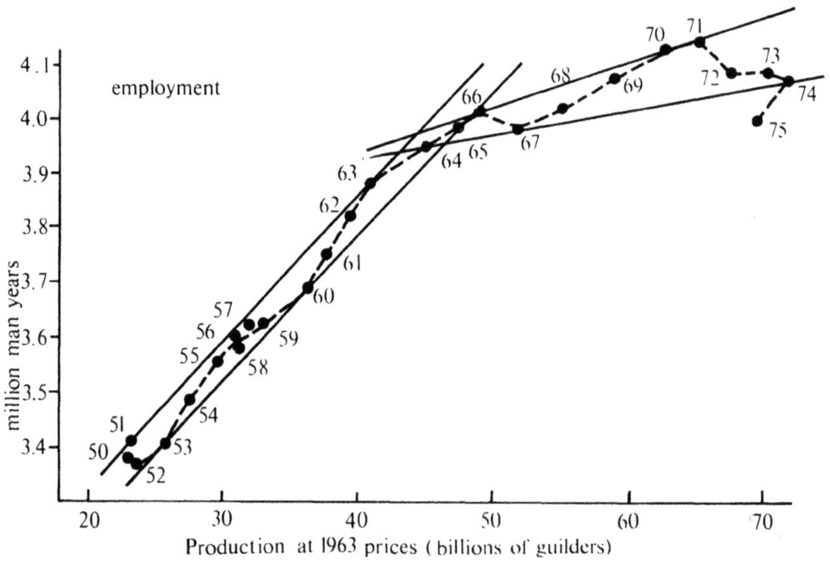

Fig. 2. Employment and production in enterprises (excl. natural gas) 1950–1975.

as refelcted in the degree of capacity utilization.

Further extensions were made at the Central Planning Bureau and another version of the model was presented under the name Vintaf-II in an Occasional Paper [2]. The model is used for medium-term projections and for the corresponding evaluation of policy alternatives. At present further improvements and reestimation of important equations are undertaken. The results of this research will probably be available in the near future.

In the following section a description of the main behavioural equations of the model will be given. A more detailed presentation of the model equations can be found in the appendix. To show the implications of the model the results of an appreciation of the Dutch guilder will be analyzed in section 3. The example is not without practical meaning as the Dutch economy had to deal with the consequences of an average yearly appreciation of about 3% over the period 1971–1977.

2. Description of the Model

Vintaf-II is a macro-economic model based on annual data. As indicated before, the emphasis lies on structural developments in the economy. Cyclical movements are taken into account, but details are omitted. In order to give an impression of the whole the following interconnected building blocks can be distinguished:

- relations explaining production capacity and labour requirements at full capacity;
- equations with regard to the demand for and supply of labour;
- wage and price relations;
- equations for the determination of expenditures and imports, from which follows by definition the level of actual production;
- institutional relations for taxation and social security payments and benefits.

Monetary variables are excluded. In spite of this the model performs fairly well with regard to the explanation of actual developments over the past. The estimation period is 1950–1973, whereas in the case of capacity and labour requirements data from the period 1959–1973 are used. The regression coefficients are obtained by OLS. The description of the model will here be restricted to the structural equations of the first four building blocks mentioned above. A more elaborate version of the model is presented in the appendix.

2.1. Production Capacity and Labour Requirements

There are no observations available for production capacity (y^*) and labour requirements (a^*) in the private production sector. Instead figures for both variables are generated with the help of a 'clay-clay' vintage sub-model. It is assumed that the capital coefficient (κ) is constant for all vintages. Successive vintages show declining labour requirements per unit of output as a result of labour savings incorporated in new equipment. Technical change proceeds at a constant rate (μ). In addition working hours (h) and technical obsolescence of equipment are accounted for. Under these assumptions the production capacity is equal to:

$$y_t^* = \frac{1}{\kappa} h_t^{\delta_1} \sum_{\tau=\nu_t}^{t} i_\tau \tag{1}$$

where y_t^* = production capacity private sector sector in year t
h_t = index of working hours in year t
i_τ = equipment of vintage τ corrected for technical obsolescence according to an a priori scheme of survival fractions
κ = capital-output ratio
ν_t = year of installation of the oldest vintage kept in operation
δ_1 = elasticity of capacity with respect to working hours

Total labour requirements (potential employment) can be related to the pattern of past investments in a similar way:

$$a_t^* = \frac{1}{\kappa}\frac{1}{\varphi} h_t^{\delta_1 - \delta_2} \sum_{\tau=\nu_t}^{t} \frac{i_\tau}{(1+\mu)^\tau} \tag{2}$$

where a_t^* = total labour requirements in year t
φ = labour productivity of the base year vintage
μ = rate of labour-saving technical progress
δ_2 = elasticity of labour requirements with respect to working hours

The labour requirement of a unit of equipment decreases with the age of the equipment. Vintages are discounted with the rate of technical change, so to say. Working hours have no influence on labour requirements, if it is assumed that the effective time of both factors of production, labour and capital, is the same ($\delta_1 = \delta_2$).

The year of installation of the oldest vintage kept in use is a variable of the model. At the margin of operation total revenue of a vintage just covers its wage bill, implying a zero quasi-rent. This condition can be written formally as:

$$p_t \cdot y_t^* = l_t a_t^* \tag{3}$$

where p_t = product price in year t
l_t = wage level per man-year in year t

The productivity of labour on the oldest vintage in operation can be expressed in terms of the parameters introduced above. So from equation (3) the following formula can be derived for the determination of ν_t:

$$\frac{l_t}{p_t} = \varphi(1+\mu)^{\nu_t} h_t^{\delta_2} \tag{4}$$

Taking logarithms on both sides of equation (4) and rearranging leads to:

$$\nu_t = \frac{\ln(l_t/p_t) - \delta_2 \ln h_t - \ln \varphi}{\ln(1+\mu)} \tag{5}$$

In the model a uniform distributed lag of three years is introduced with regard to real labour costs (l_t/p_t). According to equation (5), ν_t is measured on a time scale which is specified by choosing a base year (1948 = 0). The economic life time of equipment can be defined as $m_t = t - \nu_t$.

It is sometimes argued that the scrapping condition (3) should be replaced by a condition showing the influence of the cost of capital (see for instance Driehuis [3]). The core of the argument is that entrepreneurs have a choice with regard to marginal production activity. The last unit of output could be produced by investing in new equipment to replace units of the oldest equipment in operation *or* replacement could be postponed. The choice will then depend on the comparative costs of both options. However, J.M. Malcomson [8] and S. Nickell [9] have shown that in case of maximization of the present value of the firm, subject to a capacity relation as given in (1) and a decreasing demand curve, condition (3) still holds provided that p_t is replaced by marginal revenue. Now, if the price elasticity of demand ($-\eta$) is constant equation (3) could be written as:

$$\left(\frac{\eta - 1}{\eta}\right) p_t \cdot y_t^* = l_t a_t^* \tag{3a}$$

This extension can be dealt with in a straightforward manner.

2.2. Labour Demand and Supply

As stated above, production capacity and corresponding labour requirements are not directly observed. Both variables are applied to explain actual employment. The demand for labour (a_t) depends on the number of available jobs (a_t^*) and the degree of capacity utilization ($q_t = y_t/y_t^*$, where y_t = actual production). Assuming proportionality one could write:

$$a_t = q_t a_t^*$$

However, as could be expected Okun's law also applies in the Dutch economy. Estimation of the relation between a_t, a_t^* and q_t by OLS gives the following result:

$$a = a^* - 0.39(1 - q)a^* + 4.5 \tag{6}$$

(For reasons of convenience time subscripts are omitted from now on.) The constant term is not significant. It should be noted that the parameters μ, φ and κ of the equations (1), (2) and (3) are determined along with the estimation of equation (6). For this purpose a grid procedure is applied to the parameters φ and μ, whereas κ is determined by the assumption $y^*_{1970} = y_{1970}$.

With regard to a period of labour scarcity (rationing of demand for labour) in the early sixties equation (6) is set aside and actual employment is determined as a weighted average of labour requirements and labour supply corrected for frictional unemployment.

The supply of labour by employees (a_a) is to a large extent determined by the population of working age (a_p), which is an exogenous variable. On the other hand, there is a positive influence of (lagged) real disposable wage income per worker (l^{RD}). In addition, there is a discouraged workers' effect as appears from the inclusion of the labour market variable w/a, where w is the number of unemployed. The estimation result is as follows:

$$\dot{a}_a = \dot{a}_p + 0.19\,\dot{l}^{RD} - 18.8\left(\frac{w}{a}\right) - 53.4\left(\frac{a_a}{a_p}\right)_{-1} + 24.712$$

Variables with a dot refer to percentage changes on an annual base. The lagged participation rate is added to serve as an asymptotic variable, since participation may be subject to a limit.

2.3. *Wages and Prices*

In a situation of equilibrium growth real wages rise with the rate of technical change, which equals the increase in labour productivity. However, the purchasing power of wages depends on the price of consumer goods. The percentage change in nominal wages per employee ($\dot{l}$) may therefore be related to the percentage change in the price of consumption ($\dot{p}_c$) and the percentage increase in labour productivity. This is not all. The situation on the labour market may be of influence as A.W. Phillips observed some time ago. Attention should also be paid to the possibility that an increase in the burden of direct taxes and social security premiums may lead to a higher increase in nominal wages, because workers resist an attack on their disposable incomes.

These considerations are reflected in the following empirical equation:

$$\dot{l} = 1.00(\dot{y} - \dot{a})_{-1/2} + 1.01\,\dot{p}_{c-1/2} - 87.9\left(\frac{w}{a}\right)_{-1/2}$$

$$+ 0.47\,\dot{\mathrm{C}}\mathrm{L} + 2.00$$

where $\dot{\mathrm{C}}\mathrm{L}$ = percentage change in the burden of direct taxes plus social security premiums

Higher indirect taxes are passed on via their influence on the price of consumer goods. Direct taxes are endogenous variables, but changes in tariffs have to be considered as exogenous shifts. Social security payments are to a large extent endogenous. They are linked to (disposable minimum) wages and in case of unemployment compensation also to the number of unemployed. It is not reasonable to assume that the increase in the burden of taxes and premiums will be fully reflected in nominal wages, because workers benefit directly from certain forms of social insurance. The regression coefficient found with regard to $\dot{C}L$ confirms this view.

Relative price changes of different expenditure categories are conceived as weighted averages of the percentage changes in prices of home-produced and imported final goods, after an adjustment is made for autonomous price changes (including changes in rates of indirect taxation):

$$\dot{p}_j - \dot{p}_{jau} = (1-\epsilon_j)\dot{p}_{hj} + \epsilon_j \dot{p}_{mj} \tag{7}$$

where
$\dot{p}_j$ = price expenditure category j
$\dot{p}_{jau}$ = autonomous component in price of expenditure category j
$\dot{p}_{hj}$ = price of home produced goods in category j
$\dot{p}_{mj}$ = price of imported goods in category j
ϵ_j = share of imported final goods in total expenditure of category j at current prices ($\epsilon_j = 0$ if j stands for exports).

The price of home-produced final goods is seen as a function of costs (k_j) and the price of competing foreign goods. Further, account is taken of changes in the pressure of demand by introducing the first order difference of the degree of capacity utilization as an additional explanatory variable. The relevant formula is:

$$\dot{p}_{hj} = \dot{k}_j - \eta_{1j}(\dot{k}_j - \dot{p}_{mj}) + \eta_{2j}\Delta q + \eta_{3j}, \qquad 0 \leqslant \eta_{1j} \leqslant 1 \tag{8}$$

Again, there is a slight adaptation necessary in the case of export prices. Foreign price competition is here represented by (export) prices of competitors on markets abroad. The variable for the cost of domestic production is constructed on basis of unit labour costs and prices of imported raw materials and semi-finished products (p_{mgh}):

$$\dot{k}_j = (1-\alpha_j)\{\dot{l} - \psi_j(\dot{y} - \dot{a})\} + \alpha_j \dot{p}_{mgh} \tag{9}$$

The constant α_j stands for the cumulative input coefficient of imported raw materials and semi-finished products. The coefficient is calculated as an average over the reference period from several input-output tables. Changes in labour costs are multiplied by the complement of this coefficient. This implies that the return on capital rises in proportion with an increase in unit labour costs. The factor ψ_j accounts for the fact that the increase in labour productivity with regard to category j differs from the increase in macro-economic labour productivity.

Substitution of equation (9) in (8) and of the result in equation (7) leads to the final equation for relative price changes of expenditure category j. The share of imports ϵ_j is a predetermined running coefficient, while η_{1j}, η_{2j} and η_{3j} are OLS-estimates. Along these lines the following result for the percentage change of the price of private consumption is obtained:

$$\dot{p}_c = (1 - \epsilon_c)\{\dot{k}_c - 0.315\,(\dot{k}_c - p_{mc\,-3/4}) + 58.8\,\Delta q + 0.21\}$$
$$+ \epsilon_c \dot{p}_{mc} + 25(q - 0.97) + \dot{p}_{cau}$$

The degree of capacity utilization was included to improve the ex-post simulation results of the model over the reference period. The prices of the other expenditure categories can be found in the appendix.

2.4. Expenditures and Imports

Private consumption at current prices (C) is related to disposable wage (L_D), transfer (O_L) and non-wage income (Z_D) in the following way:

$$\Delta C = 0.89\,\Delta L_D + 0.97\,\Delta O_L + 0.35\,\Delta Z_D.$$

It appears that the marginal propensity to consume (MPC) out of disposable transfer income is somewhat higher than the MPC relating to disposable wage income.

With regard to investment in equipment (i_{ou}) a distinction is made between replacement and expansion investment. Replacement is linked to the scrap volume, calculated from the vintage sub-model. Expansion investment is explained by disposable (net) profit income and the degree of capacity utilization. Applying OLS the following result is obtained:

$$i_{ou} = 0.275\left(\frac{Z_D + D - sp_i}{p_i}\right)_{-1\frac{1}{2}} + 0.844s$$
$$- 10603(1 - q_{-1/4}) - 156$$

where i_{ou} = investment in equipment (at 1970 prices)
s = volume of scrapped equipment
Z_D = disposable non-wage income
D = depreciation allowances
p_i = price of investment in equipment

Investment in plant (i_{geb}) is related to both kinds of investment in equipment:

$$i_{geb} = 0.42(i_{ou} - s) + 0.28s - 2491\,\Delta\ln \mathrm{GC} + 793$$

As was to be expected the coefficient with regard to replacement of equipment is lower than the coefficient relating to expansion investment. A government control index (GC) was added, because some form of rationing played a role in the past.

The export of goods, excluding services, (b) depends on three factors:

- an index of world trade, reweighted in a suitable manner (m_w),
- the price of export goods in relation to the price of foreign competitors (p_b/p'_b),
- the degree of capacity utilization, indicating the home pressure of demand.

With regard to the effect of price competition a distributed lag of the Koyck type is introduced. Combination of these elements results in:

$$\ln b = 0.5 \ln b_{-1} + 1.07(\ln m_w - 0.5 \ln m_{w_{-1}})$$
$$- 0.85(\ln p_b - \ln p'_b) - 0.51(\ln q_{-1} - 0.5 \ln q_{-2}) + 5.36$$

The elasticity of exports with regard to world trade is equal to one. The long-run price elasticity amounts to: $-0.85/0.5 = -1.7$.

The volume of imported goods, excluding services, (m) is a function of:

- total expenditures, excluding invisible exports, (v),
- the price of import goods in relation to the price of expenditures (p_m/p_v),
- the degree of capacity utilization with an opposite sign compared with the export equation.

Again, a distributed lag is applied to the price variable. The corresponding regression equation is:

$$\ln m = 0.2 \ln m_{-1} + 1.11 (\ln v - 0.2 \ln v_{-1})$$
$$- 0.46 (\ln p_m - \ln p_v)$$
$$+ 0.94 (\ln q_{-1/3} - 0.2 \ln q_{-4/3}) - 1.95$$

The long-run price elasticity of imports is equal to $-0.46/0.8 = -0.58$. This elasticity is lower than the one with regard to exports. A (partial) explanation for this is the relative importance of non-competing imports in the total of imported goods.

The other components of expenditure do not need much comment. Government expenditure and investment in residential construction are exogenous. Stock building is proportional to the change in total expenditure.

3. Results of a Continuous Appreciation[1]

As observed above, the Dutch guilder appreciated substantially over the last decade. The consequences of such a continuous (effective) appreciation can be studied with the help of the Vintaf-II model. The main results of a continuous appreciation of 5% per year are summarized in table 1. The figures relate to deviations from a reference path over the period 1971–1980.

Prices determined abroad decrease at a rate of 5% because of the assumed appreciation. This leads to a fall in prices of the different expenditure

Table 1. Continuous appreciation of 5% per year. Unchanged model.

	Change in year				Cumulative effect after 10 years
	1	4	7	10	
Consumption price (%)	−2.37	−5.56	−5.36	−4.83	−49.83
Export price (%)	−3.87	−5.44	−5.29	−4.86	−50.79
Production price (%)	−1.79	−5.52	−5.71	−4.40	−48.59
Wage sum (%)	−1.45	−6.01	−6.06	−4.15	−50.91
Real labour costs (%)	0.34	−0.49	−0.35	0.25	−2.32
Consumption volume (%)	0.79	−0.42	−0.45	0.19	0.08
Investment volume (%)	0.22	−0.87	2.68	3.51	10.44
Export volume (%)	−1.04	0.09	0.61	0.10	1.12
Import volume (%)	0.86	−0.75	0.33	0.41	1.63
Production volume (%)	−0.37	0.02	0.37	0.41	1.62
Potential empl. (× 1000 m.y.)	−2.80	−2.84	5.55	23.97	68.87
Actual empl. (× 1000 m.y.)	−7.12	−2.49	9.38	19.33	64.97
Capacity utilization (%-pt.)	−0.33	0.02	0.30	−0.36	−0.29
Unemployment (× 1000 m.y.)	8.76	−0.63	−8.91	−7.59	−42.25
Balance of payments (mld. gld.)	−0.26	0.46	0.03	−2.43	−2.89

components from the first year.[2] Foreign competition plays an important role in the explanation of prices. The decline in the price of production is less than the change in price of domestic expenditure as a result of an improvement in the terms of trade. Wages follow the development of the consumption price with a lag of half a year. This explains the relatively low decline in the wage sum per worker. As a result, real labour costs increase and some potential employment opportunities get lost. The decline in actual employment is even more pronounced because of the lower degree of capacity utilization. The fall in effective demand can be attributed to lower exports and higher imports in connection with the decline in competitiveness of the economy. The difference in outcomes between actual employment and unemployment is explained by the increase in disposable real wages.

The wage-price spiral leads to a decline in wages and prices, eventually matching the rate of appreciation. The movement is reinforced by the Phillips-curve effect on nominal wages at the beginning of the period. The consequence is a fall in real labour costs, leading to a reverse development. The yearly change in employment becomes positive as appears from the figures relating to year 7. Thereafter, the Phillips-curve works the other way around. The decline in nominal wages stays behind the fall in prices as appears from the results for year 10. The consequence is a rise in real labour costs. The negative effect on employment does not yet show because of the lag in the scrapping formula. Potential employment increases considerably in year 10 under the influence of a decline in real labour costs in the years before. However, the down-swing is inevitable. Potential employment will go down again in the years ahead.

In the last column of table 1 the cumulative effects after ten years are

Table 2. Continuous appreciation of 5% per year. Model without Phillips-curve.

	Change in year				Cumulative effect after 10 years
	1	4	7	10	
Consumption price (%)	−2.31	−4.99	−4.95	−5.64	−48.12
Export price (%)	−3.82	−5.05	−4.97	−5.42	−49.55
Production price (%)	−1.71	−4.85	−5.06	−5.58	−46.21
Wage sum (%)	−1.32	−4.74	−4.96	−6.06	−46.95
Real labour costs (%)	0.39	0.11	0.10	−0.48	−0.74
Consumption volume (%)	0.84	0.10	0.08	−0.86	1.43
Investment volume (%)	0.27	−0.03	−0.07	1.02	4.64
Export volume (%)	−1.08	−0.34	−0.11	0.67	−1.31
Import volume (%)	0.90	−0.28	0.15	−0.84	1.35
Production volume (%)	−0.37	0.02	−0.12	0.25	0.10
Potential empl. (X 1000 m.y.)	−3.02	−12.02	−10.63	28.16	−4.85
Actual empl. (X 1000 m.y.)	−7.33	−10.71	−9.18	23.08	−9.80
Capacity utilization (%-pt.)	−0.33	0.10	0.08	−0.40	−0.40
Unemployment (X 1000 m.y.)	9.08	7.67	4.65	−18.66	3.15
Balance of payments (mld. gld.)	−0.28	0.02	−0.13	−1.67	−3.69

given. Appreciation checks the inflation rate. The average fall in the price level corresponds to the rate of appreciation. The cumulative effects on expenditure are moderate with the exception of investment in equipment. Unemployment decreases at an amount of 42,000 man-years, which is over 1% of the labour force. However, to draw up a balance sheet at a point in time where dynamic processes are still in full swing is somewhat arbitrary. Eventually the effects in the real part of the model may die out.

The Phillips-curve effect is disregarded at an unemployment rate above 3% in practical applications of the model. The current rate of unemployment (1979) is about 5%. Recent experience suggests a curvilinear form of the relation between the percentage of unemployed and the increase in wages. For the time being it may be worth while to analyse the consequences of a continuous appreciation in the Vintaf-II model without a Phillips-curve and compare them with the outcomes in the other case. The results of an appreciation of 5% in the truncated model are presented in table 2. The reference path is the same as before. In order to isolate the effects of an appreciation it is, of course, desirable to eliminate the Phillips-curve also on the reference path. The original path is obtained by inserting appropriate exogenous figures in the equation for the wage sum per worker. These precautions are necessary, because the model is basically non-linear, which implies that the results of variants depend to some extent on the chosen reference path.

As appears from table 2 the results in the first year are about the same as in the case of a model with Phillips-curve. However, the time path shows a different picture. The downward movement of wages takes place at a slower rate. The adaptation to the lower rate of inflation proceeds gradually. For that reason real labour costs keep on rising. In year 7 the effect is still positive.

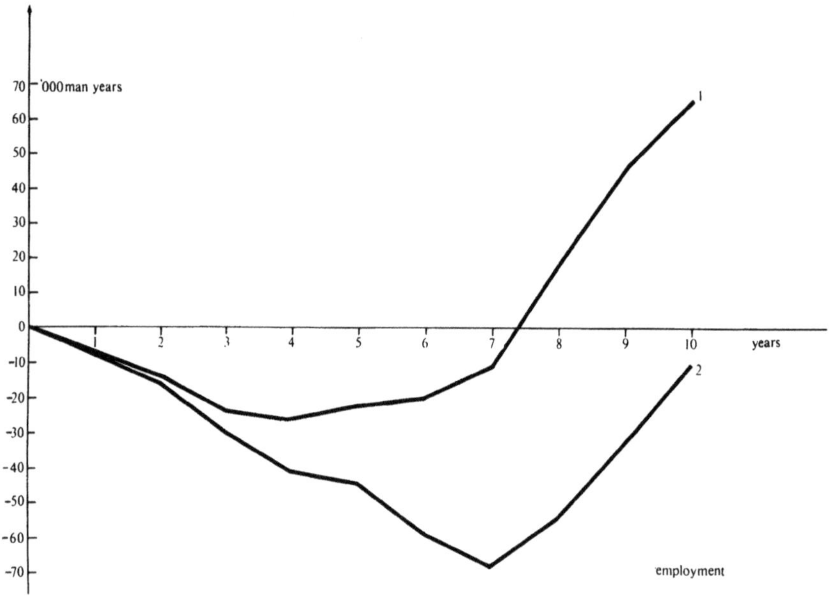

Fig. 3. Ten year appreciation of the guilder: cumulative effect on actual employment.

Labour requirements (potential employment) decline at an average rate of 10,000 man-years during this period. The gradual adaption of nominal wages implies an increase in real wages, which explains the rise in consumption. The positive influence on expenditure in general is offset by a fall in exports. The changes in the degree of capacity utilization are therefore moderate and as a matter of fact almost the same as in the case of a model with a Phillips-curve. Consequently, the fall in potential employment is reflected in the development of actual employment.

The results in year 10 deserve further comment. The decline in the wage sum per worker exceeds the decrease in the price level. As a result of this form of overshooting real labour costs fall and the expenditure and employment patterns are reversed.

The cumulative effect after 10 years with regard to labour requirements amounts to less than 5,000 man years. Actual employment decreases with almost twice this amount because of a lower degree of capacity utilization. Unemployment increases only slightly. The decline in real wages leads to some withdrawal from the labour market. The deterioration of the balance of payments on current account exceeds the result in the case with a Phillips-curve in operation.

The cumulative results of a continuous appreciation in both cases are for a few variables shown in the figures 3 to 6. The curves indicated with number 1 refer to the unchanged model, whereas the outcomes of the truncated model are marked with the number 2. It is interesting to note the main

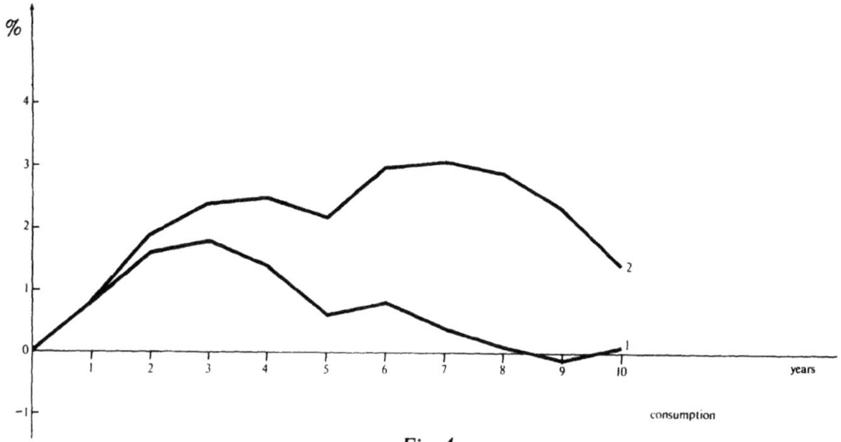

Fig. 4.

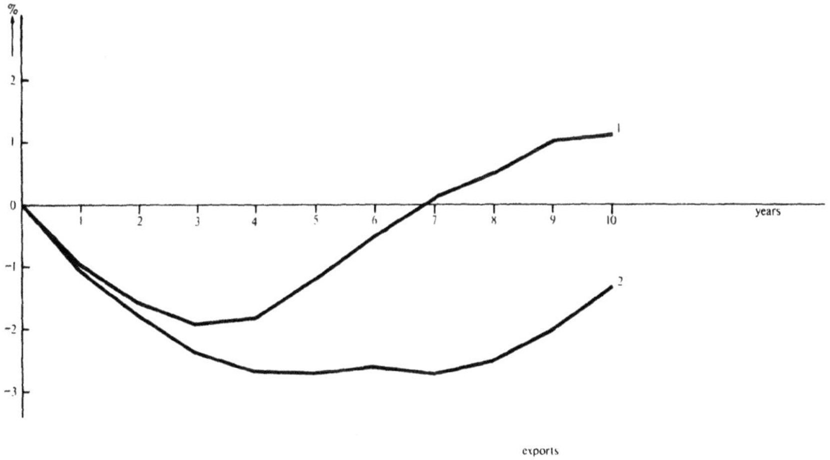

Fig. 5.

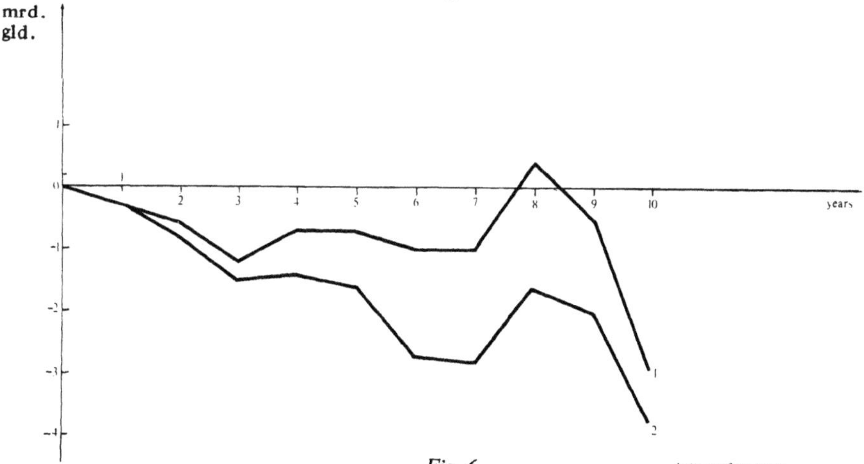

Fig. 6.

Table 3. Continuous appreciation of 5% per year. Doubling of export elasticity.

	Change in year				Cumulative effect after 10 years
	1	4	7	10	
Consumption price (%)	−2.61	−5.68	−5.41	−4.89	−50.87
Export price (%)	−4.02	−5.54	−5.32	−4.91	−51.59
Production price (%)	−2.10	−5.64	−5.79	−4.46	−49.95
Wage sum (%)	−1.74	−6.27	−6.18	−4.26	−52.88
Real labour costs (%)	0.36	−0.63	−0.39	0.20	−2.93
Consumption volume (%)	0.66	−0.54	−0.51	0.14	−0.76
Investment volume (%)	−0.06	−1.09	2.84	3.48	9.84
Export volume (%)	−2.12	0.26	0.50	0.08	0.32
Import volume (%)	0.02	−0.77	0.21	0.10	0.22
Production volume (%)	−0.66	−0.01	0.32	0.39	1.25
Potential empl. (× 1000 m.y.)	−4.32	−3.52	6.61	23.90	64.73
Actual empl. (× 1000 m.y.)	−11.88	−2.56	10.01	18.94	60.39
Capacity utilization (%-pt.)	−0.58	0.07	0.26	−0.38	−0.32
Unemployment (× 1000 m.y.)	12.49	−1.56	−9.16	−7.04	−40.78
Balance of payments (mld. gld.)	−0.45	0.55	0.01	−2.48	−3.10

differences. The movements in the real sphere are stronger in the case of no Phillips-curve effect, but there is a tendency towards 'equilibrium' at the end of the period. In the other case the market mechanism warrants a quick reaction, but now an oscillation around the reference path shows up. This is most clearly seen in the case of actual employment (figure 3). The balance of payments on current account deteriorates in both cases (figure 6), but the effect is more pronounced in the model without a Phillips-curve. This corresponds with the development of exports as illustrated in figure 5.

It was argued by T. Kloek [7] that the export elasticity found might be too low, because the explanatory variable p_b/p'_b showed little variation over the estimation period (1951–1973). It may therefore be worth while to study the consequences of an increase in this elasticity. Table 3 shows the isolated effects of a doubling of the export elasticity. The Phillips curve is *not* excluded. This implies that the outcomes should be compared with the results presented in table 1. The reference path is the same in both cases.

The volume of exports declines more than twice as much as in the case of the unchanged model in the first year. This induces an extra fall of the rate of capacity utilization. The downward wage-price spiral is reinforced during the period under consideration, because relative price changes depend on the change as well as the level of the degree of capacity utilization. The differences are nevertheless almost insignificant in the second part of the period. As appears from the last column in table 3 the lasting effects of an increase in the export elasticity are rather small. It must be concluded that the value of the export elasticity does not matter very much in the case of a continuous appreciation, at least on medium term.

The practical implications of the calculations can now be summarized.

Assuming no additional Phillips-curve effect at the actual rate of unemployment an effective appreciation of the guilder may have had the following impact over the last decade:

- a lower level of inflation in accordance with the effective rate of appreciation,
- an initial higher level of unemployment followed by a restoration at the end of the period,
- an increasing deterioration of the balance of payments on current account.

4. Appendix: The VINTAF-II Model[3]

The variables of the model generally refer to levels. Capital symbols are used to indicate values at current prices, while small symbols indicate values at constant prices (of 1970, in millions of guilders). In some cases, however, small symbols are indexes. Variables with a dot refer to (annual) percentage changes.

Variables like employment, working population etc. are in numbers (x 1000 man-years). Bold italic variables are exogenous, i.e. they are calculated from data outside the model. The subscript (*au*) also refers to exogenous, autonomous elements in the system.

The model is not fully described. The equations given below are the main reaction equations of the system; some highly relevant definition equations are also given.

4.1. Production Capacity and Potential Employment

production capacity of enterprises:

$$y^* = 0.80\,\boldsymbol{h}^{0.75} \sum_{\tau=\nu}^{t} \Omega(t-\tau)\, i_\tau. \tag{1}$$

labour requirements in enterprises:

$$a^* = 1.12 \times 0.80 \times 0.08 \times \boldsymbol{h}^0 \times \sum_{\tau=\nu}^{t} \Omega(t-\tau)\frac{i_\tau}{1.05^\tau}. \tag{2}$$

year of installation of oldest vintage in operation:

$$\nu = \frac{\ln\left[\dfrac{l + l_{-1} + l_{-2}}{(p_y + p_{y-1} + p_{y-2})}\right] - 0.75 \ln \boldsymbol{h} - \ln 12.5}{\ln(1 + 0.05)}. \tag{3}$$

4.2. Labour Market

employment in enterprises[4]:

$$a = a^* - 0.5(1-q)a^* + 4.5. \tag{4}$$

labour supply (excl. self-employed):

$$\dot{a}_a = \dot{a}_p + 0.19\,\dot{l}^{RD} - 18.8\,\frac{w}{a} - 53.4\left(\frac{a_a}{a_p}\right)_{-1} + 24.712, \tag{5}$$

where

$$\dot{l}^{RD} = 0.4\,\dot{l}^{RD} + 0.3\,\dot{l}^{RD}_{-1} + 0.3\,\dot{l}^{RD}_{-2}.$$

registered unemployment (definition):

$$w = a_a - a - a_{ov} + a_z. \tag{6}$$

4.3. Wage and Price Formation

wages in enterprises:

$$\dot{l} = 1.01\,\dot{p}_{c_{-1/2}} + 1.00\,(\dot{y} - \dot{a})_{-1/2} - 87.9\left(\frac{w}{a}\right)_{-1/2}$$

$$+ 0.47\,C\dot{l} + 2.00. \tag{7}$$

wages in government sector:

$$l^{ov} = l^{ov}_{-1}\,(1 + (\dot{l} + \dot{l}^{ov}_{au})/100). \tag{8}$$

prices of final demand components:

$$\dot{p}_c = (1 - \varepsilon_c)\{\dot{k}_c - 0.315(\dot{k}_c - \dot{p}_{mc_{-3/4}}) + 58.8\,\Delta q + 0.210\}$$

$$+ \varepsilon_c \dot{p}_{mc} + 25(q - 0.97) + \dot{p}_{cau}; \tag{9}$$

$$\dot{p}_b = \dot{k}_b - 0.461(\dot{k}_b - \dot{p}'_b) + 29.5\,\Delta q - 1.301$$

$$+ 25(q - 0.97) + \dot{p}^b_{au}. \tag{10}$$

$$\dot{p}_i = (1 - \varepsilon_i)\{\dot{k}_i - 0.386(\dot{k}_i - \dot{p}_{mi_{-1/2}}) + 37.6\,\Delta q - 1.573\}$$

$$+ \varepsilon_i \dot{p}_{mi} + 25(q - 0.97) + \dot{p}_{i,au}; \tag{11}$$

$$\dot{p}_{geb} = \dot{k}_{geb} + \dot{p}_{geb,au}; \tag{12}$$

$$\dot{p}_x = 0.35\,\dot{p}_c + 0.65\,\dot{p}_{geb}. \tag{13}$$

composition of costs, by category of final demand:

$$\dot{k}_c = 0.82\,\{\dot{l} - 0.91\,(\dot{y} - \dot{a})\} + 0.18\,\dot{p}_{mgh_{-1/4}}; \tag{14}$$

$$\dot{k}_b = 0.64\,\{\dot{l} - 1.31\,(\dot{y} - \dot{a})\} + 0.36\,\dot{p}_{mgh}; \tag{15}$$

$$\dot{k}_i = 0.73\,\{\dot{l} - 0.94\,(\dot{y} - \dot{a})\} + 0.27\,\dot{p}_{mgh_{-3/4}}; \tag{16}$$

$$\dot{k}_{geb} = 0.76\,\{\dot{l} - 0.50\,(\dot{y} - \dot{a})\} + 0.24\,\dot{p}_{mgh}. \tag{17}$$

4.4. Final Demand Components, Imports and Depreciation

business investment in equipment:

$$i_{ou} = 0.275\left[\frac{Z_{D-1}+D_{-1}-s_{-1}p_{i_{-1}}}{p_{i_{-1}}}+\frac{Z_{D-2}+D_{-2}-s_{-2}p_{i_{-2}}}{p_{i_{-2}}}\right]$$

$$+0.844\,s-10603(1-[0.75\,q+0.25\,q_{-1}])-156. \quad (18)$$

business investment in plant:

$$i_{geb} = 0.42\,(i_{ou}-s)+0.28\,s-2491\,\Delta\ln GC+793. \quad (19)$$

private consumption:

$$C = C_{-1}+0.89\,(L_D-L_{D-1})+0.35\,(Z_D-Z_{D-1})$$

$$+0.97\,(O_L-O_{L-1}). \quad (20)$$

stock formation:

$$n = 0.20\,\Delta(c+b+i_{ou}+i_{geb}+x). \quad (21)$$

export of goods (excl. services):

$$\ln b = 0.50\ln b_{-1}+1.07\,(\ln m_w-0.5\ln m_{w_{-1}})-0.85\ln\left(\frac{p_b}{p_b'}\right)$$

$$-0.51\,\{\ln q_{-1}-0.5\ln q_{-2}\}+5.36. \quad (22)$$

import of goods (excl. services):

$$\ln m = 0.2\ln m_{-1}+1.11\,(\ln v-0.2\ln v_{-1})-0.46\ln\left(\frac{p_m}{p_v}\right)$$

$$+0.94\,\{\ln q_{-1/3}-0.2\,(\ln q_{-1/3})_{-1}\}-1.95. \quad (23)$$

depreciation allowances in enterprises:

$$D = 0.965\,(Y+Y_{ag})+440. \quad (24)$$

profit (non-wage) income in enterprises:

$$Z = Y+Y_{ag}-D-L_b. \quad (25)$$

4.5. Production capacity utilization and scrap

gross value added in enterprises (at factor costs; excl. natural gas):[5]

$$y = 0.88\,(i_{ou}+i_{geb}+c+n+b+x+s_d-m-d_{ov})-y_{ag}. \quad (26)$$

degree of capacity utilization:

$$q = y/y^*. \quad (27)$$

volume of scrap:

$$s = i - \sum_{\nu_t}^{t} \Omega_{(t-T)} i_T - \sum_{\nu_{t-1}}^{t-1} \Omega_{(t-1)} i_T. \tag{28}$$

4.6. Taxes and Premiums

indirect taxes minus subsidies:

$$T_{k-s} = 0.1485 (C + xp_x) - 460 + T_{k-s}^{au}. \tag{29}$$

direct taxes on wage and transfer income:

$$T_L = 0.1854 (L_b + L_{ov} + T_R + U_L - P_L) - 10299.34 \frac{U_L + T_R}{L_b + L_{ov} - P_L} + 1450 + T_L^{au}. \tag{30}$$

direct taxes on profit (non-wage) income:

$$T_z = 0.407 (Z + Z_{au} - TLZ) + \frac{T_L'}{L_b + L_{ov}} \cdot TLZ - 456 + T_z^{au}. \tag{31}$$

social security premium payments (total), equal (total) benefits, apart from policy changes (P_{au}^s) and fluctuations in the unemployment fund ($U_{ww}^s - P_{ww}^s$):

$$P^s = 1.0\, U^s - 1.0 (U_{ww}^s - P_{ww}^s) + P_{au}^s. \tag{32}$$

life insurance plus pension premiums:

$$P^{lp} = 0.205 (1.1\, L_{ov}) + 0.065 \frac{a}{a - a_z} (L_b - 0.1\, L_{ov}) - 57.32\, l. \tag{33}$$

4.7. Social Security Benefits and Transfer Payments

components of social security benefits:

$$U^s = \sum_c U^{sc}. \tag{34}$$

The numerous equations for the individual components of the social security payments system are not presented. In general, volumes in this sphere are considered as exogenous, with unemployment benefits as the obvious exception, since the number of unemployed is an endogenous variable.

Endogenous, too, are all 'prices' in the social security system, since benefit levels are more or less closely linked to (disposable minimum) wage incomes in the enterprise sector.

There remain transfers paid by the government which are considered as fully endogenous

$$T_R = 0.041 \times p_y \times y + 0.81 \times l \times w' \quad (34)$$

where w' is part of total unemployment not falling under the unemployment act.

Finally, life insurance plus pension payments follow from

$$U^{lp} = 3330 p_c PEN \quad (35)$$

Taxes and premiums on the one hand, social security benefits, transfers and other payments on the other hand are of importance in the model when disposable incomes have to be defined as they appear, for example, in the consumption equation. This requires an additional number of relations, among them the distribution of taxes and premiums between income groups. In fact, the number of equations of the complete model amounts to 110.

5. List of Symbols

a	employment, enterprise sector
a^*	labour requirements, enterprise sector
a_{ov}	employment, government sector
a_z	self-employed working population
a_a	labour supply, excl. self-employed
a_p	population of working age
B, b	export of goods
C, c	private consumption
Cl	variable representing the burden of direct taxes plus social premiums
D, d	depreciation allowances, enterprise sector
D_{ov}, d_{ov}	depreciation allowances, government sector
GC	government control on plant investment
h	hours worked
I_{geb}, i_{geb}	business investment in plant
I_{ou}, i_{ou}	business investment in equipment (incl. transport)
k_c	total costs, private consumption
k_b	total costs, exports
k_i	total costs, equipment investment
k_{geb}	total costs, plant investment
l	wage level, enterprise sector
l^{ov}	wage level, government sector
l^{RD}	real disposable wage income
L_b	wage bill, enterprise sector
L_{ov}	wage bill, government sector
L_D	disposable wage income (incl. imputed wage income of self-employed)
m_w	world trade

M, m	import of goods (excl. services)
N, n	stock formation
O_L	disposable transfer income (incl. pensions and social security benefits)
p_b	price level, exports
p_b'	price level, competitive exports
p_c	price level, private consumption
p_{geb}	price level, plant investment
p_i	price level, equipment investment
p_m	price level, imports
p_{mc}	price level, imported consumption goods
p_{mi}	price level, imported investment goods
p_{mgh}	price level, imported raw materials plus semi-finished products
p_v	price level, total expenditure
p_x	price level, autonomous expenditure (incl. investment in housing)
p_y	price level, enterprise production (at factor costs, excl. gas)
P_L	social security plus pension premiums
P^s	social security premiums
p^s_{ww}	unemployment premiums
p^{lp}	life insurance and pension premiums
PEN	number of pensioners
q	degree of capacity utilization
s	scrap (equipment)
s_d	invisible trade (net)
T_{k-s}	indirect taxes minus subsidies
T_L	direct taxes on wage and transfer income
T_L'	direct taxes on wage income
TLZ	inputed wage income, self-employed
T_R	transfer payments (government)
T_Z	taxes on profit income
U_L	social security benefits plus pension and life insurance payments
U^{lp}	life insurance plus pension payments
U^s	social security benefits
U^{sc}	components of social security benefits[1]
U^s_{ww}	unemployment benefits
v	total expenditures (excl. stock formation and export of services)
w	registered unemployment
w'	registered unemployment, paid by the government
x	autonomous expenditure (incl. housing)
y^*	production capacity, enterprise sector (excl. natural gas)
Y, y	production, enterprise sector
Y_{ag}, y_{ag}	production, natural gas
Z	profit income, incl. income of self-employed
Z_D	disposable profit income, excl. imputed disposable wage income of self-employed

References

1. Beld, C.A. van den (1977), Employment growth in the Collective Sector versus the Enterprise Sector (with special reference to the Netherlands economy). Paper presented at an OECD conference on Structural determinants of employment and unemployment (Paris).
2. Central Planning Bureau (1977), Een macro-model voor de Nederlandse economie op middellange termijn (Vintaf-II), Occasional Paper no. 12 (The Hague).
3. Driehuis, W. (1977), Capital-labour substitution and other potential determinants of structural employment and unemployment, Research Memorandum no. 7708, University of Amsterdam.
4. Hartog, H. den and Tjan, H.S. (1974), Investeringen, lonen, prijzen en arbeidsplaatsen, CPB Occasional Paper no. 2 (The Hague).
5. Hartog, H. den and Tjan, H.S. (1976), 'Investments, wages, prices and demand for labour (A clay-clay vintage model for the Netherlands), De Economist', Vol. 124, no. 1/2, 1976.
6. Hartog, H. den, Klundert, Th. van de and Tjan, H.S. (1975), "De structurele ontwikkeling van de werkgelegenheid in macro-economisch perspectief" in: Werkloosheid; aard, omvang, structurele oorzaken en beleidsalternatieven, Preadviezen van de Vereniging voor de Staatshuishoudkunde (The Hague).
7. Kloek, T. (1977), Vintaf-II bezien tegen de achtergrond van eerdere Planbureau-modellen, Economisch Statistische Berichten, 26 October 1977.
8. Malcomson, J.M. (1975), 'Replacement and the rental value of capital equipment subject to obsolescence, Journal of Economic Theory', February, 1975.
9. Nickell, S. (1975), 'A closer look at replacement investment', Journal of Economic Theory', February, 1975.

Endnotes

1. I am indebted to Dr. A. van Schaik and Miss Joan Strijk for their valuable help with regard to the computations made.
2. A negative (positive) figure will be interpreted as a decline (rise) of the relevant variable regardless of the value on the reference path. This is done for the sake of convenience. The reader should keep in mind that all results relate to deviations from the reference path.
3. Adapted from C.A. van den Beld [1].
4. The regression coefficient was set at 0.5 on the basis of ex-post simulations over the estimation period. The OLS coefficient amounted to 0.39.
5. Gross value at current prices (Y) is defined in a similar way. The factor price of production (p_y) – appearing in equation 3 – then follows from Y/y.

INTERPLAY, A LINKED MODEL FOR ECONOMIC POLICY IN THE EEC

A Modified Version, 1953–1975

JOSEPH E.J. PLASMANS[1]

1. Introduction

INTERPLAY is a linked econometric model for six countries of the European (Economic) Community, i.e. Belgium (*B*), France (*F*), the Federal Republic of Germany (*FRG*, or *D*), Italy (*I*), the Netherlands (*NL*) and the United Kingdom (*UK*), based on a postwar sampling period (1953–1975).

Each country model comprises about thirty structural equations, of which eleven are behavioural: two for private expenditure (private consumption and private investments); two for labour market quantities (unemployment and employment); two describing foreign trade (commodity exports and imports); and five price equations (prices of commodity exports, government expenditure on goods, private consumption, private investments and the private wage rate[2]).

In constructing the model, special attention has been paid to the economic specification and the exact empirical evidence of the structural relationships, taking account of multicollinearity and stability of parameter estimates within the sampling period (checked by successively deleting observations). The six submodels are linked to each other by means of the bilateral trade flows and by the corresponding prices.

In the *first part* of this study, the structural submodels of the six economies are specified and empirically tested. The basic statistics employed are Student t ratios of ordinary least squares estimates, F statistics on multicollinearity (about the significance of squared multiple correlation coefficients among explanatory variables), the equation's multiple correlation coefficient and the Durbin–Watson statistic.[3] In a further version of this paper, autoregressive simultaneous estimation methods (such as autoregressive 3SLS) will be applied on the submodels selected.

The *second part* is the linking of the estimated submodels via bilateral trade flows and prices; it stresses the global functioning of the model. Since the model is basically a system of (linearized) difference equations, the linked model can be used to compute (simulate) time paths for the endogenous variables, by choosing a set of initial values for the lagged endogenous variables and for the exogenous variables.

1.1. List of Symbols

With uppercase letters we (usually) mean variables at current prices; lowercase letters (usually) represent a deflated variable. Price variables always start with uppercase *P*. All variables are relative yearly growth rates except for those with a tilde (~), which represent the true value instead of the relative annual increase. Further (*p*) means private, (*h*) households, (*g*) government, (*c*) corporations, (*d*) disposable, and (*NW*) non-wage. For instance $EM(g) = EMg$ is employment by the government. With Δ we mean the first difference and with Δ2 the second difference. The base year for price conversion is 1970.

$C(p), C(g), c(p), c(g), Pc(p), Pc(g)$	consumption
CR	central rate (official exchange rate)
CS	capital stock
DU_t	dummy with value 1 in year *t* and 0 elsewhere
$D(p), D(g), d(p), d(g)$	depreciation
$E1, e1$	total expenditures
$E2, e2, Pe2$	*E*1 less stocks and net invisibles
Eg, eg, Peg	expenditures of government
$EM(p), EM(g)$	employment
$EMps$	*EMp* plus self-employed
EMR	immigrants
Fg	financing shortage of the government
$Gvamp(p), Gvamp(g), gvamp(p), gvamp(g), Pgvamp(p), Pgvamp(g)$	gross value added at market prices
H	unit labour costs
$I(p), I(g), i(p), i(g), Pi(p), Pi(g)$	investment
ia	autonomous investment, defined as investment by the government plus investment in dwellings, transport and communication
Ipa	private investment abroad
$L1$	primary liquidities
$L2$	secondary liquidities
$L23$	secondary liquidities and savings deposits
$L123$	total liquidities
Mg, mg, Pmg	import of goods
MR	market rate divided by central rate (actual exchange rate)
Ms, ms	import of services
$NW(h), NW(c), NW(d)$	non-wage income (households) (corporations) (disposable)
POd, POP	(dependent working) population

$POwa$	population at working age
PR	parity
Pxc	price index of competitive exports
q	rate of utilization of capacity
q^+, q^-	max $\{0, q\}$, min $\{0, q\}$
$Rl, Rs, \Delta\tilde{R}l, \Delta\tilde{R}s$	long-run and short-run interest rates
$Rtb, \Delta\tilde{R}tb$	interest rate on treasury bills
Sc	savings of corporations
Sh	savings of households
SO	relative market share
SU	subsidies
ST, st	stocks
STR	strikes
$T(d), T(i), T(w), T(nw)$	taxes (direct) (indirect) (on wages) (on non-wages)
$TR(w)$	transfers (wages) defined as $\tilde{T}d$ on wages plus $\tilde{T}R$ of wages to government ($= \tilde{T}Rwg$) minus $\tilde{T}R$ of government to households ($= \tilde{T}Rgh$) minus $\tilde{T}R$ of the rest of the world to households ($= \tilde{T}Rrh$)
TS	indirect taxes minus subsidies
$un, \Delta\widetilde{un}$	unemployment rate
$W(p), W(g), W(r)$	wage income (private) (government) (rest of the world)
Wd	disposable wage income, $\tilde{W} - \tilde{T}Rw$
$WEQI$	world export quantum index
w	wage per labourer in the private sector, $\tilde{W}p/E\tilde{M}p$
Xg, xg, Pxg	export of goods
Xs, xs	export of services
Xpa	total private income from abroad
$Y(h), Y(d)$	income (households) (disposable)
y	per capita volume of gross value added at market prices
Yr	income from the rest of the world

2. The Structural Submodels of INTERPLAY

The six national submodels of the linked model INTERPLAY are discussed now for each type of behavioural equation. The definitional equations are selected in such a way that certain types of variables are endogenized (total expenditures, gross value added at market prices of the private sector, labour productivity, unit labour costs, and so on), and that the national submodel is 'closed' as much as possible. Only the behavioural equations will be discussed in this section.

2.1. Private Consumption

Starting from a simple Keynesian consumption model in nominal terms and allowing for the dichotomy of the disposable national income of private households into disposable wage and non-wage income:

$$\tilde{Cp} := \alpha + \beta \tilde{Y}hd, \tag{2.1}$$

$$\tilde{Y}hd := \tilde{W}d + \widetilde{NW}hd, \tag{2.2}$$

$$\tilde{Cp} := \widetilde{CW} + \widetilde{CNW}, \tag{2.3}$$

where $\widetilde{CW}$ and $\widetilde{CNW}$ can be briefly denoted as workers' and capitalists' consumption respectively. The percentage year to year changes of private consumption can be approximated by:

$$Cp = \beta \frac{\Delta \tilde{Y}hd}{\tilde{Cp}_{-1}} \approx \eta_{CW,\,Wd} \cdot \gamma \cdot Wd + \eta_{CNW,\,NWhd} \cdot (1 - \gamma) \cdot NWhd, \tag{2.4}$$

where the η parameters are the labour and non-labour income elasticities of private consumption respectively. The disaggregation of disposable income into disposable wage and non-wage income allows for trendwise changes in the distribution of income and its impact on aggregate private consumption, γ being the average relative share of workers' consumption in total private consumption.

Other explanatory factors for aggregate private consumption are:

- a quasi-accelerator $\Delta cp_{-\tau}$ to account for stabilizing or destabilizing forces in the pattern of consumption;
- liquid assets, implying principally short-run changes in income, and, hence, in private consumption;
- the rate of interest, determining the savings ratio of households.

The growth rates of the volume of postwar private consumption in *Belgium* can be explained quite satisfactorily by means of a generalized partial adjustment process with regard to consumption, by an anticipatory income distribution process, by the demand prices of consumption and by the lagged changes in long term-interest rates:

$$\begin{array}{lll} \widehat{cp}_{(B)} = & 0.676(Wd - Pcp)_{-1/2} & + 0.314(NWd - Pcp)_{-1/2} \\ (t) & (16.29) & (5.48) \\ [F] & [0.37] & [1.85] \end{array}$$

$$\begin{array}{lll} - 0.267\,\Delta cp_{-1} & - 0.157\,\Delta Pcp & - 2.142\,\Delta \tilde{R}l_{-3/4}, \\ (-2.46) & (-2.03) & (-4.63) \\ [2.69] & [0.43] & [0.71] \end{array}$$

$$R = 0.981, \quad s^2 = 0.812, \quad DET = 0.558, \tag{2.5}$$

where the figures between brackets are t and F statistics on significance and multicollinearity respectively; R is the equation's multiple correlation coefficient, s^2 the residual variance and DET the determinant of the correlation matrix of the explanatory variables.[4] Due to the occurrence of the lagged quasi-accelerator Δcp_{-1} (built-in stabilizer), the short-run weighted elasticities exceed those of the long run.[5] The impact of the quasi-accelerator ΔPcp is rather sensitive to the first part of the sampling period: deleting the first four observations of this period, the absolute value of its coefficient falls from 0.157 to 0.102 (with a t value of 1.39).

The weighted (per capita) labour income elasticity of postwar private consumption in *France* seems fairly low. Its contribution, however, is amended by the growth of employed and self-employed persons in the private sector, which may serve as an indicator for the ultimate effect of an increase (decrease) in the real wage bill of the French economy as a whole. If, for example, the volume of labour employed in the private sector and the real wage both increase at a rate of 0.5% per year, the long-run effect on consumption will be approximately 0.7% per year.

The ultimately estimated stable relationship shows as follows:

$$\begin{array}{llll}
\widehat{cp}_{(F)} & = 0.452(w - Pcp)_{-1/2} & + 1.170 EMps_{-1/4} \\
(t) & \quad (4.50) & \quad (5.07) \\
[F] & \quad [1.30] & \quad [0.19] \\
 & + 0.323(\tilde{R}l - Pe2) & + 0.178 L1_{-1}, \\
 & \quad (5.27) & \quad (4.43) \\
 & \quad [0.07] & \quad [1.41]
\end{array}$$

$$R = 0.992, \quad s^2 = 0.494, \quad DET = 0.810, \quad DW = 1.505,$$

$$\hat{\rho} = 0.175, \tag{2.7}$$

where DW is the familiar Durbin–Watson statistic and $\hat{\rho}$ the (estimated) first-order autocorrelation coefficient.

The sign of the real interest elasticity is positive and, hence, has to be interpreted as a more than complete offset of the substitution effect against savings; it may serve as an indicator for a larger expected non-wage income.

Postwar private consumption in *Germany* satisfies the relationship:

$$\begin{array}{lllll}
\widehat{cp}_{(D)} & = 1.644 & + 0.620(Wd - Pcp) & + 0.126(NWhd - PcP)_{-1/2} \\
(t) & \quad (2.64) & \quad (8.54) & \quad (2.92) \\
[F] & \quad [-] & \quad [8.77] & \quad [7.10] \\
 & -0.201 Pcp, \\
 & \quad (-2.09) \\
 & \quad [5.06]
\end{array}$$

$$R = 0.970, \quad s^2 = 0.597, \quad DET = 0.41, \quad DW = 2.51,$$

$$\hat{\rho} = -0.28. \tag{2.8}$$

The weighted income elasticities imply an average marginal propensity to consume of 0.96, being not significantly different from unity; the F ratios however indicate slight multicollinearity.

Postwar *Italian* private consumption satisfies:

$$\begin{array}{llll} \widehat{cp}_{(I)} & = -1.918 & + 0.100w & - 0.980\Delta\tilde{R}l_{-1/4} \\ (t) & (-2.46) & (2.32) & (-3.01) \\ [F] & [-] & [8.10] & [9.12] \end{array}$$

$$\begin{array}{l} + 0.951(gvampp - EMps)_{-1/2}, \\ (9.84) \\ [1.47] \end{array}$$

$$R = 0.9, \quad s^2 = 0.678, \quad DET = 0.469, \quad DW = 2.01,$$

$$\hat{\rho} = -0.203, \tag{2.9}$$

from which it seems that the bulk of the explanatory power lies in the labour productivity variable: an increase in the productivity of labour is nearly fully transmitted into consumption with a delay of about half a year; this phenomenon can also be made clear from the functioning of the wage–price spiral in the postwar Italian economy. Notice, equally, the impact of the multicollinear set of variables, being indicators for labour and non-linear income. This impact has been relevant only in the seventies.

In the *Netherlands*, the aggregate wage income elasticity of private consumption is rather low, and explains, therefore, the falling consumption quota in the postwar Dutch economy, which shows the following stable picture:

$$\begin{array}{lll} \widehat{cp}_{(NL)} & = 0.654(Wd - Pcp) & + 0.162(L1 - Pe2)_{-1}, \\ (t) & (15.16) & (3.53) \\ [F] & [1.40] & [1.40] \end{array}$$

$$R = 0.982, \quad s^2 = 1.243, \quad DET = 0.937, \quad DW = 2.601,$$

$$\hat{\rho} = -0.301. \tag{2.10}$$

The elasticity of real primary liquidities is rather high and suggests a considerably effective monetary policy with regard to consumers' expenditures in the Netherlands. The Durbin–Watson statistic points to an inconclusive region, so we cannot state whether significant negative autocorrelation is present.

Real disposable wages, the acceleration of the treasury bill rate and the relative price increase of imported goods with regard to the domestic price level of total expenditures are the principal ingredients for the postwar private consumption in the *United Kingdom:*

$$\widehat{cp}_{(UK)} = \underset{\substack{(5.74)\\ [-]}}{1.412} + \underset{\substack{(6.76)\\ [2.07]}}{0.412}(Wd - Pcp) - \underset{\substack{(-5.02)\\ [5.73]}}{0.500}\Delta\tilde{R}tb_{-1} - \underset{\substack{(-6.84)\\ [4.21]}}{0.102}(Pmg - Pe2)_{-1},$$

(t), $[F]$

$$R = 0.995, \quad s^2 = 0.215, \quad DET = 0.59, \quad DW = 1.84,$$

$$\hat{\rho} = -0.08. \tag{2.11}$$

The significant contribution of the relative price variable follows from the large share of consumption goods in British imports.

2.2. Private Investments

Investment decisions of (private) firms will generally be based on optimal (ex-ante) plans, being derived for a dynamic stochastic model of the firm, in which uncertainty and technical change play a predominant role. Actual investment rates are built up with the help of realization and completion functions.

Under a number of conditions, the investment demand function can be expressed as [17]:

$$\widetilde{ip} = \phi\left(\tilde{R}l, \tilde{T}dc, \frac{\tilde{P}ip}{\tilde{P}e}, \frac{\tilde{w}}{\tilde{P}e}, t, \tilde{q}, \widetilde{NW}c, \tilde{L}\right), \tag{2.12}$$

where various variables can occur in the form of some transformation (for example unit labour costs $H := w - (gvampp - EMps)_{-1/2}$ instead of the wage rate w), and where $\tilde{q}$ is an appropriate measure for capacity utilization (sometimes approximated by the rate of unemployment $\widetilde{un}$). The deflator for the factor prices $\tilde{w}$ and $\tilde{P}ip$ is the price of total expenditures ($\tilde{P}e$) in (2.12); it can also be the price of output or the price of private consumption. Assuming a log-linear relationship for (2.12), which is quite conceivable for Constant Elasticity of Substitution (C.E.S.) production technologies (Plasmans [17]), the ultimately selected postwar investment functions for the six private EEC economies are now discussed.

The government financing shortage plays a peculiar role in postwar *Belgian* investments. Its short-run impact is negative because the money stock, being necessary to finance this governmental shortage, is competitive with respect to the capital which is necessary for financing private investments. In contrast, the lagged effect of governmental shortage on private investments is positive because of the stimulating effect of official orders on private investments. The long-run effect, however, remains negative (about -0.019), which highlights the disadvantageous influence of the growing budget deficits of the Belgian governments in the seventies. Moreover, productivity growth has a stimulating effect on private Belgian (rationalization) investments, which becomes clear from the following equation selected:

$$\begin{array}{lllll}
\widehat{ip}_{(B)} = & 0.292\Delta ip_{-1} & -0.051 Fg & +0.033 Fg_{-1} & +0.206 Sh \\
(t) & (2.95) & (-4.42) & (2.76) & (3.52) \\
[F] & [1.24] & [2.19] & [1.41] & [1.59]
\end{array}$$

$$\begin{array}{l}
+0.682(gvampp - EMps)_{-1/4}, \\
(2.44) \\
[2.11]
\end{array}$$

$$R = 0.927, \quad s^2 = 11.722, \quad DET = 0.470. \tag{2.13}$$

The lagged changes of the relative indirect tax rates are an important instrument in the execution or consideration of new investment projects in the postwar *French* economy:

$$\begin{array}{lll}
\widehat{ip}_{(F)} = & -1.505(w - Pcp)_{-1/2} & -0.983(TI - E2)_{-1} \\
(t) & (-2.38) & (-4.34) \\
[F] & [2.27] & [1.19]
\end{array}$$

$$\begin{array}{lll}
-0.699 Pip & +2.229 gvamp_{-3/4} & +0.690(L1 - Pe2)_{-1} \\
(-5.26) & (4.63) & (4.79) \\
[1.20] & [2.18] & [2.42]
\end{array}$$

$$\begin{array}{ll}
+2.774\Delta\tilde{R}l & +23.034 DU'59, \\
(3.34) & (7.32) \\
[1.69] & [-]
\end{array}$$

$$R = 0.963, \quad s^2 = 6.105, \quad DET = 0.195, \quad DW = 2.03,$$

$$\hat{\rho} = -0.01. \tag{2.14}$$

The negatively elastic impact of the real wage rate implies that cost increases are very unfavourable for the level of general activity, which is related to the modest substitutability in the postwar French economy. The positive influence of the long-term interest rate stands for an increased degree of profit anticipation, since monetary authorities switch over to stimulating self-financing when debt financing becomes too expensive. This relationship is shown to be very stable over the sample period.

Labour productivity and the (anticipated) pressure of private consumption demand both have an elastic impact on postwar *German* fixed capital formation:

$$\begin{array}{llll}
\widehat{ip}_{(D)} = & -13.048 & +1.539(gvampp - EMps) & +1.971\, cp_{-1/4}, \\
(t) & (-6.49) & (3.62) & (6.19) \\
[F] & [-] & [7.40] & [7.40]
\end{array}$$

$$R = 0.943, \quad s^2 = 10.400, \quad DET = 0.739, \quad DW = 2.032,$$

$$\hat{\rho} = -0.056. \tag{2.15}$$

Note also the considerable technological progress in the postwar private German economy; it is involved in the labour productivity variable (endogenous rationalization investments) as well as in the large negative intercept (exogenous technical change).

The following stable clay-clay investment relationship (without ex-ante and ex-post factor substitution) is ultimately accepted for the private *Italian* economy during the (abbreviated) sampling period 1954–1975:

$$\begin{array}{lllll} \widehat{ip}_{(I)} & = 4.828 & -0.698w_{-1} & +0.460ip_{-1} & +0.565(L12-Pip)_{-1}, \\ (t) & (1.62) & (-4.08) & (3.93) & (3.73) \\ [F] & [-] & [3.01] & [0.18] & [3.12] \end{array}$$

$$R = 0.947, \quad s^2 = 12.352, \quad DET = 0.75. \tag{2.16}$$

Notice that the short-term impact of the labour cost variable is inelastic, while its long-run impact is elastic.

The volume of private investments in the *Netherlands* is principally determined by the rate of unused capacity, measured by the rate of unemployment, the real unit cost of the substitutive production factor, the equity financial capital and the financing shortage of the government. In contrast with the Belgian case in (2.13), the net impact of the financing shortage is a positive stimulus on private investments, particularly in the seventies, but not before.

$$\begin{array}{lllll} \widehat{ip}_{(NL)} & = -5.707 & -6.577\Delta\widetilde{un} & +1.590(w-Pe2) & +0.331NWc \\ (t) & (-2.690) & (-7.176) & (5.155) & (4.877) \\ [F] & [-] & [1.29] & [1.30] & [1.80] \end{array}$$

$$\begin{array}{ll} +0.0025\Delta\widetilde{Fg}_{-1/2} & -17.829DU'69, \\ (2.777) & (-5.800) \\ [2.40] & [-] \end{array}$$

$$R = 0.956, \quad s^2 = 8.354, \quad DET = 0.471, \quad DW = 2.53,$$

$$\hat{\rho} = -0.302. \tag{2.17}$$

The introduction of the tax on value added in 1969 in the Netherlands was responsible for a sudden fall in investment volume, although the economic activity was at a top level (overestimation of the growth of private investments by almost 18%).

The ultimate specification of the demand for the volume of private investments in the *United Kingdom* rests on the (change of) utilization of productive capacity and on the cost development of the factor inputs, labour and capital:

$$
\begin{array}{llll}
\widehat{ip}_{(UK)} & = \; 1.902 + 2.070q_{-1/4} & + \; 1.304(w - Pip), \\
(t) & \quad (1.507) \; (7.031) & \quad (4.612) \\
[F] & \qquad [-] \quad [0.42] & \quad [0.42]
\end{array}
$$

$$R = 0.923, \quad s^2 = 6.856, \quad DET = 0.98, \quad DW = 1.40,$$

$$\hat{\rho} = 0.28. \tag{2.18}$$

2.3. The Labour Market: Supply and Demand for Labour

It is commonly known that labour markets are almost permanently in disequilibrium; either there exists a shortage of labour (overemployment) or there is excess labour supply (considerable unemployment) as nowadays. Over the postwar sampling period, various disequilibrium regimes have occurred, so the problem of switching regimes has to be tackled.

In general, the distinction between notional and effective demands is critical in disequilibrium analysis. Notional demands and supplies are calculated by individuals and firms on the assumption that they can buy and sell as much as they want of any 'good' at prevailing prices. This assumption can only be true in (Walrasian) equilibrium, where the quantities are obtained as the result of a trade-off between, for example the households' utility-maximizing behaviour and the entrepreneurs' profit-maximizing or cost-minimizing behaviour. In disequilibrium, there are constraints on the amounts of some goods an individual can buy or sell. Effective demands are calculated conditionally on the quantity constraints, or any other non-price constraints the individual perceives on other markets. For instance, if there is an excess supply of labour, the effective demand for goods by an individual who cannot sell as much labour as he wants is less than the notional demand for goods at prevailing prices. Hence, his demand for goods in that situation will be a function of the amount of labour he can sell.[6] Further, it is assumed that individuals express demands in each market which are based on the quantity constraints perceived in other markets. Thus, the effective supply of labour, when the individual is constrained only in the labour market, is the notional supply of labour.

Considering only the product and labour markets, the type of disequilibrium characteristic for the postwar aggregate EEC economies is principally the case of 'Keynesian unemployment', where there is excess supply on both markets, resulting in an effective demand for labour (being dependent, among other things, on a limited supply of output) and a Walrasian supply of labour. Hence the difficult estimation problem of simultaneous switching of various regimes can be circumvented.

Summarizing, and allowing for execution delays, for example as a consequence of limited financial means, the private demand for labour ($\widetilde{EMp}$) can be expressed as:

$$\widetilde{EMp} = \phi_1(\tilde{w}, \widetilde{Pip}, \widetilde{Pe}, \widetilde{Rl}, t, \widetilde{gvampp}, \widetilde{NWc}, \tilde{L}), \tag{2.19}$$

where the same remarks regarding particular variables can be made as for (2.12).

Since Walrasian supply of labour only depends on (relative) prices and time, the excess supply of labour (unemployment: $\widetilde{UN}$) can be expressed as a function of private employment; also purely demographic variables such as the dependent working population are important for this quantity, or, basically:

$$\widetilde{un} = \phi_2(\widetilde{EMp}, \widetilde{POd}) \tag{2.20}$$

The postwar private labour market in *Belgium* shows factor substitution and substitution of debt capital by equity capital for financing private employment. The more expensive debt capital becomes, the more employment decisions are financed through equity capital (increased degree of profit anticipation, as for French private investments). The private employment relationship, being stable over the sampling period, satisfies:

$$\begin{array}{llll}
\widehat{EMp}_{(B)} = & -0.208 H_{-1}^{(-1/2)} & +0.912 \Delta\tilde{R}l & +0.362 gvampp_{-3/4}, \\
(t) & (-5.27) & (3.08) & (7.23) \\
[F] & [0.86] & [0.85] & [0.06]
\end{array}$$

$$R = 0.894, \quad s^2 = 0.633, \quad DET = 0.919, \quad DW = 2.35,$$

$$\hat{\rho} = -0.23, \tag{2.21}$$

where the spillover effect, originating from the excess supply product market, has been estimated significantly at 0.362: if the producers expect to sell 10% more within three-quarters of a year, then they are willing to increase their current labour demand by 3.62%.

The postwar Belgian unemployment relationship is directly related to (2.21):

$$\begin{array}{lll}
\widehat{\Delta\widetilde{un}}_{(B)} = & -0.552 EMp_{-1/4} & +0.093 H_{-1/2}^{(-1/4)}, \\
(t) & (-16.17) & (10.81) \\
[F] & [0.08] & [0.08]
\end{array}$$

$$R = 0.967, \quad s^2 = 0.051, \quad DET = 0.965, \quad DW = 2.044,$$

$$\hat{\rho} = -0.031. \tag{2.22}$$

Combining (2.21) and (2.22), the entrepreneurs' 'dismissal elasticity' of employment force, due to increased wage costs, is about 0.2%.

In *France* too, the postwar labour and product markets are characterized by the Keynesian unemployment disequilibrium situation, with the product spillover coefficient in the labour demand function being somewhat comparable to that for Belgium:[7]

$$\begin{array}{lll}
\widehat{EMp}_{(F)} = & -0.181 (w - Pip)_{-1/4} & +0.626 el_{-1/2} \\
(t) & (-5.82) & (9.83) \\
[F] & [1.04] & [2.09]
\end{array}$$

$$
\begin{aligned}
&-0.292(gvamp - EMps), \\
&(-3.98) \\
&[1.47]
\end{aligned}
$$

$$R = 0.960, \quad s^2 = 0.277, \quad DET = 0.797, \quad DW = 1.65,$$

$$\hat{\rho} = 0.10. \tag{2.23}$$

A stable unemployment equation for the postwar French economy is obtained as:

$$
\begin{aligned}
\widehat{\Delta \widetilde{un}}_{(F)} &= 0.670 - 0.296 EMp - 0.048 ip_{-1/4} \\
(t) \quad & \quad (6.68)(-7.80) \quad (-4.71) \\
[F] \quad & \quad [-] \quad [0.07] \quad [1.25] \\
& + 0.141 \, [(\Delta \widetilde{PO}wa - \Delta \widetilde{EM}g)/\widetilde{PO}d_{-1}]_{-1/2} \\
& \quad (2.38) \\
& \quad [1.26]
\end{aligned}
$$

$$R = 0.913, \quad s^2 = 0.045, \quad DET = 0.885, \quad DW = 1.634,$$

$$\hat{\rho} = 0.182, \tag{2.24}$$

where the occurrence of the demand for private investment implies substitutability with private employment.

In the *Federal Republic of Germany* the private employment changes are almost completely explained by the aggregate expenditure less increase in stocks and non-invisibles, with a strong spillover effect:

$$
\begin{aligned}
\widehat{EMp}_{(D)} &= -3.533 + 0.727 e2_{-1/4}, \\
(t) \quad & \quad (-9.25) \; (13.59)
\end{aligned}
$$

$$R = 0.956, \quad s^2 = 0.681, \quad DW = 2.31, \quad \hat{\rho} = -0.172. \tag{2.25}$$

The negative time trend seems to be connected to a considerable labour-augmenting technological progress during the postwar sampling period. The German unemployment relationship is simple:

$$
\begin{aligned}
\widehat{\Delta \widetilde{un}}_{(D)} &= 0.201 - 0.335 EMp, \\
(t) \quad & \quad (2.40)(-10.78)
\end{aligned}
$$

$$R = 0.923, \quad s^2 = 0.135, \quad DW = 1.12, \quad \hat{\rho} = 0.402, \tag{2.26}$$

with a slight autonomous increase of 0.2% per year.

The postwar *Italian* private employment equation shows, in the short run, complementary behaviour between capital investments and labour employment, which is fully compatible with the clay-clay character of the investment relationship: installation of new machines and new buildings attracts labour (half a year later) and does not replace it:

$$\widehat{EMp}_{(I)} = \underset{\substack{(4.02) \\ [-]}}{1.164} - \underset{\substack{(-3.55) \\ [1.32]}}{0.156}(w - Pip)_{-1/4} + \underset{\substack{(6.85) \\ [4.30]}}{0.162}ip_{-1/2}$$

$$+ \underset{\substack{(3.83) \\ [3.17]}}{0.061}(mg - xg)_{-1/4},$$

(t) and [F] rows as above.

$R = 0.962$, $s^2 = 0.66$, $DET = 0.314$, $DW = 1.72$,

$\hat{\rho} = 0.10.$ (2.27)

Note also the positive impact of the foreign exchange rate: the Italian imports are more employment-creating than are Italian exports. The postwar Italian unemployment equation has a very good fit:

$$\widehat{\Delta \widetilde{un}}_{(I)} = - \underset{\substack{(-7.71) \\ [-]}}{3.630} - \underset{\substack{(-7.60) \\ [2.33]}}{0.450}EMp + \underset{\substack{(2.11) \\ [1.97]}}{0.086}(gvampp - EMps)_{-1}$$

$$+ \underset{\substack{(7.38) \\ [1.38]}}{0.490}\widetilde{SO} + \underset{\substack{(2.34) \\ [0.59]}}{0.048}(Pxg - Pxc)_{-1} + \underset{\substack{(11.84) \\ [-]}}{4.231}DU'56,$$

$R = 0.981$, $s^2 = 0.091$, $DET = 0.46$, $DW = 1.842$,

$\hat{\rho} = 0.023.$ (2.28)

Increase of domestic labour productivity leads to the expulsion of labour: this may indicate either that, through expansion investments, labour is not fully absorbed after the replacement of older machines by more productive ones, or, that the labour process itself is organized in an increasingly more efficient way. The composite export price variable points out that a deterioration (amelioration) of the relative competitive position leads to an increase (decrease) of unemployment. Finally, the dummy variable $DU'56$ stands for a sudden increase in unemployment in 1956, owing to the Suez crisis, when many Italian ports went through a disastrous period.

A typical Keynesian unemployment situation is found for the *Netherlands,* where the demand function for private employment can be specified as:

$$\widehat{EMp}_{(NL)} = \underset{\substack{(2.38) \\ [-]}}{1.529} - \underset{\substack{(-4.81) \\ [1.73]}}{0.198}w_{-1} + \underset{\substack{(4.08) \\ [2.34]}}{0.225}e2_{-1/4} + \underset{\substack{(2.89) \\ [0.63]}}{0.287}EMp_{-1},$$

$R = 0.956$, $s^2 = 0.445$, $DET = 0.802.$ (2.29)

This relationship, which shows a very stable picture over the post-war sampling period, implies a long-run product spillover effect of 0.316; hence, if producers expect to sell 10% more within a time horizon of one quarter, the short-run demand for private employment will be increased by 2.25% and the long-run demand will be adjusted by 3.16%. The autonomous increase in Dutch private employment is estimated at 1.53% per year.

The postwar Dutch version of the unemployment function (2.20) looks like this:

$$\widehat{\Delta \tilde{un}}_{(NL)} = -0.458 EMp + 0.283\,[(\Delta \widetilde{PO}wa - \Delta \widetilde{EM}g)/\widetilde{PO}d_{-1}],$$
$$\begin{array}{lll} (t) & (-12.52) & (9.67) \\ [F] & [0.11] & [0.11] \end{array}$$

$$R = 0.940, \quad s^2 = 0.071, \quad DET = 0.995, \quad DW = 1.900,$$
$$\hat{\rho} = 0.001, \qquad (2.30)$$

which shows a very stable pattern over the sampling period.

In the *United Kingdom*, employment in enterprises developed completely differently before and after 1967: in the period 1950–1966, private employment increased at an average rate of 0.8% per year, but in the period 1967–1975 it decreased at about 1% per year on average. This evolution was accompanied by a very large decrease in the degree of capacity utilization from 1966 on (the decrease in the degree of utilization of productive capacity was about 9% from 1966 to 1975). The demand function for British private employment satisfies:

$$\widehat{EMp}_{(UK)} = 1.720 + 0.840 q_{-1/4} - 0.602(gvampp - EMps)$$
$$\begin{array}{llll} (t) & (6.05) & (12.55) & (-8.86) \\ [F] & [-] & [5.40] & [5.40] \end{array}$$
$$+ 0.062\, WEQI,$$
$$\begin{array}{l} (2.02) \\ [3.43] \end{array}$$

$$R = 0.977, \quad s^2 = 0.235, \quad DET = 0.52, \quad DW = 1.84$$
$$\hat{\rho} = 0.014, \qquad (2.31)$$

from which it seems that a unit increase in labour productivity reduces the private demand for employment by 0.6% per year. The sensitivity of British private employment to changes in world trade activity is illustrated by the inference of the world export quantum index.

The importance of British exports to private employment is illustrated again by the unemployment function:

$$\widehat{\Delta \tilde{un}}_{(UK)} = 0.311 - 0.047 xg - 0.249\, EMp,$$
$$\begin{array}{llll} (t) & (4.96) & (-4.43) & (-7.96) \\ [F] & [-] & [2.21] & [2.21] \end{array}$$

$$R = 0.926, \quad s^2 = 0.043, \quad DET = 0.905, \quad DW = 1.65,$$
$$\hat{\rho} = 0.11. \qquad (2.32)$$

During the last years, about 84% of exported goods in the United Kingdom have been 'manufactured goods', with the most important component being 'machinery and transport equipment' (about 48%). Employment in the total 'manufacturing industries' is about 40% of the total number of employed people and the share of exported 'manufactured goods' in the total of 'manufacturing' is about 50%. About one third of unemployed persons were in the 'manufacturing industries' (*Annual Abstract of Statistics,* 1977). Hence, exports of goods have been determining the unemployment level, especially during the seventies.

2.4. International Trade: Exports and Imports of Goods

Heckscher [11] and Ohlin [16] developed the classical theories of factor price equalization and factor abundancy, roughly saying that those products which are relatively less scarce and cheaper outside than in the domestic markets will be imported. The international differences in factor endowments are the critical and sole factor determining a comparative advantage. A country's exports use intensively the most abundant factor of production available in that country. Kravis [13] developed the availability theory, which states that a country tends to import products that are unavailable at home: availability is determined by natural resources, technological progress and product differentiation. Barker [3] amended this theory with the variety hypothesis.

Posner [21] advanced the technological gap theory, which stresses the temporary monopoly of a country after successful product innovation. Drèze [8, 9] put forward the demand theory of international trade: economies of scale and thresholds to trade across the border mean especially that small countries are specializing in nationally differentiated goods, whereas large countries will be specializing in internationally standardized goods.

In fact, these newer theories, except for the availability theory, stress the comparative advantage in supply, while the earlier theories additionally emphasize the effects of real income and its growth on international trade. Hence, import demand studies generally stress the importance of the Marshallian concept of import price elasticity and the Keynesian concept of import income elasticity. The quantity of imports purchased by any consumer will thus also depend on the price of all other commodities, approximated by $\widetilde{Pe}$, so that the basic import demand equation looks like this:

$$\widetilde{mg} = \psi_1(\tilde{e}, \widetilde{Pmg}, \widetilde{Pe}). \tag{2.33}$$

Exports are demanded by foreign countries, depending on the relative price (cost) advantage, labour productivity and structural components such as relative availability, relative specialization, and so on, as indicated above, or:

$$\widetilde{xg} = \psi_2\,[(\widetilde{Pxg}/\widetilde{Pxc}), (\widetilde{gvampp}/\widetilde{EMps})]\,, \tag{2.34}$$

where $\tilde{P}xc$ is the price index of competitive exports.[8]

The postwar *Belgian* relationships for imports and exports of goods are respectively:

$$\begin{array}{lllll}
\widehat{mg}_{(B)} & = 2.016cp_{-1/4} & +\,0.291ip & -\,0.475Pmg_{-1}, & \\
(t) & (10.81) & (3.16) & (-5.81) & \\
[F] & [0.76] & [1.28] & [1.57] & \\
\end{array}$$

$$R = 0.970, \quad s^2 = 7.074, \quad DET = 0.835, \quad DW = 2.47,$$

$$\hat{\rho} = -0.31; \tag{2.36}$$

and

$$\begin{array}{lll}
\widehat{xg}_{(B)} & = -\,0.805H_{-1}^{(-1/2)} & +\,1.981(gvampp - EMps) \\
(t) & (-4.48) & (4.74) \\
[F] & [0.67] & [3.42] \\
 & +\,1.050cp_{-1/2}, & \\
 & (2.16) & \\
 & [3.30] & \\
\end{array}$$

$$R = 0.953, \quad s^2 = 11.659, \quad DET = 0.736, \quad DW = 2.682,$$

$$\hat{\rho} = -0.341. \tag{2.37}$$

The pressure of demand variables in the import equation have a large impact; private consumption and private investment need raw materials, which are not available at home (viz. availability theory). Unit labour costs are embarassing costs for Belgian exports; private consumption plays the role of a cyclical variable of pressure of demand, being only important in the first part of the sampling period.[9]

The postwar foreign sector of *France* is summarized in the following pair of equations:

$$\begin{array}{llll}
\widehat{mg}_{(F)} & = -\,10.693 & -\,0.419(Pmg - Pe2) & +\,0.889Pcp \\
(t) & (-3.767) & (-3.530) & (3.407) \\
[F] & [-] & [1.78] & [2.52] \\
 & -\,4.713\Delta\widetilde{un} & +\,2.090WEQI_{-1/4}, & \\
 & (-2.451) & (7.566) & \\
 & [2.81] & [2.62] & \\
\end{array}$$

$$R = 0.978, \quad s^2 = 12.047, \quad DET = 0.517, \quad DW = 2.095,$$

$$\hat{\rho} = -0.089; \tag{2.38}$$

and

$$\begin{array}{llll}
\widehat{xg}_{(F)} & = -\,10.113 & +\,0.703(Pxg - Pxc)_{-1} & +\,0.713Pe2_{-1/4} \\
(t) & (-3.586) & (5.368) & (2.847) \\
[F] & [-] & [1.59] & [1.87] \\
\end{array}$$

$$+ 2.030 WEQI_{-1/2} + 6.999 \Delta\widetilde{un}_{-1/4} - 12.712 DU'56$$
$$(7.514) \qquad (3.133) \qquad (-3.712)$$
$$[1.82] \qquad [-] \qquad [-]$$

$$R = 0.974, \quad s^2 = 9.071, \quad DET = 0.442, \quad DW = 2.188,$$

$$\hat{\rho} = -0.129. \tag{2.39}$$

The price variables in the import equation indicate substitution effects between foreign and home-produced goods. The dummy variable in the export equation is introduced to take care of the influence of the Suez crisis of July 1956. Notice that French exports are growing much faster than world exports. The positive elasticity of the relative export price variable is an indicator for an accelerated growth in current exports when a deterioration of the French relative export competitivity is expected next year.

The ultimate equations for *German* imports and exports of goods are:

$$\widehat{mg}_{(D)} = 1.888 + 1.529 e1 + 11.251 DU'54,$$
$$(t) \qquad (1.59) \quad (9.05) \qquad (3.60)$$

$$R = 0.979, \quad s^2 = 9.043, \quad DW = 2.20, \quad \hat{\rho} = -0.204; \tag{2.40}$$

and

$$\widehat{xg}_{(D)} = 13.382 - 1.187 H^{(-1/4)}_{-1/4} + 0.749 (Pmg - Pe2)$$
$$(t) \qquad (8.70)(-4.45) \qquad (4.49)$$
$$[F] \qquad [-] \quad [0.67] \qquad [0.35]$$

$$+ 0.498 ip_{-3/4},$$
$$(4.22)$$
$$[0.78]$$

$$R = 0.964, \quad s^2 = 12.673, \quad DET = 0.913, \quad DW = 1.964,$$

$$\hat{\rho} = -0.049. \tag{2.41}$$

The dummy variable $DU'54$ is introduced to account for the cancellation of important German tariffs on imports in 1954, which led to an 'importation explosion' (see also the Dutch import equation). Private investment serves as an indicator for the German business cycle. The trend term is needed to account for the very fast growth of German exports.

The postwar *Italian* foreign sector satisfies:

$$\widehat{mg}_{(I)} = -5.642 + 2.588 e2 + 26.205 DU'60,$$
$$(t) \qquad (-2.78) \quad (7.83) \qquad (5.94)$$

$$R = 0.967, \quad s^2 = 17.66, \quad DET = 0.95, \quad DW = 2.220,$$

$$\hat{\rho} = -0.115; \tag{2.42}$$

and

$$\widehat{xg}_{(I)} = \underset{\substack{(7.55)\\ [-]}}{16.276} - \underset{\substack{(-5.77)\\ [0.73]}}{1.670}(Pxg - Pxc)_{-1/4} - \underset{\substack{(-2.52)\\ [2.07]}}{0.346}(H^{(-1/4)} - Pxg)$$

$$- \underset{\substack{(-2.54)\\ [2.81]}}{0.742}\, WEQI_{-1} + \underset{\substack{(1.88)\\ [2.53]}}{0.185}\, mg_{-1} + \underset{\substack{(2.84)\\ [-]}}{12.422} DU'65,$$

(t), $[F]$

$$R = 0.974, \quad s^2 = 12.830, \quad DET = 0.436, \quad DW = 1.98,$$

$$\hat{\rho} = -0.068. \qquad (2.43)$$

Like Japan's and Germany's, Italian exports are expanding almost explosively, so the trend term amounts to more than 16%. Very interesting is the 'profit liability' variable $(H - Pxg)$. If 'internal' costs (H) are rising more rapidly compared with 'external gains', symbolized by Pxg, then firms are apt to withdraw from the export market.

Postwar *Dutch* foreign trade can be expressed as follows:

$$\widehat{mg}_{(NL)} = \underset{(-2.09)}{1.518} + \underset{(16.39)}{1.608} e1 + \underset{(3.12)}{6.111} DU'54,$$

(t)

$$R = 0.989, \quad s^2 = 3.355, \quad DET = 0.914, \quad DW = 2.467,$$

$$\hat{\rho} = -0.272; \qquad (2.44)$$

and

$$\widehat{xg}_{(NL)} = \underset{\substack{(2.15)\\ [-]}}{3.786} - \underset{\substack{(-3.88)\\ [0.41]}}{0.668} Pip_{-1/2} + \underset{\substack{(4.66)\\ [0.42]}}{1.132}(e2 - EMps)_{-1/2}$$

$$+ \underset{\substack{(6.40)\\ [0.07]}}{10.558}\, \Delta\widetilde{SO}_{-1},$$

(t), $[F]$

$$R = 0.980, \quad s^2 = 5.403, \quad DET = 0.958, \quad DW = 1.867,$$

$$\hat{\rho} = -0.002. \qquad (2.45)$$

Imports are completely determined by those of Germany (see 2.40), where there was a general decrease of import duties in 1954.

The postwar foreign trade of the *United Kingdom* can be summarized as follows:

$$\widehat{mg}_{(UK)} = \underset{\substack{(-3.36)\\ [-]}}{-12.356} + \underset{\substack{(2.86)\\ [0.41]}}{2.609} CS + \underset{\substack{(5.36)\\ [0.73]}}{2.403} cp + \underset{\substack{(2.84)\\ [1.08]}}{2.045}\, \Delta\widetilde{RI}_{-1/4},$$

(t), $[F]$

$$R = 0.90, \quad s^2 = 12.377, \quad DET = 0.896, \quad DW = 2.31,$$

$$\hat{\rho} = -0.267; \qquad (2.46)$$

and

$$
\begin{array}{llll}
\widehat{xg}_{(UK)} & = -0.294(Pxg-Pmg) & -0.212(Pmg-Pe2)_{-1} & \\
(t) & (-3.05) & (-3.19) & \\
[F] & [3.05] & [2.26] & \\
 & +0.395\,WEQI_{-1/2} & +0.089\,Ipa_{-1\frac{1}{4}} & -0.323MR, \\
 & (4.66) & (3.15) & (-2.04) \\
 & [2.39] & [3.37] & [1.29]
\end{array}
$$

$$R = 0.978, \quad s^2 = 4.077, \quad DET = 0.313, \quad DW = 2.464,$$

$$\hat{\rho} = -0.23. \tag{2.47}$$

The significant contribution of the lagged terms of trade on the volume of British exports is sensitive in the boom years 1974 and 1975 only. Direct investments abroad (*Ipa*) generate a flow of goods which are supplementary to those investments (Reddaway [23]), and increase, thereby, British exports of goods.

2.5. *Prices and Wages*

What are the factors that influence price policy? First of all, there are the primary costs like labour costs, capital costs, prices of goods and services necessary for the production of goods (intermediary goods), taxes, and so on, which may bring about cost inflation. Since labour unions try to keep the total wage bill at least at the same rate, it is in their interests to keep wages rising at the same rate as labour productivity. As regards relative prices, technological progress, and its endogenous measure, labour productivity, has a reducing effect. Above these costs, there is a mark-up (share of profits): this mark-up is partly based on the need for cash flows to finance the planned investment expenditures and partly based on the price-setting behaviour of other firms. Now, there are two possibilities regarding demand: first, if the firms are operating on the elastic part of the demand curve, then changes in demand, which can also be measured by changing capacity utilization, will lead to price changes (demand-pull inflation); on the other hand, if the firms are operating on the inelastic part, then changes in demand will not lead to changes in prices.

Finally, liquidity creation within the economy may lead to price increases (monetary inflation). Summarizing for linearized functions in relative growth rates:

$$
\begin{aligned}
P_t = {} & \alpha_0 + \alpha_1(B)w_t + \alpha_2(B)Pip_t + \alpha_3(B)Pmg_t + \alpha_4(B)\Delta\tilde{R}l_t \\
& + \alpha_5(B)(gvampp - EMps)_t + \alpha_6(B)q_t + \alpha_7(B)e_t \\
& + \alpha_8(B)L_t + \alpha_9(B)P_{t-1} + \epsilon_{1,t},
\end{aligned}
\tag{2.48}
$$

where $\alpha_i(\cdot)$ $(i = 1, 2, \ldots, 9)$ are polynomials in the lag operator B.

As to nominal wages per labourer in the private sector, the principal determinants are prices of private consumption (price compensation), labour productivity and the change of unemployment (weak version of the Phillips curve), or:

$$w_t = \beta_0 + \beta_1(B)P_t + \beta_2(B)(gvampp - EMps)_t + \beta_3(B)\Delta\widetilde{un}_t + \beta_4(B)w_{t-1} + \epsilon_{2,t}. \qquad (2.49)$$

For the postwar *Belgian* economy, the following price–wage picture is obtained:

(a) *Prices of exports of goods:*

$$\begin{array}{llll} \hat{P}xg_{(B)} = & -3.208 & +1.227Pmg_{-1/4} & +0.834(mg - e1), \\ (t) & (-3.68) & (10.84) & (4.83) \\ [F] & [-] & [0.65] & [0.65] \end{array}$$

$$R = 0.933, \quad s^2 = 9.775, \quad DET = 0.970, \quad DW = 1.965,$$

$$\hat{\rho} = -0.102. \qquad (2.50)$$

(b) *Prices of government expenditures:*

$$\begin{array}{llll} \hat{P}eg_{(B)} = & -1.168 & +0.983Pip_{-1/4} & +0.236NWh, \\ (t) & (-2.12) & (11.88) & (2.60) \\ [F] & [-] & [7.70] & [7.70] \end{array}$$

$$R = 0.983, \quad s^2 = 1.402, \quad DET = 0.732, \quad DW = 2.33,$$

$$\hat{\rho} = -0.27. \qquad (2.51)$$

(c) *Prices of private consumption:*

$$\begin{array}{llll} \hat{P}cp_{(B)} = & 0.692w_{-1/4} & -0.343(gvampp - EMps) & -0.064Sh, \\ (t) & (12.46) & (-3.02) & (-3.67) \\ [F] & [0.80] & [0.03] & [0.83] \end{array}$$

$$R = 0.964, \quad s^2 = 1.894, \quad DET = 0.923, \quad DW = 2.18,$$

$$\hat{\rho} = -0.105. \qquad (2.52)$$

(d) *Prices of private investments:*

$$\begin{array}{lll} \hat{P}ip_{(B)} = & 2.907 & +0.653Pmg_{-1/2}, \\ (t) & (8.37) & (11.06) \end{array}$$

$$R = 0.966, \quad s^2 = 2.446, \quad DW = 1.315, \quad \hat{\rho} = 0.278. \qquad (2.53)$$

(e) *Private wages per labourer:*

$$\begin{array}{lll} \hat{w}_{(B)} = & 1.385Pcp_{-1/2} & +0.969(gvampp - EMps)_{-1/2} \\ (t) & (13.10) & (8.55) \\ [F] & [0.17] & [0.54] \end{array}$$

$$-1.853\Delta\widetilde{un}_{-1} \quad -4.310DU'61,$$
$$(-4.35) \qquad (-2.76)$$
$$[0.77] \qquad [-]$$

$$R = 0.990, \quad s^2 = 2.161, \quad DET = 0.866, \quad DW = 1.822,$$
$$\hat{\rho} = 0.054. \tag{2.54}$$

Because of the high multicollinearity between the wage variable and the price of imports of goods, only the last variable was used for explaining the Belgian price of exports. The effect of this variable thus partly accounts for the effect of wages. The increasing necessity for imports, which means for Belgian imports of raw materials and half-fabricats, has a large positive effect on the price of exports. It corrects our theoretical equation (2.48) for shifts in supply and product differentiation which have taken place during the sampling period.

Non-wage income of households is important for the Belgian prices of government expenditures only in the early mid-seventies (1972–1975). Also, the influence of labour productivity on prices of private consumption depends completely on the last two years of the sampling period. Further, the savings of households are an indicator for preferences of future consumption.

Remarkable are the rather high fluctuations in the price elasticity, depending on the estimation period of the wage equation:

period	1953–1973	1953–1969	1957–1975	1957–1969
coefficient	1.606	1.419	1.294	1.016
t statistic	(6.91)	(6.58)	(13.26)	(4.72)

The dummy variable $DU'61$ stands for the elimination of the three-month political strike in 1961 against Prime Minister Eyskens Unit Law.

For the period 1953–1975, prices and wages in *France* satisfy:

(a) *Prices of exports of goods:*

$$\hat{P}xg_{(F)} = 0.501w_{-1/4} + 0.380Pmg$$
$$(t) \qquad (4.914) \qquad (8.319)$$
$$[F] \qquad [2.11] \qquad [2.98]$$

$$-0.673(gvamp - EMps)_{-1/4} + 0.183MR_{-1/4},$$
$$(-3.327) \qquad (2.650)$$
$$[1.24] \qquad [0.55]$$

$$R = 0.970, \quad s^2 = 2.932, \quad DET = 0.612, \quad DW = 2.127,$$
$$\hat{\rho} = -0.096. \tag{2.55}$$

(b) *Prices of government expenditures:*

$$\begin{array}{lllll} \hat{Peg}_{(F)} & = 7.159 + 0.224ip_{-1/2} & -1.547(\widetilde{Rl} - Pe2) & -0.313eg, \\ (t) & (8.04) \quad (2.16) & (-8.08) & (-6.21) \\ [F] & [-] \quad [0.12] & [0.87] & [0.96] \end{array}$$

$$R = 0.963, \quad s^2 = 4.454, \quad DET = 0.910, \quad DW = 1.855,$$

$$\hat{\rho} = 0.057. \qquad (2.56)$$

(c) *Prices of private consumption:*

$$\begin{array}{lll} \hat{Pcp}_{(F)} & = 0.677w_{-1/4} & -0.994(gvamp - EMps) \\ (t) & (8.96) & (-6.41) \\ [F] & [2.65] & [0.89] \end{array}$$

$$\begin{array}{ll} +0.182TS & +0.049L2_{-3/4}, \\ (2.80) & (2.11) \\ [1.95] & [0.19] \end{array}$$

$$R = 0.984, \quad s^2 = 1.447, \quad DET = 0.688, \quad DW = 1.921,$$

$$\hat{\rho} = -0.164. \qquad (2.57)$$

(d) *Prices of private investments:*

$$\begin{array}{llll} \hat{Pip}_{(F)} & = 5.445 + 0.181Pmg & +0.486TI & -0.783ip_{-1/2}, \\ (t) & (4.10) \quad (4.10) & (3.71) & (-7.76) \\ [F] & [-] \quad [0.49] & [1.33] & [1.05] \end{array}$$

$$R = 0.968, \quad s^2 = 3.832, \quad DET = 0.878, \quad DW = 2.495,$$

$$\hat{\rho} = -0.254. \qquad (2.58)$$

(e) *Private wages per labourer:*

$$\begin{array}{lll} \hat{w}_{(F)} & = 1.130Pcp & +0.890(gvamp - EMps), \\ (t) & (12.59) & (8.02) \\ [F] & [6.98] & [6.98] \end{array}$$

$$R = 0.988, \quad s^2 = 3.016, \quad DET = 0.751, \quad DW = 2.326,$$

$$\hat{\rho} = -0.279. \qquad (2.59)$$

The last explanatory variable in the equation for export prices is the exchange rate (market rate divided by the parity central rate), indicating the influence of monetary unrest. The private investment variable is important for the explanation of the prices of government expenditures for the first three years of the sampling period only.

From the small price–money elasticity in the equation for prices of private consumption, it follows that the direct effect of monetary inflation is minor; its main effect probably rests on an increase of the pressure of (private) demand, and, indirectly, on prices. Prices of French private investments were much influenced in 1974 and 1975 by the import cost variables (oil prices!), much more than previously. The influence of the unit labour costs is probably measured by the large intercept.

Typical for the French wage equation is the 'elasticity reversal' in 1974: elastic price compensation ('overcompensation') in 1974 and 1975, inelastic before; inelastic impact of labour productivity in 1974 and 1975, elastic influence before.

Prices and wages in the *Federal Republic of Germany* for 1953–1975 satisfy the following relations.

(a) *Prices of exports of goods:*

$$\begin{array}{llllll} \hat{P}xg_{(D)} & = -1.726 & +0.421w_{-1/2} & +0.636Pmg_{-1/2} & -0.186Pxg_{-1}, \\ (t) & (-1.83) & (3.86) & (11.21) & (-2.40) \\ [F] & [-] & [2.96] & [6.21] & [4.74] \end{array}$$

$$R = 0.970, \quad s^2 = 1.22, \quad DET = 0.54. \qquad (2.60)$$

(b) *Prices of government expenditures:*

$$\begin{array}{llll} \hat{P}eg_{(D)} & = -6.983 & +1.174w_{-1/2} & -7.599DU'58, \\ (t) & (-4.07) & (6.13) & (-3.37) \end{array}$$

$$R = 0.907, \quad s^2 = 4.730, \quad DW = 1.403, \quad \hat{\rho} = 0.121. \qquad (2.61)$$

(c) *Prices of private consumption:*

$$\begin{array}{llll} \hat{P}cp_{(D)} & = 2.470 & +0.538(w-e2)_{-1/4} & -0.261cp_{-1/2}, \\ (t) & (4.57) & (9.51) & (-3.67) \\ [F] & [-] & [3.51] & [3.51] \end{array}$$

$$R = 0.981, \quad s^2 = 0.568, \quad DET = 0.86, \quad DW = 1.155.$$

$$\hat{\rho} = 0.40, \qquad (2.62)$$

(d) *Prices of private investments:*

$$\begin{array}{lllll} \hat{P}ip_{(D)} & = -2.357 & +0.874H^{(-1/4)} & +0.277NWh_{-1/4} & +0.085eg, \\ (t) & (-3.62) & (12.16) & (4.20) & (2.16) \\ [F] & [-] & [0.02] & [0.07] & [0.08] \end{array}$$

$$R = 0.979, \quad s^2 = 1.094, \quad DET = 0.992, \quad DW = 1.349,$$

$$\hat{\rho} = 0.233. \qquad (2.63)$$

(e) *Wages per private labourer:*

$$\begin{array}{llll} \hat{w}_{(D)} & = 2.425 & +0.580(gvampp - EMps)_{-3/4} & +0.902Pip_{-1/4}, \\ (t) & (2.37) & (3.22) & (9.21) \\ [F] & [-] & [0.11] & [0.11] \end{array}$$

$$R = 0.992, \quad s^2 = 1.527, \quad DET = 0.995, \quad DW = 1.531,$$

$$\hat{\rho} = 0.229. \qquad (2.64)$$

If we regard in the price equation for German exports of goods the composite variable $\alpha Pmg + (1-\alpha)w$ minus the constant term (as a correction for productivity increase) as the approximate unit costs, we then have the mark-up price relation exactly. The impact of the one-year-lagged export price represents the competitors' influence.

The negative elasticity of private consumption in (2.62) reflects a monopolistic element in price-setting behaviour: inverse demand relationship as was the case for French government expenditure prices.

The influence of government expenditures in the price equation of German private investments becomes clear from the following. At first sight, one may think that government investment expenditures compete with private investments, thereby causing an upward shift in the price level of private investments. But if this mechanism existed, regression of the price on the volume of private investments should yield equivalent or better results, which is not the case. German government consumption, at 1970 prices, is performing slightly better than German government investments, but causes the contribution of the price of imports to diminish to a level not significantly different from zero. The government part in the gross value added of the private sector at market prices shows an upward trend during the fifties and sixties; this ratio, 9.96% in 1953 growing to 13.32% in 1966, has been (relatively) constant since that time. This suggests a slight demand-pull inflation owing to the rigidity of government expenditures.

Since nominal private investment is a quite stable part of the gross value added at market prices of the private sector, investment price and gross value added price keep in line. Hence, *Pip* reflects output price in the German wage equation. On the other hand, the investment price can be just the best description of the outcome of the wage-bargaining process with respect to prices (with nearly full compensation).

The *Italian* price and wage equations can be estimated for the period 1954–1975 as follows.

(a) *Prices of exports of goods:*

$$\begin{array}{llll} \hat{P}xg_{(I)} & = -0.986 & + 0.817 Pmg_{-1/4} & + 0.216(mg - el)_{-1/4}, \\ (t) & (-1.63) & (20.65) & (3.05) \\ [F] & [-] & [1.36] & [1.36] \end{array}$$

$$R = 0.980, \quad s^2 = 4.913, \quad DET = 0.939, \quad DW = 1.67,$$

$$\hat{\rho} = 0.049. \qquad (2.65)$$

(b) *Prices of government expenditures:*

$$\begin{array}{llll} \hat{P}eg_{(I)} & = 0.962 Pcp_{-1/2} & - 0.789 eg_{-1/4} & - 0.002 st_{-1} \\ (t) & (6.64) & (-5.73) & (-2.78) \\ [F] & [3.58] & [4.28] & [2.10] \end{array}$$

$$+ 0.554(L12 - Pe2)_{-1},$$
$$(4.66)$$
$$[1.57]$$

$$R = 0.917, \quad s^2 = 15.176, \quad DET = 0.501, \quad DW = 2.19,$$

$$\hat{\rho} = -0.136. \qquad (2.66)$$

(c) *Prices of private consumption:*

$$\hat{Pcp}_{(I)} = -1.095 + 1.177(0.4295 w_{-1/4} + 0.1824 Pmg)_{-1/4},$$
$$(t) \qquad (-2.16) \; (15.70)$$

$$R = 0.982, \quad s^2 = 2.101, \quad DW = 1.535, \quad \hat{\rho} = -0.032. \qquad (2.67)$$

(d) *Prices of private investments:*

$$\hat{Pip}_{(I)} = 0.905 H^{(-1/4)} + 0.312(Pmg - Pe2) + 0.014 STR_{-1/4},$$
$$(t) \qquad (19.30) \qquad (6.61) \qquad (2.31)$$
$$[F] \qquad [2.17] \qquad [2.12] \qquad [0.62]$$

$$R = 0.984, \quad s^2 = 3.523, \quad DET = 0.79, \quad DW = 1.137,$$

$$\hat{\rho} = 0.405. \qquad (2.68)$$

(e) *Private wages per labourer:*

$$\hat{w}_{(I)} = 1.327 Pcp_{-1/2} + 0.773(gvampp - EMps)_{-1/4}$$
$$(t) \qquad (19.91) \qquad (10.22)$$
$$[F] \qquad [9.97] \qquad [9.93]$$

$$+ 0.0187 STR_{-1},$$
$$(4.32)$$
$$[0.14]$$

$$R = 0.991, \quad s^2 = 3.365, \quad DET = 0.50, \quad DW = 1.631,$$

$$\hat{\rho} = 0.177. \qquad (2.69)$$

The effect of $(mg - e1)$ in the price equation for exports is that an increase in imports, being necessary for the production of goods, pushes up the price for finished products, which are exported. The influence of import price changes is principally a last years' influence, owing to the imported inflation from the oil-producing countries. The observations on the price of government expenditures in Italy are very remarkable: starting in 1953 at a level of 77.5, this price becomes 63.7 in 1961; since that time, it has risen very steeply, so that the 'explanation' of the relative differences is a hard job. Moreover, this time series has two 'breaks', namely in 1960 and 1970. The break in 1960 is caused by a change of definition of government consumption, while in 1970 government employment was redefined.[10] The impact of the private consumption price plays a part principally in the last two years. Since gross wages per labourer and prices of imports of goods are highly multicollinear, they are combined into a composite cost variable in the price equation of private consumption:

$$K := 0.4295 w_{-1/4} + 0.1824 Pmg$$

or

$$K' := 0.702 w_{-1/4} + 0.298 Pmg \tag{2.70}$$

The above weights were found after studying the combined influence on *Pcp* over several periods. It would of course be more correct to base our weights on data of the input–output tables, but we do believe that our approximation is reasonable.

The relative price of imported goods in the price equation for private investments, being important only in the last two years of the sampling period, is an indicator for cost increase from abroad. The inference of the number of strikes in this price equation measures the direct cost effect of strikes. In this country of many strikes, the strikes have also an indirect influence via the unit labour cost variable $H^{(-1/4)} = w - (gvampp - EMps)_{-1/4}$, since *STR* also occurs in wage equation (2.69).

The Italian wage equation shows multicollinearity between consumption prices and labour productivity; this interrelationship, however, is caused by the last observation (1975) only and the coefficients do not change when this observation is deleted. This stability of coefficients over the sampling period is observed for all coefficients, including that for strikes.

In the *Netherlands*, the ordinary least squares estimated equations for prices and wages for the period 1953–1975 are:

(a) *Prices of exports of goods:*

$$\hat{P}xg_{(NL)} = 0.793 Pmg,$$
$$(t) \quad (29.95)$$

$$R = 0.988, \quad s^2 = 1.098, \quad DW = 1.720, \quad \hat{\rho} = 0.100. \tag{2.71}$$

(b) *Prices of government expenditures:*

$$\hat{P}eg_{(NL)} = 1.150 Pip - 0.320 eg + 0.276(mg - e2),$$
$$(t) \quad (12.45) \quad (-8.11) \quad (2.43)$$
$$[F] \quad [2.78] \quad [1.18] \quad [2.35]$$

$$R = 0.951, \quad s^2 = 5.560, \quad DET = 0.737, \quad DW = 1.408,$$

$$\hat{\rho} = 0.288. \tag{2.72}$$

(c) *Prices of private consumption:*

$$\hat{P}cp_{(NL)} = 1.279 + 0.653 H^{(-1/4)} + 0.168(TS - e2)_{-1/2},$$
$$(t) \quad (4.30) \quad (12.00) \quad (3.75)$$
$$[F] \quad [-] \quad [3.21] \quad [3.21]$$

$$R = 0.987, \quad s^2 = 0.922, \quad DET = 0.867, \quad DW = 1.242,$$

$$\hat{\rho} = 0.351. \qquad (2.73)$$

(d) *Prices of private investments:*

$$\begin{array}{lllll} \hat{Pip}_{(NL)} & = 0.844(0.695w + 0.305Pmg)_{-1/4} & & & \\ (t) & (17.01) & & & \\ [F] & [2.45] & & & \\ & & -0.202(e2 - EMps)_{-1/4} & -0.110(L2 - Pe2)_{-1/2}, & \\ & & (-3.30) & (-5.24) & \\ & & [0.20] & [2.26] & \end{array}$$

$$R = 0.983, \quad s^2 = 1.193, \quad DET = 0.803, \quad DW = 1.554,$$

$$\hat{\rho} = 0.198. \qquad (2.74)$$

(e) *Private wages per labourer:*

$$\begin{array}{lllll} \hat{w}_{(NL)} & = 1.278Pcp_{-1/4} & +0.758(e2 - EMps)_{-1/4} & -1.114(\Delta\widetilde{un})_{-1}, \\ (t) & (19.03) & (13.19) & (-3.41) \\ [F] & [1.02] & [0.94] & [0.14] \end{array}$$

$$R = 0.995, \quad s^2 = 1.367, \quad DET = 0.902, \quad DW = 1.592,$$

$$\hat{\rho} = 0.187. \qquad (2.75)$$

A better picture than equation (2.71), which shows the utmost international interdependence of the Dutch economy, hardly exists. Price equation (2.72) is an inverse demand relationship, principally during the first four years. The tension variable $(mg - e2)$ influences prices of Dutch government expenditures during the first two years of the sampling period, but much less thereafter. Owing to the inflationary tendencies of the postwar period, indirect taxes less grants corrected for total expenditure $(TS - e2)$ have a considerable and stable influence on the price of private consumption. Since the critical DW value is 1.15 at the 95% confidence level, the positive autocorrelation in (2.73) is not significant.

Note the considerable impact of the composite cost variable on the price of Dutch private investments. The impact of real secondary liquidities is more indirect, via the demand for investment goods, than direct, on prices. Hence the estimated relationship in fact is also an inverse demand function. Because of the lack of sufficient Dutch statistical data, $e2$ is used instead of *gvampp* in the measure for labour productivity. Relationship (2.75) is a weak version of the Phillips curve, but the Dutch wage equation could be estimated equally well (and even somewhat more stably) without the change of unemployment:

$$\begin{array}{lll} \hat{w}_{(NL)} & = 1.145Pcp_{-1/4} & + 0.862(e2 - EMps)_{-1/2}, \\ (t) & (16.16) & (14.06) \\ [F] & [0.50] & [0.50] \end{array}$$

$$R = 0.995, \quad s^2 = 1.348, \quad DET = 0.977, \quad DW = 1.630,$$

$$\hat{\rho} = 0.14. \qquad (2.76)$$

From both equations (2.75) and (2.76), it becomes clear that prices are overcompensated and labour productivity is undercompensated in private wages in the postwar Dutch economy. For simultaneity reasons, (2.75) is preferred.

Finally, the *United Kingdom* shows the following price and wage equations:

(a) *Prices of exports of goods:*

$$\begin{array}{llll} \hat{P}xg_{(UK)} = & 1.969 + 0.623Pmg_{-1/4} & -0.495(Pxg - Pxc)_{-1} & \\ (t) & (5.44) \quad (19.35) & (-5.47) & \\ [F] & [-] \quad [0.89] & [0.93] & \\ & + 4.119DU'56, & & \\ & (2.67) & & \\ & [-] & & \end{array}$$

$$R = 0.994, \quad s^2 = 2.26, \quad DET = 0.91. \qquad (2.77)$$

(b) *Prices of government expenditures:*

$$\begin{array}{lllll} \hat{P}eg_{(UK)} = & 3.584 + 0.554Pmg_{-1/2} & -0.606\Delta 2e2_{-1/2} & + 0.223eg, \\ (t) & (7.32) \quad (11.43) & (-1.97) & (2.38) \\ [F] & [-] \quad [3.24] & [4.75] & [1.32] \end{array}$$

$$R = 0.990, \quad s^2 = 3.91, \quad DET = 0.67, \quad DW = 2.02,$$

$$\hat{\rho} = -0.03. \qquad (2.78)$$

(c) *Prices of private consumption:*

$$\begin{array}{lll} \hat{P}cp_{(UK)} = & -1.502 + 0.895w_{-1/4} & -0.357(gvampp - EMps), \\ (t) & (-2.46) \quad (21.56) & (-3.05) \\ [F] & [-] \quad [3.68] & [3.68] \end{array}$$

$$R = 0.993, \quad s^2 = 0.913, \quad DET = 0.85, \quad DW = 1.85,$$

$$\hat{\rho} = 0.07. \qquad (2.79)$$

(d) *Prices of private investments:*

$$\begin{array}{ll} \hat{P}ip_{(UK)} = & -0.462 + 1.036(0.750H^{(-1/4)} + 0.259Pmg)_{-1/2}, \\ (t) & (-1.03) \quad (18.86) \end{array}$$

$$R = 0.983, \quad s^2 = 2.56, \quad DW = 1.85, \quad \hat{\rho} = 0.05. \qquad (2.80)$$

(e) *Private wages per labourer:*

$$\begin{array}{lll} \hat{w}_{(UK)} = & 1.647 + 1.189Pcp & + 0.361(gvampp - EMps), \\ (t) & (2.05) \quad (17.95) & (2.00) \\ [F] & [-] \quad [6.60] & [6.60] \end{array}$$

$$R = 0.983, \quad s^2 = 1.94, \quad DET = 0.76, \quad DW = 2.31,$$
$$\hat{\rho} = -0.17. \tag{2.81}$$

The United Kingdom is the only EEC country (of the six investigated) where the external market conditions have a direct influence on the price of exports of goods. $DU'56$ was necessary to cover internal (strikes and large wage demands) and external (Suez crisis) unrest. Here too, wages and import prices are highly multicollinear and it is not necessary for the fitting to use both variables. The positive constant can be looked upon as a partial adjustment for the absence of the wage variable.

The price of British government expenditures on goods depends on cost factors and on cyclical factors; the latter varies, as e.g. the second differences in the growth of total expenditures, explain mainly the first years' variation of the price of government expenditures.

When we were first modelling the British economy, our estimation period was 1953–1973. The best ordinary least squares consumption price equation for this period was:

$$\begin{array}{llll} \hat{P}cp_{(UK)} & = -1.900 & + 0.752 w_{-1/2} & - 0.380 q^-, \\ (t) & (4.15) & (12.49) & (-2.31) \\ [F] & [-] & [1.15] & [1.15] \end{array}$$
$$R = 0.97, \quad s^2 = 0.44. \tag{2.82}$$

The last explanatory variable stands for the negative increases in the degree of utilization of productive capacity: $q_t^- := \min\{0, q_t\}$. The reason for this was to investigate whether negative changes of the degree of utilization of capacity have a more significant effect than the degree of utilization itself;[11] this appeared to be so, indeed. Reestimation of this equation over the complete sample period 1953–1975 yielded:

$$\begin{array}{llll} \hat{P}cp_{(UK)} & = -3.030 & + 0.875 w_{-1/2} & - 0.740 q^-, \\ (t) & (-7.07) & (13.93) & (-3.88) \\ [F] & [-] & [29.44] & [29.44] \end{array}$$
$$R = 0.94, \quad s^2 = 0.81. \tag{2.83}$$

To avoid high multicollinearity, we tried several approximations to q^-, but none of these were satisfying. The result chosen was:

$$\begin{array}{lll} \hat{P}cp & = -2.932 & + 0.944 w_{-1/4}, \\ (t) & (-6.33) & (20.87) \end{array}$$
$$R = 0.96, \quad s^2 = 1.275, \quad DW = 1.85, \quad \hat{\rho} = 0.07. \tag{2.84}$$

Finally, equation (2.79), with a strong price-reducing labour productivity impact, has been selected.

Note the important influence of the composite cost variable for British prices of private investments, which is fairly stable over the complete sampling period. The wage determination in the United Kingdom is nearly the same as in the Netherlands, although the low influence of labour productivity is remarkable, the more so as its impact mainly rests only on the crisis years 1974 and 1975; this is compensated, however, by the significantly positive (overall) constant term. In spite of what one would expect, there is no significant influence of strikes on United Kingdom wages.

3. Definitional Equations, Linking and Stability of the Model

In this section, the functioning of the complete model INTERPLAY will be shortly discussed. A comprehensive simulation study, however, tracing the effects of changing monetary exchange rates, fiscal policy variables, other monetary policy variables and government expenditures on the time paths of the principal endogenous variables will be deferred to a subsequent paper. The same can be said as regards decentralized economic policy measures using solution concepts of linear-quadratic six-person nonzero-sum difference games.

3.1. Definitional Equations

To 'close' the submodels and to take important endogenized variables into consideration, the national submodels are completed with definitional equations for, among other things:

- real disposable wage income $(Wd - Pcp)$;
- total expenditures, $e1, e2$;
- prices of total expenditures, $Pe2$;
- labour productivity $(gvampp - EMps)$;
- unit labour costs $H^{(-i)} := w - (gvampp - EMps)_{-i}$;
- lagged endogenous variables with fractional lags smaller than unity.

Some 'definitional' equations in relative growth rates are approximated as linear combinations with weights equal to the average shares over the sampling period of the corresponding right-hand-side variables, as follows.

3.1.1. Belgium

$$(Wd - Pcp)_{(B)} = 0.787w + 0.787EMp + 0.187Wg + 0.015Wr + 0.011TRw - Pcp \quad (3.1)$$

$$e1_{(B)} = 0.551cp + 0.153ip + 0.057eg + 0.231xg + st + (xs - ms) \quad (3.2)$$

The variables st and $(xs - ms)$ are defined as $(\Delta\widetilde{st}/\widetilde{e1}_{-1})$ and $(\Delta(\widetilde{xs} - \widetilde{ms})/\widetilde{e1}_{-1})$ respectively, in order to prevent violent fluctuations in the observation series.

$$(gvampp - EMps)_{(B)} = 1.295e1 - 0.295mg - 0.749EMp - 0.251EMs \quad (3.3)$$

3.1.2. France

$$e2_{(F)} = 0.633cp + 0.183ip + 0.082eg + 0.102xg \quad (3.4)$$

$$Pe2_{(F)} = 0.614Pcp + 0.187Pip + 0.087Peg + 0.112Pxg \quad (3.5)$$

$$e1_{(F)} = 0.970e2 + st + (xs - ms) \quad (3.6)$$

$$(gvamp - EMps)_{(F)} = 1.009e1 + 0.098wg - 0.107mg - 0.701EMp - 0.299EMs \quad (3.7)$$

3.1.3. Federal Republic of Germany

$$(Wd - Pcp)_{(D)} = 0.853w + 0.853EMp + 0.167(Wg + Wr) + 0.252(TRgh + TRrh) - 0.272(TRwg + TDw) - Pcp \quad (3.8)$$

$$e2_{(D)} = 0.539cp + 0.214ip + 0.101eg + 0.146xg \quad (3.9)$$

$$Pe2_{(D)} = 0.540Pcp + 0.194Pip + 0.102Peg + 0.164Pxg \quad (3.10)$$

$$e1_{(D)} = 0.991e2 + st + (xs - ms) \quad (3.11)$$

$$(gvampp - EMps)_{(D)} = 1.120e1 - 0.120mg - 0.765EMp - 0.235EMs \quad (3.12)$$

$$(W - e2)_{(D)} = 0.837w + 0.837EMp + 0.163(Wg + Wr) - e2 \quad (3.13)$$

3.1.4. Italy

$$e2_{(I)} = 0.658cp + 0.196ip + 0.050eg + 0.096xg \quad (3.14)$$

$$Pe2_{(I)} = 0.604Pcp + 0.175Pip + 0.115Peg + 0.106Pxg \quad (3.15)$$

$$e1_{(I)} = 0.977e2 + st + (xs - ms) \quad (3.16)$$

$$(gvampp - EMps)_{(I)} = 1.124e1 - 0.124mg - 0.630EMp - 0.370EMs \quad (3.17)$$

3.1.5. The Netherlands

$$(Wd - Pcp)_{(NL)} = 0.838w + 0.838EMp + 0.211Wg + 0.001Wr - 0.050TRw - Pcp \quad (3.18)$$

$$e2_{(NL)} = 0.504cp + 0.168ip + 0.073eg + 0.255xg \quad (3.19)$$

$$Pe2_{(NL)} = 0.472Pcp + 0.159Pip + 0.075Peg + 0.294Pxg \quad (3.20)$$

$$el_{(NL)} = 0.946e2 + st + (xs - ms) \quad (3.21)$$

$$(e2 - EMps)_{(NL)} = e2 - 0.774EMp - 0.226EMs \quad (3.22)$$

3.1.6. The United Kingdom

$$(Wd - Pcp)_{(UK)} = 0.848w + 0.848EMp + 0.199Wg - 0.047TRw - Pcp \quad (3.23)$$

$$e2_{(UK)} = 0.632cp + 0.116ip + 0.112eg + 0.140xg \quad (3.24)$$

$$Pe2_{(UK)} = 0.628Pcp + 0.124Pip + 0.100Peg + 0.148Pxg \quad (3.25)$$

$$el_{(UK)} = 0.992e2 + st + (xs - ms) \quad (3.26)$$

$$(gvampp - EMps)_{(UK)} = 1.161el - 0.161mg - 0.913EMp - 0.087EMs \quad (3.27)$$

3.2. Linking of the National Submodels

On average, EEC member countries have a trade flow with other member countries of 60% of its total trade. Hence, from an EEC point of view, the measurement of the impact of economic fluctuations from one member country to another is of paramount importance. What happens in one country is felt in the others. While the member countries of the EEC have formally retained a high degree of freedom for their economic policies, such policies can only be effective if they take into account the policies of the partner countries. The need for coordinated action manifests itself more and more.

In order to perform such studies,[12] a set of interrelated macroeconomic models for the EEC countries is necessary to have a clear insight into the consequences of available alternatives. Therefore, the six national submodels will be linked to each other. Important links are bilateral trade flows, prices of bilateral trade flows, bilateral capital flows and labour migrations. Attention is concentrated on trade flows and the corresponding prices.[13] According to Ranuzzi [22], there are three types of linkage models:

(i) *direct linkage based on bilateral trade flows,* where the bilateral flows of goods are supposed to depend positively on the domestic demand (demand of the importing country) and negatively on the export prices of the individual suppliers (exporting countries);[14] this type of linkage presumes the assumption that all countries linked together form one market, so that a more direct influence of the transmission mechanism among member countries can be shown;[15]

(ii) *import allocation models,* where a separation is performed between the determination of domestic production and imported goods on the one hand and the allocation of total imports over the various exporting countries on the other hand; hence the problem is separated into two steps, the first being an allocation of expenditures between domestic commodities and foreign commodities[16] and the second the distribution of commodities according to their origin, given the total imports determined in the first step;[17]

(iii) *the world trade approach,* where bilateral trade is not directly explained but where:
- the volume of imports of a country is determined by domestic factors and the ratio between the import price and the domestic price,
- the volume of world trade is determined as a weighted average of the individual countries' import volumes,
- the volume of exports of a country is determined by the global volume of world trade, the ratio between the export price and the competitive export price, and other factors.[18]

The linking of the INTERPLAY national submodels is of the import allocation type. If, for example, a generalized C.E.S. utility function is maximized subject to an import addivity constraint per country, or

$$\max_{\{\widetilde{mg}\$_{ij}\}} U_i := \left(\sum_j \delta_{ij} \widetilde{mg}\$_{ij}^{\rho_i}\right)^{\nu_i/\rho_i}$$

subject to

$$\widetilde{Mg}\$_i = \widetilde{mg}\$_i \cdot \widetilde{Pmg}\$_i = \sum_j \widetilde{mg}\$_{ij} \cdot \widetilde{Pmg}\$_{ij}$$
$$\rho_i < 1, \quad \nu_i > 0; \quad \forall_j : \delta_{ij} > 0 \tag{3.28}$$

yields a 'basically log-linear' import allocation relationship, being homogeneous of degree zero in both prices and homogeneous of degree one in total commodity imports, but with variable 'shares', which are non-linear in the bilateral prices, i.e.

$$\widetilde{mg}\$_{ij} = \alpha_{ij} \cdot \widetilde{mg}\$_i \cdot \left(\frac{\widetilde{Pmg}\$_{ij}}{\widetilde{Pmg}\$_i}\right)^{-1} \tag{3.29}$$

with non-constant shares α_{ij} being equal to:[19]

$$\alpha_{ij} := \frac{\left(\dfrac{\widetilde{Pmg}\$_{ij}^{\rho_i}}{\delta_{ij}}\right)^{1/\rho_i - 1}}{\sum_k \left(\dfrac{\widetilde{Pmg}\$_{ik}^{\rho_i}}{\delta_{ik}}\right)^{1/\rho_i - 1}} = \frac{\widetilde{mg}\$_{ij} \widetilde{Pmg}\$_{ij}}{\widetilde{mg}\$_i \widetilde{Pmg}\$_i} \tag{3.30}$$

where $\widetilde{Mg}\$_{ij}$ is the value of the commodity imports of country i from country j, measured in dollars;

$\widetilde{Mg}\$_i$ is the value of the total imports of goods of country i, measured in dollars;

$\widetilde{Pmg}\$_i$ is the dollar price index of total imports (1970 = 100); and

$\widetilde{Pmg}\$_{ij}$ is the dollar price index of bilateral imports $Mg\$_{ij}$ (1970 = 100).

Since $\widetilde{Pmg}\$_i$ and $\widetilde{Pmg}\$_{ij}$ are price indices (and not real prices) with base year 1970, the volumes of commodity imports are measured in dollar prices of 1970, or

$\widetilde{mg}\$_{ij}$ is the volume of imports of goods of country i from country j, measured in 1970 dollars, and

$\widetilde{mg}\$_i$ is the volume of the total imports of goods of country i, measured in 1970 dollars.

Further relevant variables can be introduced, such as:

- the gross domestic product per capita ($\tilde{y}\$$) – the higher per capita income is, the more the demand for foreign commodities will be diversified [15];
- the long-term interest rate ($\widetilde{Rl}$), as a cost variable for the importer – cost of credit warranty on exports and imports;
- the per capita wage rate of the private sector ($\tilde{w}\$$), which is an income variable – a (relative) wage increase is demand rising.

Assuming a general log-linear relationship for the bilateral trade flows and allowing for general polynomial lags in the lag operator B, we have:

$$mg\$_{ij,t} = \alpha_0 + \alpha_1(B)(Pmg\$_{ij} - Pmg\$_i)_t + \alpha_2(B)mg\$_{i,t} + \alpha_3(B)y\$_{i,t} + \alpha_4(B)\Delta\widetilde{Rl}_{i,t} + \alpha_5(B)w\$_{i,t} + \epsilon_{ij,t}. \tag{3.31}$$

Now, the bilateral prices have to be specified, since direct observation is very cumbersome.[20]

Taking into account that import flows are measured in c.i.f. prices and export flows are measured in f.o.b. prices and allowing for price discrimination among various alternative importing countries, the bilateral trade flow price can be approximated by a geometric mean in import and export prices, or

$$\Delta \ln \widetilde{Pmg}\$_{ij,t} = \alpha_{ij}\Delta \ln \widetilde{Pmg}\$_{i,t} + (1-\alpha_{ij})\Delta \ln \widetilde{Pxg}\$_{j,t}, \tag{3.32}$$

where α_{ij} is the relative market share of country j in the total commodity imports of country i, measured in value terms and supposed to be approximately constant over time.[21]

Since in general:

$$\Delta \ln \tilde{X}_t = \ln \tilde{X}_t - \ln \tilde{X}_{t-1} = \ln \frac{\tilde{X}_t}{\tilde{X}_{t-1}} = \ln\left(1 + \frac{\Delta\tilde{X}_t}{\tilde{X}_{t-1}}\right)$$

$$= \ln(1 + X_t) \approx X_t = \frac{\Delta\tilde{X}_t}{\tilde{X}_{t-1}}, \tag{3.34}$$

if $|X_t| \ll 1$, we find for (3.32) in relative annual changes:

$$Pmg\$_{ij,\,t} \approx \alpha_{ij} Pmg\$_{i,\,t} + (1-\alpha_{ij}) Pxg\$_{j,\,t}. \tag{3.35}$$

Since the importing price $\widetilde{Pmg}\$_i$ can be defined as a weighted arithmetic mean of the bilateral price indices:

$$\widetilde{Pmg}\$_{i,\,t} = \sum_{j \neq i} \frac{\widetilde{mg}\$_{ij,\,t}}{\widetilde{mg}\$_{i,\,t}} \cdot \widetilde{Pmg}\$_{ij,\,t}, \tag{3.36}$$

the relative growth rates of the import prices can be expressed as:

$$\begin{aligned} Pmg\$_{i,\,t} &= \frac{\widetilde{Pmg}\$_{i,\,t}}{\widetilde{Pmg}\$_{i,\,t-1}} - 1 = \sum_{j \neq i} \frac{\widetilde{mg}\$_{ij,\,t} \cdot \widetilde{Pmg}\$_{ij,\,t}}{\widetilde{mg}\$_{i,\,t} \cdot \widetilde{Pmg}\$_{i,\,t-1}} - 1 \\ &= \sum_{j \neq i} \frac{\widetilde{mg}\$_{ij,\,t}}{\widetilde{mg}\$_{i,\,t}} \cdot \frac{\widetilde{Pmg}\$_{ij,\,t-1}}{\widetilde{Pmg}\$_{i,\,t-1}} (1 + Pmg\$_{ij,\,t}) - 1 \\ &= \sum_{j \neq i} \frac{\widetilde{mg}\$_{ij,\,t}}{\widetilde{mg}\$_{i,\,t}} \cdot \frac{\widetilde{Pmg}\$_{ij,\,t-1}}{\widetilde{Pmg}\$_{i,\,t-1}} - 1 \\ &\quad + \sum_{j \neq i} \frac{\widetilde{mg}\$_{ij,\,t}}{\widetilde{mg}\$_{i,\,t}} \cdot \frac{\widetilde{Pmg}\$_{ij,\,t-1}}{\widetilde{Pmg}\$_{i,\,t-1}} \cdot Pmg\$_{ij,\,t}. \end{aligned} \tag{3.37}$$

Assuming that successive relative prices do not change too much,[22] i.e., if

$$\frac{\widetilde{Pmg}\$_{ij,\,t}}{\widetilde{Pmg}\$_{i,\,t}} \approx \frac{\widetilde{Pmg}\$_{ij,\,t-1}}{\widetilde{Pmg}\$_{i,\,t-1}}. \tag{3.38}$$

the first term on the right-hand side of (3.37) is approximately the relative market share of country j in the total commodity imports of country i, measured in dollar value terms.

So the assumed constancy over time of this relative market share, as considered in (3.32), transforms (3.37) into an expression where in the relative growth rates of the import prices are approximated by a convex combination of the relative growth rates of the bilateral trade prices, the weights being the relative market shares α_{ij}, or:

$$Pmg\$_{i,\,t} \approx \sum_{j \neq i} \alpha_{ij} Pmg\$_{ij,\,t}. \tag{3.39}$$

Substituting (3.35) into (3.39), and replacing the approximation signs by equalities, the import price changes of country i can be expressed as a convex combination of the export price changes of all the (other) exporters, or:

$$\begin{aligned} Pmg\$_{i,\,t} &= Pmg\$_{i,\,t} \sum_{j \neq i} \alpha_{ij}^2 + \sum_{j \neq i} \alpha_{ij}(1-\alpha_{ij}) Pxg\$_{j,\,t} \\ &= \sum_{j \neq i} \gamma_{ij} Pxg\$_{j,\,t},^{23} \end{aligned} \tag{3.40}$$

with relative weights γ_{ij} given by

$$\gamma_{ij} := \frac{\alpha_{ij}(1-\alpha_{ij})}{1-\sum_{j\neq i}\alpha_{ij}^2} > 0 \quad \text{and} \quad \sum_{j\neq i}\gamma_{ij} = 1. \tag{3.41}$$

Now, the relative growth rates of the prices of the bilateral trade flows $\widetilde{mg\$}_{ij}$ can be expressed as a function of the individual growth rates of the export prices by substituting (3.40) into (3.35):

$$\begin{aligned} Pmg\$_{ij,t} &= \alpha_{ij}\left(\gamma_{ij}Pxg\$_{j,t} + \sum_{\substack{k\neq i\\k\neq j}}\gamma_{ik}Pxg\$_{k,t}\right) + (1-\alpha_{ij})Pxg\$_{j,t} \\ &= (1-\alpha_{ij})\,\frac{1-\sum_{\substack{k\neq i\\k\neq j}}\alpha_{ik}^2}{1-\sum_{k\neq i}\alpha_{ik}^2}\,Pxg\$_{j,t} \\ &\quad + \alpha_{ij}\sum_{\substack{k\neq i\\k\neq j}}\gamma_{ik}Pxg\$_{k,t}. \end{aligned} \tag{3.42}$$

Since the weights of all export price changes in (3.42) also sum to unity, the relative price changes of the bilateral trade flows can be approximated as a convex combination of all the exporters' relative price changes of their commodity exports.[24]

Some important results of these computations will now be presented for the sampling period, together with a computation of (3.40),[25] taking account of the fact that the 'unit value index world export, all commodities' is considered as a valid approximation to the export price index of the rest of the world ($\widetilde{Pxg\$}_R$).[26]

Belgium–Luxembourg:

$$\begin{aligned} Pmg\$_{B,F} &= 0.868Pxg\$_F + 0.036Pxg\$_D + 0.006Pxg\$_I \\ &\quad + 0.032Pxg_{NL} + 0.011Pxg\$_{UK} + 0.047Pxg\$_R, \end{aligned} \tag{3.43}$$

$$\begin{aligned} Pmg\$_{B,D} &= 0.039Pxg\$_F + 0.827Pxg\$_D + 0.008Pxg\$_I \\ &\quad + 0.045Pxg\$_{NL} + 0.016Pxg\$_{UK} + 0.065Pxg\$_R, \end{aligned} \tag{3.44}$$

$$\begin{aligned} Pmg\$_{B,NL} &= 0.033Pxg\$_F + 0.043Pxg\$_D + 0.007Pxg\$_I \\ &\quad + 0.847Pxg\$_{NL} + 0.014Pxg\$_{UK} + 0.056Pxg\$_R, \end{aligned} \tag{3.45}$$

$$\begin{aligned} Pmg\$_B &= 0.175Pxg\$_F + 0.226Pxg\$_D + 0.035Pxg\$_I \\ &\quad + 0.201Pxg\$_{NL} + 0.071Pxg\$_{UK} + 0.291Pxg\$_R, \end{aligned} \tag{3.46}$$

$$Pxg\$_B = Pxg_B - MR_B \quad \text{and} \quad Pmg = Pmg\$_B + MR_B. \tag{3.47}$$

France:

$$Pmg\$_{F,B} = 0.923Pxg\$_B + 0.022Pxg\$_D + 0.010Pxg\$_I + 0.005Pxg\$_{NL} + 0.005Pxg\$_{UK} + 0.035Pxg\$_R, \tag{3.48}$$

$$Pmg\$_{F,D} = 0.025Pxg\$_B + 0.858Pxg\$_D + 0.021Pxg\$_I + 0.011Pxg\$_{NL} + 0.011Pxg\$_{UK} + 0.075Pxg\$_R, \tag{3.49}$$

$$Pmg\$_{F,I} = 0.010Pxg\$_B + 0.018Pxg\$_D + 0.935Pxg\$_I + 0.004Pxg\$_{NL} + 0.004Pxg\$_{UK} + 0.029Pxg\$_R, \tag{3.50}$$

$$Pmg\$_{F,NL} = 0.005Pxg\$_B + 0.010Pxg\$_D + 0.004Pxg\$_I + 0.963Pxg\$_{NL} + 0.002Pxg\$_{UK} + 0.015Pxg\$_R, \tag{3.51}$$

$$Pmg\$_F = 0.131Pxg\$_B + 0.247Pxg\$_D + 0.109Pxg\$_I + 0.060Pxg\$_{NL} + 0.059Pxg\$_{UK} + 0.395Pxg\$_R, \tag{3.52}$$

$$Pxg\$_F = Pxg_F - MR_F \quad \text{and} \quad Pmg_F = Pmg\$_F + MR_F. \tag{3.53}$$

Federal Republic of Germany:

$$Pmg\$_{D,B} = 0.924Pxg\$_B + 0.012Pxg\$_F + 0.010Pxg\$_I + 0.016Pxg\$_{NL} + 0.004Pxg\$_{UK} + 0.034Pxg\$_R, \tag{3.54}$$

$$Pmg\$_{D,F} = 0.011Pxg\$_B + 0.923Pxg\$_F + 0.011Pxg\$_I + 0.016Pxg\$_{NL} + 0.004Pxg\$_{UK} + 0.035Pxg\$_R, \tag{3.55}$$

$$Pmg\$_{D,NL} = 0.016Pxg\$_B + 0.017Pxg\$_F + 0.015Pxg\$_I + 0.896Pxg\$_{NL} + 0.006Pxg\$_{UK} + 0.050Pxg\$_R, \tag{3.56}$$

$$Pmg\$_D = 0.129Pxg\$_B + 0.132Pxg\$_F + 0.120Pxg\$_I + 0.181Pxg\$_{NL} + 0.044Pxg\$_{UK} + 0.393Pxg\$_R, \tag{3.57}$$

$$Pxg\$_D = Pxg_D - MR_D \quad \text{and} \quad Pmg_D = Pmg\$_D + MR_D. \tag{3.58}$$

Italy:

$$\begin{aligned} Pmg\$_{I,D} &= 0.008Pxg\$_B + 0.025Pxg\$_F + 0.886Pxg\$_D \\ &\quad + 0.011Pxg\$_{NL} + 0.007Pxg\$_{UK} + 0.062Pxg\$_R, \end{aligned} \tag{3.59}$$

$$\begin{aligned} Pmg\$_I &= 0.056Pxg\$_B + 0.172Pxg\$_F + 0.230Pxg\$_D \\ &\quad + 0.075Pxg\$_{NL} + 0.049Pxg\$_{UK} + 0.418Pxg\$_R, \end{aligned} \tag{3.60}$$

$$Pxg\$_I = Pxg_I - MR_I \quad \text{and} \quad Pmg_I = Pmg\$_I + MR_I. \tag{3.61}$$

The Netherlands:

$$\begin{aligned} Pmg\$_{NL,B} &= 0.873Pxg\$_B + 0.013Pxg\$_F + 0.043Pxg\$_D \\ &\quad + 0.006Pxg\$_I + 0.011Pxg\$_{UK} + 0.055Pxg\$_R, \end{aligned} \tag{3.62}$$

$$\begin{aligned} Pmg\$_{NL,F} &= 0.012Pxg\$_B + 0.942Pxg\$_F + 0.017Pxg\$_D \\ &\quad + 0.002Pxg\$_I + 0.004Pxg\$_{UK} + 0.022Pxg\$_R, \end{aligned} \tag{3.63}$$

$$\begin{aligned} Pmg\$_{NL,D} &= 0.049Pxg\$_B + 0.022Pxg\$_F + 0.809Pxg\$_D \\ &\quad + 0.010Pxg\$_I + 0.018Pxg\$_{UK} + 0.092Pxg\$_R, \end{aligned} \tag{3.64}$$

$$\begin{aligned} Pmg\$_{NL} &= 0.187Pxg\$_B + 0.084Pxg\$_F + 0.276Pxg\$_D \\ &\quad + 0.036Pxg\$_I + 0.067Pxg\$_{UK} + 0.349Pxg\$_R, \end{aligned} \tag{3.65}$$

$$\begin{aligned} Pxg\$_{NL} &= Pxg_{NL} - MR_{NL} \quad \text{and} \\ Pmg_{NL} &= Pmg\$_{NL} + MR_{NL}. \end{aligned} \tag{3.66}$$

United Kingdom:

$$\begin{aligned} Pmg\$_{UK} &= 0.064Pxg\$_B + 0.112Pxg\$_F + 0.151Pxg\$_D \\ &\quad + 0.063Pxg\$_I + 0.151Pxg\$_{NL} + 0.459Pxg\$_R, \end{aligned} \tag{3.67}$$

$$\begin{aligned} Pxg\$_{UK} &= Pxg_{UK} - MR_{UK} \quad \text{and} \\ Pmg_{UK} &= Pmg\$_{UK} + MR_{UK} \end{aligned} \tag{3.68}$$

The smaller the relative market share of a particular exporting country on a specific importing market is, the nearer to unity is the coefficient belonging to the export price of the exporting country ('diagonal element') and the more other linkage studies can be approximated. Inspecting the above definitional equations, the dominating impact of the German export market is striking, principally for Dutch imports, but also for the other EEC-importing markets. The influence of 'the rest of the world' is particularly important for UK import prices.

Very small influences can be observed of Italian export price changes on Belgian bilateral price changes, Dutch and UK export prices on French (bilateral) importing prices, UK export prices on German bilateral prices and Italian export prices on Dutch bilateral prices. Remarkable also is that the postwar Dutch economy seems to have a larger impact on German imports than the postwar French economy has (principally in the beginning and at the end of the sampling period).

Note that the more the particular EEC markets are integrated, the less are the weights belonging to the 'export price change of the rest of the world'; since integration is progressing, one may expect these coefficients to be continually decreasing. This, indeed, has been observed for the last sampling years, during the seventies; together with this increasing 'integration effect', the impact of the German export market on all other EEC import markets considered has still risen.[27]

How has intra-Community trade reacted to the hectic oil price increases in 1973? To study this phenomenon, consider table 3.69, where the increase (+) or the decrease (–) of a weight belonging to $Pxg\$_j$ in the definitional equation of $Pmg\$_i$ is shown when extending the sampling period from 1953–1973 to 1953–1975.

Table 3.69. Change of 'integration effect' due to 1974 and 1975.

i	*j*						
	BL	F	D	I	NL	UK	Rest
BL	–	0.041	0.026	0.009	0.034	0.000	–0.109
F	0.033	–	0.005	0.012	0.001	–0.013	–0.037
D	0.002	–0.016	–	0.009	0.019	–0.006	–0.012
I	–0.002	0.010	0.006	–	0.007	–0.016	–0.007
NL	–0.014	0.029	0.026	0.009	–	0.001	–0.050
UK	0.014	0.005	0.020	0.009	–0.037	–	–0.013

Hence, extension of the sampling period to 1974 and 1975 teaches us that:

- EEC integration advances and the impact of the rest of the world recedes;
- the impacts of the German and Italian exporting markets increase on all the EEC importing markets studied;
- the French influence on EEC import price increases has also risen, except for the important German importing market;
- the Dutch impact on the other EEC markets is also increasing, except for a

steep decrease on the UK importing market; and

– UK membership of the EEC had not yet had very much effect in 1974 and 1975.

The behavioural and other definitional equations of the linking block of INTERPLAY are briefly discussed now. For this a variable $Pmg\$_{i\backslash j}$ is defined as the (average) increase of the import prices of country i, except for the influence of the import price increase of a trade flow originating from country j. Mathematically:

$$Pmg\$_{i\backslash j,\,t} = \sum_{\substack{k\neq i\\ k\neq j}} \frac{\alpha_{ik}}{1-\alpha_{ij}}\, Pmg\$_{ik,\,t}. \tag{3.70}$$

Hence the variable $(Pmg\$_{ij,\,t} - Pmg\$_{i\backslash j,\,t})$, representing the measure by which bilateral prices increase faster than the (average) import prices of the trade flows originating from the other exporting countries, can be rewritten, using (3.39) and (3.35) respectively, as:

$$(Pmg\$_{ij,\,t} - Pmg\$_{i\backslash j,\,t}) = Pmg\$_{ij,\,t} - \sum_{\substack{k\neq i\\ k\neq j}} \frac{\alpha_{ik}}{1-\alpha_{ij}}\, Pmg\$_{ik,\,t}$$

$$\overset{(3.39)}{=} Pmg\$_{ij,\,t} - \frac{Pmg\$_{i,\,t} - \alpha_{ij} Pmg\$_{ij,\,t}}{1-\alpha_{ij}}$$

$$= \frac{Pmg\$_{ij,\,t} - Pmg\$_{i,\,t}}{1-\alpha_{ij}}$$

$$\overset{(3.35)}{=} \frac{\alpha_{ij} Pmg\$_{i,\,t} + (1-\alpha_{ij}) Pxg\$_{j,\,t} - Pmg\$_{i,\,t}}{1-\alpha_{ij}}$$

$$= Pxg\$_{j,\,t} - Pmg\$_{i,\,t}, \tag{3.71}$$

or the change of the relative competitiveness of the bilateral trade can be measured by the changing terms of trade.[28] which should have a negative impact on the changing volume of the bilateral trade considered.

In order to estimate relationship (3.31) for the bilateral trade flows, the observations of these flows have to be computed first from the observed nominal bilateral trade flows, divided by the bilateral prices, being computed as indicated in (3.42) (see (3.43–3.68)). Ordinary least squares estimation for the complete sampling period 1973–1975 yields the following.

3.2.1. The Belgian–Luxembourg Economic Union (BLEU)

$$\widehat{mg\$}_{BL,\,F} = -\,1.349(Pxg\$_F - Pmg\$_B) + 1.385\, mg\$_{BL}$$

(t)	$(-\,3.90)$	(16.87)
$[F]$	$[4.52]$	$[0.30]$

$$- 5.213\,\Delta\tilde{R}l_F,$$
$$(-4.08)$$
$$[4.33]$$

$$R = 0.97, \quad DET = 0.68, \quad DW = 1.96. \qquad (3.72)$$

$$\widehat{mg\$}_{BL,\,D} = \underset{\substack{(2.47)\\ [-]}}{6.000} - \underset{\substack{(-2.35)\\ [4.11]}}{0.388} Pxg\$_{D_{-1}} + \underset{\substack{(4.77)\\ [4.11]}}{0.892}\, mg\$_{BL} - \underset{\substack{(-2.51)\\ [-]}}{11.344} DU'59,$$

(t), [F]

$$R = 0.96, \quad DET = 0.70, \quad DW = 1.77. \qquad (3.73)$$

$$\widehat{mg\$}_{BL,\,I} = \underset{\substack{(9.38)\\ [-]}}{14.434} - \underset{\substack{(-3.71)\\ [0.15]}}{2.172}(Pxg\$_I - Pmg\$_B) - \underset{\substack{(-2.78)\\ [0.15]}}{0.487} Pmg\$_{B_{-1}} + \underset{\substack{(2.66)\\ [-]}}{19.036} DU'57,$$

(t), [F]

$$R = 0.93, \quad DET = 0.96, \quad DW = 1.35. \qquad (3.74)$$

$$\widehat{mg\$}_{BL,\,NL} = \underset{\substack{(4.50)\\ [0.50]}}{0.407}\, mg\$_{BL,\,NL_{-1}} + \underset{\substack{(5.44)\\ [0.50]}}{0.528}\, mg\$_{BL} + \underset{\substack{(4.00)\\ [-]}}{11.648} DU'71, \qquad (3.75)$$

(t), [F]

$$R = 0.97, \quad DET = 0.95.$$

$$\widehat{mg\$}_{BL,\,UK} = \underset{\substack{(3.41)\\ [1.97]}}{0.784}\, mg\$_{BL} + \underset{\substack{(1.99)\\ [1.97]}}{0.882}(w\$_B - w\$_{UK}),$$

(t), [F]

$$R = 0.74, \quad DET = 0.91, \quad DW = 2.51. \qquad (3.76)$$

If French long-term interest rates increase, the cost of exporting credits becomes greater, so less can be exported from France (e.g. to BLEU). Belgian imports from the United Kingdom vary very irregularly, such that explanation is very hard; the relative wage advantage variable should be viewed as a relative income advantage for Belgian importers, or, alternatively, as a lower wage cost for UK products so that UK exports to the BLEU are being stimulated.

3.2.2. France

$$\begin{array}{llll} \widehat{mg\$}_{F,BL} = & 7.028 - 0.626 Pmg\$_{F,B_{-1}} & + 1.044 mg\$_F & \\ (t) & (3.22)(-4.20) & (5.88) & \\ [F] & [-] \quad [2.35] & [2.57] & \\ & + 0.485(w\$_F - w\$_B) & - 13.091 DU'59, & \\ & (1.77) & (-2.01) & \\ & [0.65] & [-] & \end{array}$$

$$R = 0.97, \quad DET = 0.62, \quad DW = 2.17. \qquad (3.77)$$

$$\begin{array}{llll} \widehat{mg\$}_{F,D} = & 6.662 - 0.481 Pmg\$_{F,D_{-1}} & + 0.876 mg\$_F & \\ (t) & (3.80)(-3.27) & (6.48) & \\ [F] & [-] \quad [4.57] & [3.39] & \\ & -2.287(\Delta\tilde{R}l_F - \Delta\tilde{R}l_D), & & \\ & (2.22) & & \\ & [1.02] & & \end{array}$$

$$R = 0.97, \quad DET = 0.68, \quad DW = 1.55. \qquad (3.78)$$

$$\begin{array}{llllll} \widehat{mg\$}_{F,I} = & -7.221 & + 1.856 mg\$_F & + 1.558 y\$_{F_{-1}} & - 7.518 \Delta\tilde{R}l_F & \\ (t) & (-2.05) & (7.01) & (3.28) & (-2.82) & \\ [F] & [-] & [1.15] & [0.25] & [1.53] & \\ & + 43.534 DU'59, & & & & \\ & (4.41) & & & & \\ & [-] & & & & \end{array}$$

$$R = 0.95, \quad DET = 0.73, \quad DW = 1.18. \qquad (3.79)$$

$$\begin{array}{llll} \widehat{mg\$}_{F,NL} = & -0.375 Pmg\$_F & + 1.135 mg\$_F & + 1.180 y\$_{NL}, \\ (t) & (-1.76) & (4.45) & (1.86) \\ [F] & [0.15] & [0.87] & [0.90] \end{array}$$

$$R = 0.88, \quad DET = 0.91, \quad DW = 1.89. \qquad (3.80)$$

$$\begin{array}{lll} \widehat{mg\$}_{F,UK} = & 1.243 mg\$_F & - 25.227 DU'57, \\ (t) & (6.53) & (-2.41) \end{array}$$

$$R = 0.83, \quad DW = 2.28. \qquad (3.81)$$

In 1959, there seems to have been a substitution of Belgian exports to France by Italian exports (EEC or De Gaulle effect?); this is also illustrated by the very elastic response of French–Italian bilateral imports when France is increasing its total imports.

3.2.3. Federal Republic of Germany

$$\begin{array}{llll} \widehat{mg\$}_{D,BL} = & 3.436 y\$_D & - 7.936 \Delta\tilde{R}l_B & - 27.069 DU'56, \\ (t) & (9.93) & (-2.38) & (-2.90) \\ [F] & [0.22] & [0.22] & [-] \end{array}$$

$$R = 0.91, \quad DET = 0.98, \quad DW = 1.30. \tag{3.82}$$

$$\begin{array}{llll} \widehat{mg\$}_{D,F} = & -0.273 Pxg\$_F & +0.636 mg\$_D & +2.059 y\$_D \\ (t) & (-1.89) & (3.31) & (4.63) \\ [F] & [1.90] & [5.45] & [4.57] \end{array}$$

$$\begin{array}{ll} -2.473 \Delta\tilde{R}l_D & -21.693 DU'56, \\ (-1.76) & (-3.63) \\ [1.60] & [-] \end{array}$$

$$R = 0.97, \quad DET = 0.30, \quad DW = 1.80. \tag{3.83}$$

$$\begin{array}{llllll} \widehat{mg\$}_{D,I} = & 6.861 & -0.686 Pxg\$_I & +0.874 mg\$_D & +24.385 DU'65, \\ (t) & (2.14) & (-3.16) & (3.92) & (3.40) \\ [F] & [-] & [2.52] & [2.52] & [-] \end{array}$$

$$R = 0.95, \quad DET = 0.80, \quad DW = 2.16. \tag{3.84}$$

$$\begin{array}{llll} \widehat{mg\$}_{D,NL} = & 7.819 & -0.336 Pmg\$_{D_{-1}} & +0.579 mg\$_D \\ (t) & (3.43) & (-2.63) & (3.43) \\ [F] & [-] & [4.14] & [6.01] \end{array}$$

$$\begin{array}{l} -3.418 (\Delta\tilde{R}l_D - \Delta\tilde{R}l_{NL})_{-1}, \\ (-1.98) \\ [2.00] \end{array}$$

$$R = 0.96, \quad DET = 0.59, \quad DW = 1.22. \tag{3.85}$$

$$\begin{array}{llll} \widehat{mg\$}_{D,UK} = & 12.889 & -0.906 Pmg\$_{D_{-1}} & -0.196 mg\$_{D,UK_{-1}} \\ (t) & (5.11) & (-4.27) & (-1.27) \\ [F] & [-] & [3.03] & [0.16] \end{array}$$

$$\begin{array}{l} -6.457 (\Delta\tilde{R}l_D - \Delta\tilde{R}l_{UK})_{-1}, \\ (-3.89) \\ [2.95] \end{array}$$

$$R = 0.88, \quad DET = 0.76. \tag{3.86}$$

If German importers experience an unfavourable interest cost development, they try to postpone imports until a later period, or, alternatively, they try to substitute trade flows.

3.2.4. Italy

$$\begin{array}{lll} \widehat{mg\$}_{I,BL} = & 1.299 mg\$_I & -7.566 \Delta\tilde{R}l_B, \\ (t) & (10.05) & (-2.26) \end{array}$$

$$R = 0.91, \quad DET = 1.00, \quad DW = 1.36. \tag{3.87}$$

$$\begin{array}{lll} \widehat{mg\$}_{I,F} = & 1.245 mg\$_I & +63.314 DU'59, \\ (t) & (7.65) & (5.24) \end{array}$$

$$R = 0.91, \quad DW = 1.87. \tag{3.88}$$

$$\widehat{mg\$}_{I,D} = -8.812 + 1.227\, mg\$_I + 1.840\, y\$_{I_{-1}} - 3.437\, \Delta\tilde{R}l_D,$$
$$\begin{array}{llll} (t) & (-2.41)\ (10.79) & (2.80) & (-2.34) \\ [F] & [-]\quad [1.91] & [0.30] & [1.75] \end{array}$$

$$R = 0.96, \quad DET = 0.84, \quad DW = 2.26. \qquad (3.89)$$

$$\widehat{mg\$}_{I,NL} = 0.504\, mg\$_I + 2.743\, y\$_{NL} + 1.111\,(w\$_I - w\$_{NL}),$$
$$\begin{array}{llll} (t) & (3.61) & (5.75) & (2.92) \\ [F] & [2.31] & [1.42] & [1.25] \end{array}$$

$$R = 0.94, \quad DET = 0.81, \quad DW = 2.46. \qquad (3.90)$$

$$\widehat{mg\$}_{I,UK} = 7.769 + 0.945\, mg\$_I + 0.997(w\$_I - w\$_{UK})$$
$$\begin{array}{llll} (t) & (-2.26) & (4.64) & (1.81) \\ [F] & [-] & [0.63] & [0.92] \end{array}$$
$$- 4.409(\Delta\tilde{R}l_I - \Delta\tilde{R}l_{UK})_{-1} + 36.456\, DU'53,$$
$$\begin{array}{ll} (-2.12) & (3.24) \\ [0.36] & [-] \end{array}$$

$$R = 0.88, \quad DET = 0.86, \quad DW = 2.01. \qquad (3.91)$$

As was already indicated for French imports from Italy, the bilateral trade between France and Italy was considerably increased in 1959, when President De Gaulle had been just a few months in power and when the European Commission began its activities. Relative wage costs are important for Dutch and British exports to Italy.

3.2.5. The Netherlands

$$\widehat{mg\$}_{NL,BL} = -0.251\, Pmg\$_{NL} + 1.027\, mg\$_{NL} + 17.486\, DU'72,$$
$$\begin{array}{llll} (t) & (-2.44) & (10.49) & (3.25) \\ [F] & [1.55] & [1.55] & [-] \end{array}$$

$$R = 0.93, \quad DET = 0.89, \quad DW = 1.57. \qquad (3.92)$$

$$\widehat{mg\$}_{NL,F} = 1.349\, mg\$_{NL} + 32.256\, DU'59,$$
$$\begin{array}{lll} (t) & (7.27) & (3.19) \end{array}$$

$$R = 0.89, \quad DW = 2.71, \quad \hat{\rho} = -0.356. \qquad (3.93)$$

$$\widehat{mg\$}_{NL,D} = 2.601 - 0.268\, Pxg\$_D + 1.168\, mg\$_{NL}$$
$$\begin{array}{llll} (t) & (2.19) & (-2.88) & (12.87) \\ [F] & [-] & [1.37] & [1.37] \end{array}$$
$$- 5.697\, DU'65,$$
$$\begin{array}{l} (-1.93) \\ [-] \end{array}$$

$$R = 0.99, \quad DET = 0.89, \quad DW = 2.09. \qquad (3.94)$$

$$\widehat{mg\$}_{NL,I} = \underset{\substack{(1.56)\\ [-]}}{7.405} - \underset{\substack{(-4.04)\\ [0.79]}}{0.841} Pxg\$_I + \underset{\substack{(2.65)\\ [0.79]}}{2.155} y\$_{I_{-1}} + \underset{\substack{(2.20)\\ [-]}}{15.999} DU'56,$$

$R = 0.95, \quad DET = 0.93, \quad DW = 1.58.$ (3.95)

$$\widehat{mg\$}_{NL,UK} = -\underset{\substack{(-2.28)\\ [1.97]}}{0.993} (Pxg\$_{UK} - Pmg\$_{NL}) + \underset{\substack{(5.76)\\ [0.86]}}{0.816} mg\$_{NL}$$

$$-\underset{\substack{(-1.89)\\ [2.84]}}{3.091} (\Delta\tilde{R}l_{NL} - \Delta\tilde{R}l_{UK})_{-1},$$

$R = 0.84, \quad DET = 0.78, \quad DW = 2.58.$ (3.96)

The EEC effect and the 'De Gaulle' effect are present, this time for the Dutch imports from France in 1959. The very good fit for the important German exports to the Netherlands is striking; it is also a good example of a pure import allocation model.

The Suez crisis in 1956 stimulates the Italian economy to look for other selling markets (e.g. the Netherlands), to be attained via the sea ports. As Dutch (long-term) interest costs have increased more quickly than UK interest costs, the (relative) financing burden for Dutch importers from the United Kingdom has become heavier.

3.2.6. The United Kingdom

$$\widehat{mg\$}_{UK,BL} = \underset{(3.35)}{1.183} mg\$_{UK_{-1}} + \underset{(2.20)}{25.889} DU'72,$$

$R = 0.68, \quad DW = 1.75.$ (3.97)

$$\widehat{mg\$}_{UK,F} = \underset{\substack{(2.58)\\ [2.72]}}{0.852} mg\$_{UK} + \underset{\substack{(3.90)\\ [0.18]}}{1.273} y\$_{F_{-1}}$$

$$+ \underset{\substack{(2.68)\\ [2.11]}}{5.324} (\Delta\tilde{R}l_{UK} - \Delta\tilde{R}l_F) - \underset{\substack{(-3.17)\\ [-]}}{27.070} DU'56,$$

$R = 0.89, \quad DET = 0.69, \quad DW = 1.65.$ (3.98)

$$\widehat{mg\$}_{UK,D} = -\underset{\substack{(-1.68)\\ [0.85]}}{0.538} (Pxg\$_D - Pmg\$_{UK}) + \underset{\substack{(3.62)\\ [0.28]}}{1.022} mg\$_{UK}$$

$$+ \underset{\substack{(2.52)\\ [0.60]}}{0.700} mg\$_{UK_{-1}} + \underset{\substack{(1.92)\\ [0.72]}}{0.458} w\$_{UK_{-1}},$$

The rows labelled (t) and [F] give the t-values and F-values, respectively, beneath each coefficient.

$$R = 0.87, \quad DET = 0.85, \quad DW = 2.34. \tag{3.99}$$

$$\begin{aligned}
\widehat{mg}\$_{UK, I} &= 1.717(Pxg\$_I - Pmg\$_{UK}) + 6.864y\$_{UK} \\
(t) \quad & \quad (-1.92) \qquad\qquad\qquad (4.82) \\
[F] \quad & \quad [1.48] \qquad\qquad\qquad [0.93] \\
& \qquad -1.861(w\$_I - w\$_{UK})_{-1} \\
& \qquad (-2.24) \\
& \qquad [1.04] \\
& \qquad -9.755(\Delta\tilde{R}l_I - \Delta\tilde{R}l_{UK})_{-1}, \\
& \qquad (-3.10) \\
& \qquad [1.00]
\end{aligned}$$

$$R = 0.83, \quad DET = 0.73, \quad DW = 2.66. \tag{3.100}$$

$$\begin{aligned}
\widehat{mg}\$_{UK, NL} &= 4.802 - 1.143(Pxg\$_{NL} - Pmg\$_{UK}) \\
(t) \quad & \quad (1.71)(-1.72) \\
[F] \quad & \quad [-] \quad [2.75] \\
& \qquad + 2.105y\$_{UK_{-1}} - 14.240DU'69, \\
& \qquad (2.23) \qquad\quad (-1.78) \\
& \qquad [2.75] \qquad\quad [-]
\end{aligned}$$

$$R = 0.84, \quad DET = 0.84, \quad DW = 2.32. \tag{3.101}$$

The United Kingdom entered the EEC in 1972; the change stimulated UK imports from the BLEU, but not so clearly from the other EEC markets.

Now the linkage model has to be completed, so we have to assume that the differences between the c.i.f. and f.o.b. values of the bilateral flows (i.e. freight and insurance costs) are fixed parts of the f.o.b. values of bilateral imports. Since, moreover, (f.o.b.) exporting values $\tilde{X}g\$_{ij,\,t}$ are assumed to be proportional to these f.o.b. values of bilateral imports, we can derive that the export price changes are approximated by a convex combination of bilateral import prices (analogously to (3.39); see Janssens, [12], pp. 100–103)

$$Pxg\$_{j,\,t} \approx \sum_{i \neq j} \beta_{ji} Pmg\$_{ij,\,t} \tag{3.102}$$

with weights

$$\beta_{ji} := \frac{1}{T} \sum_{t=0}^{T-1} \frac{\tilde{X}g\$_{ji,\,t}}{\tilde{X}g\$_{j,\,t}},$$

and that the relative growth rates of the various export demands satisfy approximately:

$$xg\$_{j,\,t} \approx \sum_{i \neq j} \beta_{ji}\, mg\$_{ij,\,t}, \tag{3.103}$$

where the bilateral import flows are measured in c.i.f. prices.

Hence, our behavioural export equations can be conveniently substituted by definitional equations such as (3.103), in which supplementary linkage properties are provided; if these export equations are transferred to the national currencies, we have:

$$xg_{j,\,t} = \sum_{i \neq j} \beta_{ji}\, mg\$_{ij,\,t} + MR_{j,\,t}. \tag{3.104}$$

To 'close' the complete INTERPLAY model, the following equations are added: (3.104), (3.42) where necessary, and transfers to national currencies:

$$mg\$_{BL} = 0.930\, mg_B + 0.070\, mg_{LUX} - MR_B,^{29} \tag{3.105}$$

$$\begin{aligned} xg_B = {} & 0.157\, mg\$_{F,\,BL} + 0.191\, mg\$_{D,\,BL} + 0.039\, mg\$_{I,\,BL} \\ & + 0.221\, mg\$_{NL,\,BL} + 0.060\, mg\$_{UK,\,BL} \\ & + 0.417\, mg\$_{R,\,BL} + 1.085\, MR_B - 0.085\, xg_{LUX}, \end{aligned} \tag{3.106}$$

$$w\$_B - w\$_{UK} = w_B - MR_B - w_{UK} + MR_{UK}, \tag{3.107}$$

$$mg\$_F = mg_F - MR_F, \tag{3.108}$$

$$\begin{aligned} xg_F = {} & 0.090\, mg\$_{BL,\,F} + 0.154\, mg\$_{D,\,F} + 0.075\, mg\$_{I,\,F} \\ & + 0.039\, mg\$_{NL,\,F} + 0.053\, mg\$_{UK,\,F} \\ & + 0.589\, mg\$_{R,\,F} + MR_F, \end{aligned} \tag{3.109}$$

equations (3.48) and (3.49),

$$w\$_F - w\$_B = w_F - MR_F - w_B + MR_B, \tag{3.110}$$

$$y\$_F = gvamp_F - POP_F - MR_F, \tag{3.111}$$

$$mg\$_D = mg_D - MR_D, \tag{3.112}$$

$$\begin{aligned} xg_D = {} & 0.073\, mg\$_{BL,\,D} + 0.100\, mg\$_{F,\,D} + 0.070\, mg\$_{I,\,D} \\ & + 0.096\, mg\$_{NL,\,D} + 0.041\, mg\$_{UK,\,D} \\ & + 0.620\, mg\$_{R,\,D} + MR_D, \end{aligned} \tag{3.113}$$

$$y\$_D = 0.900\, gvampp_D + 0.100\, wg_D - POP_D - MR_D, \tag{3.114}$$

$$mg\$_I = mg_I - MR_I, \tag{3.115}$$

$$\begin{aligned} xg_I = {} & 0.032\, mg\$_{BL,\,I} + 0.099\, mg\$_{F,\,I} + 0.173\, mg\$_{D,\,I} \\ & + 0.035\, mg\$_{NL,\,I} + 0.057\, mg\$_{UK,\,I} \\ & + 0.604\, mg\$_{R,\,I} + MR_I, \end{aligned} \tag{3.116}$$

$$w\$_I - w\$_{NL} = w_I - MR_I - w_{NL} + MR_{NL}, \tag{3.117}$$

$$w\$_I - w\$_{UK} = w_I - MR_I - w_{UK} + MR_{UK}, \quad (3.118)$$

$$y\$_I = 0.887 gvampp_I + 0.113 wg_I - POP_I - MR_I, \quad (3.119)$$

$$mg\$_{NL} = mg_{NL} - MR_{NL}, \quad (3.120)$$

$$\begin{aligned} xg_{NL} = {} & 0.146 mg\$_{BL,\,NL} + 0.077 mg\$_{F,\,NL} + 0.247 mg\$_{D,\,NL} \\ & + 0.039 mg\$_{I,\,NL} + 0.097 mg\$_{UK,\,NL} \\ & + 0.394 mg\$_{R,\,NL} + MR_{NL}, \end{aligned} \quad (3.121)$$

$$\begin{aligned} y\$_{NL} = {} & 1.175 el_{NL} + 0.151 wg_{NL} - 0.326 mg_{NL} \\ & - POP_{NL} - MR_{NL}, \end{aligned} \quad (3.122)$$

$$mg\$_{UK} = mg_{UK} - MR_{UK}, \quad (3.123)$$

$$\begin{aligned} xg_{UK} = {} & 0.031 mg\$_{BL,\,UK} + 0.037 mg\$_{F,\,UK} + 0.046 mg\$_{D,\,UK} \\ & + 0.026 mg\$_{I,\,UK} + 0.040 mg\$_{NL,\,UK} \\ & + 0.820 mg\$_{R,\,UK} + MR_{UK}, \end{aligned} \quad (3.124)$$

$$w\$_{UK} = w_{UK} - MR_{UK}, \quad (3.125)$$

$$y\$_{UK} = 0.878 gvampp_{UK} + 0.122 wg_{UK} - POP_{UK} - MR_{UK}. \quad (3.126)$$

Now, the INTERPLAY model comprises completely linked national submodels; links are provided by the bilateral trade flows, the bilateral prices when they occur, the import price equations and the commodity export equations. Some stability properties and concluding remarks will be stated in the next section.

3.3. Stability Properties of INTERPLAY and Some Concluding Remarks

The complete INTERPLAY model as it is presented in this paper is not (globally) stable since the largest moduli of the eigenvalues of the coefficient matrix belonging to the lagged endogenous variables are not lower than unity, because the five largest moduli are 1.488, 1.290, 0.703, 0.695 and 0.692.[30] The instability of the model is illustrated by the two eigenvalues with modulus larger than one.

In order to obtain stability of the INTERPLAY model, the sensitivity of the model specification presented has been studied with respect to changes in the stability properties. If we change the wage–price spiral in the UK submodel in such a way that the coefficient of private wages per labourer in price equation (2.79) of private consumption is reduced from 0.895 to 0.81 and the price-compensation elasticity in wage equation (2.81) is reduced from 1.189 to 1.1, the five largest eigenvalue moduli of the endogenous coefficient matrix become 1.488, 0.705, 0.692, 0.686 and 0.672.[31]

Since the positive eigenvalue 1.488 was observed to originate from the

French submodel, particularly from the coefficient of $gvamp_{-3/4}$, the INTERPLAY model has been computed in which two (minor) modifications have been introduced with respect to the original model presented in this study, i.e., the output elasticity of the French investment equation (2.14) has been reduced from 2.229 to 1.1 and the price elasticity of the UK's wage equation (2.81) has been reduced from 1.189 to 1.1 too.

The resulting model is globally stable then, with largest moduli of eigenvalues of the coefficient martix, belonging to the lagged endogenous variables, being 0.973, 0.937, 0.698, 0.686 and 0.593.[32] The average cycle length of all complex eigenvalues is about 8 years.

Concluding, we can say that the linked INTERPLAY model is slightly unstable, but with very minor modifications has been transformed to become stable. The basic characteristics of the model do not change by introducing the two modifications; moreover, the modifications lie within the 90% confidence interval of the particular point estimators (certainly for the price coefficient in the UK wage equation).

The model should now be tested on its global functioning by tracing the consequences of changes in the policy variables, for example, exchange rates, government expenditures, fiscal policy variables, liquidities, interest policy variables, and so on, on the time paths of the endogenous variables. The impact of exogenous changes such as oil price increases, strikes and so on could also be studied. Such 'policy simulation' analyses will be deferred to a subsequent study.

The model presented in this study differs in many aspects from other known linked models for the European Community; for example, the main differences from COMET [4] are (1) the use of relative annual growth rates for the variables instead of logarithmic-level variables; (2) the differing specification per type of equation; (3) the bilateral prices being supposed to follow a weighted (geometric) average of importing and exporting prices and not simply equal to the respective exporting prices; (4) the endogeneity and, hence, the linking property of importing prices; (5) the typical specification of the other ('z-') variables in the linking model; and (6) the observation period (INTERPLAY, 1953–1975; COMET, 1959–1975).

References

1. Adams, F.G., Eguchi, H. and Meyer zu Schlochtern, H. (1969), An Econometric Analysis of International Trade. Paris: OECD.
2. Ball, R.J., ed. (1973), International Linkage of National Economic Models. Amsterdam: North-Holland.
3. Barker, T.S. (1977), 'International trade and economic trade growth: an alternative to the neoclassical approach'. Cambridge Journal of Economics, 153–172.
4. Barten, A.P., d'Alcantara, G. and Carrin, G.J. (1976), 'Comet, a medium term macro-economic model for the European Economic Community'. European Economic Review, 63–115.
5. Bhagwati, J. (1964), 'The pure theory of international trade'. Economic Journal, March 1964.

6. Blair, J.M. (1972), Economic Concentration, Structure Behaviour and Public Policy. New York: Harcourt Brace.
7. Dramais, A. (1976), 'Desmos III'. Cahiers économiques de Bruxelles, 64, 473–514; 65, 53–108; 66, 201–260.
8. Drèze, J. (1960), 'Quelques Réflections sur l'Adaptation de l'Industrie Belge au Marché Commun'. Comptes-Rendus de Travaux de la Société Royale de l'Economie Politique de la Belgique, 275.
9. Drèze, J. (1961). 'Les Exportations intra CEE anno 1955 et la Position Belge'. Recherches Economiques de Louvain, 27.
10. Durbin, J. (1970), 'Testing for serial correlations in least squares regression when some of the regressors are lagged dependent variables'. Econometrica, 38.
11. Heckscher, E.F. (1919). 'Utrikes Hanelens Ferkan På Inkomstförelningen' (Foreign Trade and its Impact on National Income Changes'). Economisk Tidskrift, 4.
12. Janssens, M. (1980), 'Terms of probation report'. Mimeographed paper, Catholic University of Tilburg.
13. Kravis, I.B. (1956), 'Availability and other influences on the commodity composition of trade'. Journal of Political Economy, 64.
14. Levison, C. (1971), Capital, Inflation and the Multinationals. New York: Harcourt Brace.
15. Linneman, H. (1966), An Econometric Study of International Trade Flows. Amsterdam: North-Holland.
16. Ohlin, B. (1933). Interregional and International Trade, Cambridge Massachusetts: Harvard University Press.
17. Plasmans, J. (1975a), Production Investment Behaviour. Tilburg: Tilburg University Press.
18. Plasmans, J. (1975b), 'Een heterogeen Arbeidsvraagmodel'. Maandschrift Economie, 40, 24–37.
19. Plasmans, J.E.J. and de Zeeuw, A.J. (1980a), 'Nash, Pareto and Stackelberg solutions in macro-economic policy models with a decentralized decision structure'. Paper presented at the Ifac workshop on differential games, Sochi, USSR, April 1980.
20. Plasmans, J.E.J. and de Zeeuw, A.J. (1980b), 'Incentives to cooperate in linear quadratic difference games'. International Journal of Systems Science, 11, 607–619.
21. Posner, M.V. (1961). 'International Trade in Technical Change'. Oxford Economic Papers, 13.
22. Ranuzzi, P. (1976), 'Notes on a bilateral model for the real sector', Internal note, European Community, Brussels.
23. Reddaway, W.D. (1967), Effects of UK Direct Investments Overseas. Cambridge: Cambridge University Press.
24. Resnick, S. (1968), 'An empirical study of economic policy in the Common Market', in Studies in Economic Stabilization. Washington D.C.: Brookings, pp. 184–214.

Endnotes

1. The author wishes to thank T. Dunnewijk, W. Groenendaal, M. Janssens and C. van Zundert for very helpful advice and computations; and Mrs G. van Gorp for quick and skilful typing. Obviously only the author is responsible for any remaining deficiencies.
2. Provisionally, interest rates are kept exogenous, but estimated reaction equations are already available for the countries investigated.
3. If no constant term occurs in the structural equation, the F and Durbin-Watson statistics will be computed as if a constant intercept were present. If lagged endogenous variables occur, the Durbin–Watson statistic is not calculated because it should then be adjusted (Durbin [10]). Further details about statistics utilized can be found in Plasmans [17], ch. 4, pp. 184–197.
4. The lags in the variables are defined as linear interpolations, e.g.:

$$\tilde{Rl}_{-3/4} := 0.25\tilde{Rl} + 0.75\tilde{Rl}_{-1}. \quad (2.6)$$

5. The long-run weighted disposable wage income elasticity of private consumption is 0.534 and the weighted disposable non-wage income elasticity of private consumption amounts to 0.248.
6. To be precise, it is supposed that individuals can never be prescribed to sell more labour services than they want to sell, although they may be forced for lack of buyers to sell less than they desire.
7. Notice that the volume of private gross value added at market prices is not available for the postwar French economy, so the gross value added at market prices for the whole economy is employed instead.
8. $\widetilde{Pxc}$ is computed for each country as follows, taking into account the twenty most important competitors on that country's twenty most important export markets:

$$\widetilde{Pxc} := \sum_{j=1}^{20} \frac{\widetilde{xg}_j}{\sum_{k=1}^{20} \widetilde{mg}_{jk}} \widetilde{Pmg}_j, \tag{2.35}$$

where $\widetilde{xg}_j$ is a country's export to country j and $\widetilde{mg}_{jk}$ is the import of country j from country k.
9. This phenomenon is contradictory to the familiar 'Zijlstra effect', saying that exports fall when domestic expenditure grows ('home pressure of demand').
10. These changes of definition had the following numerical consequences: in 1960, cg, at 5207 (billion lire) was revised to 5074 (billion lire); in 1970 $\widetilde{EMg}$, at 1,794,000, was revised to 2,091,000 (= 16.6% difference).
11. If it is true that the changes of the degree of utilization of capital stock can be transmitted to the price of private consumption, then it is very rational, from the entrepreneur's point of view to do so only if it has a positive effect on the product price; in other words, if there is an increase of the degree of utilization, then it is better for him to leave the price unchanged. Levison [14] and Blair [6] agree that prices are adjusted upwards if the degree of utilization of productive capacity falls.
12. Decentralized economic policies can be evaluated by means of linear-quadratic difference games (Plasmans and de Zeeuw [19]). The problem of coordination among players (= countries) is discussed in Plasmans and de Zeeuw [20].
13. Bilateral capital flows among EEC countries are being studied by the European Monetary Project Group (1980).
14. The individual export prices are related to those of all other member countries, including the importing country itself.
15. Examples of this direct linkage approach are Resnick [24] and the *Euro* (1974) EC project.
16. This allocation is not of concern in the linkage model, because the demand for tradeable (domestic and foreign) goods is already established in each national submodel (see the equations *cp/ip* and *mg*).
17. Examples of import allocation models are those of Barten et al [4] and Dramais [7].
18. Examples of the world trade approach are the project LINK, of L.R. Klein et al. (see R. Ball [2]), and the project METEOR of the European Community at Brussels (not published).
19. Under the assumption of a Cobb–Douglas utility function ($\rho_i := 0$), the shares become constant and equal to the (relative) utility elasticities of trade flows $\widetilde{mg\$}_{ij}$.
20. The United Nations commodity trade statistics show quarterly figures for bilateral flows of commodity groups at the three-digit level of the Standard International Trade Classification (SITC code: 155 commodity groups). Since the necessary computations would be very time-consuming (at least two man-years for the period 1959–1975) and, moreover, since quantity statistics do not exist for the period before 1959, bilateral prices will be specified according to a presumed economic model.

21. Obviously, this invariancy over time of the relative market shares is a very simplified hypothesis; for some particular (ij) combinations, the following linear trends can be estimated over the sampling period:

$$\underset{(t)}{\hat{\alpha}_{FI,t}} = \underset{(1.39)}{0.0062} + \underset{(13.45)}{0.0044t} \quad \text{and} \quad \underset{(t)}{\hat{\alpha}_{UKD,t}} = \underset{(7.46)}{0.0160} + \underset{(13.92)}{0.0022t} \qquad (3.33)$$

In order to avoid very large and very undesirable non-linearities, the constancy hypothesis, however, has been retained (see also (3.38–3.39)).

22. This hypothesis is not too strong, as might be seen from direct data inspection, for those particular cases where (quarterly and annual) data on bilateral prices were available (see also footnote 20).
23. Hence the import prices, exogenous in the national submodels, are endogenized by (3.40).
24. Note that Barten et. al. [4] simply substitute bilateral price changes $Pmg\$_{ij,t}$ by export price changes $Pxg\$_{i,t}$ for the COMET model of the EEC.
25. See Janssens ([12], pp. 25 ff.) for a full report of the results, where the coefficients are averages over the period 1953–1975.
26. See United Nations, *Yearbook of International Trade Statistics*, Special Table C.
27. This is clarified from the inspection of the coefficients of $Pxg\$_D$ in the various import price equations for the periods 1953–1973 and 1953–1975 respectively:

	BL	F	I	NL	UK
1953–1973	0.200	0.242	0.224	0.250	0.131
1953–1975	0.226	0.247	0.230	0.276	0.151

28. Note that equations (3.35) and (3.39) imply constant market shares.
29. Separation of Belgian and Luxembourg imports according to their average shares over the sampling period in total BLEU imports. Equation (3.106) is the same for exports.
30. The latter modulus belongs to a complex pair of eigenvalues: $0.491 \pm 0.487i$ (period length of eight years). The average cycle length, derived from the complex eigenvalues, is 7.5 years in this case. Notice that the cycle length is easily computed as $2\pi/\text{arctg}(\text{Im}/\text{Re})$.
31. This time none of these five moduli correspond with complex eigenvalues.
32. The fifth modulus belongs to a complex pair of eigenvalues: $0.359 \pm 0.472i$ with a cycle length of 6.8 years.

INDEX

GPSR Compliance

The European Union's (EU) General Product Safety Regulation (GPSR) is a set of rules that requires consumer products to be safe and our obligations to ensure this.

If you have any concerns about our products, you can contact us on ProductSafety@springernature.com

In case Publisher is established outside the EU, the EU authorized representative is:

Springer Nature Customer Service Center GmbH
Europaplatz 3
69115 Heidelberg, Germany

Batch number: 10512295

Printed by Printforce, the Netherlands